"We often hear about work/life balance, but Stew Friedman takes it two steps further. He breaks life into four parts: work, home, community, and the private realm of mind, body, and spirit. *Leading the Life You Want* illustrates through compelling biographies the skills you need to act with authenticity, integrity, and creativity—helping you lead a life that truly blends meaning and happiness."

—Melinda Gates, Co-chair,
Bill & Melinda Gates Foundation

"*Leading the Life You Want* delivers a much-needed surge of inspiration. He crafts detailed, motivating profiles of high performers who've learned how to be real, be whole, and be innovative. Anyone who has struggled to find harmony between work, family, community, and inner spirit will benefit from this book."

—Tom Gardner, CEO, The Motley Fool

"Stew Friedman shows how to harness your passions to pursue four-way wins—in your work, home, community, and most importantly, for yourself."
—Billie Jean King, sports icon and social justice pioneer

"Stew Friedman makes the idea of finding harmony between work and life not only possible, but practicable. *Leading the Life You Want* is a brainy yet conversational guide that offers inspired, effective solutions."
—Neil Blumenthal, Co-founder and Co-CEO, Warby Parker

"In this absolutely wonderful book, Stew Friedman tells us how to put an end to the zero-sum mentality that keeps us from leading the life we want. Read it, and you will be inspired to live and work like never before."
—Herminia Ibarra, Professor, INSEAD;
author, *Act Like a Leader, Think Like a Leader*

"The speed of change and the 24/7 connected world we're experiencing have made Stew Friedman's book a particularly important read. Incessantly increasing options, opportunities, and obligations have made becoming conscious of what matters most to us something that should matter most to us. This is a great manifesto for getting it done. Bravo!"
—David Allen, author of the international
bestseller, *Getting Things Done*

"Stew Friedman understands that pitting our passions and responsibilities against each other is a losing battle. Instead, as he powerfully illustrates in this great new book, he teaches a masterful strategy to integrate self, career, family, and community—an approach that has allowed me to grow as a CEO, mother, and community activist."

—Julie Smolyansky, President and CEO, Lifeway Foods

"Great stuff! Teddy Roosevelt famously said, 'The best prize that life offers is the chance to work hard at work worth doing.' In this engaging, instructive, and insatiably useful book, Stew Friedman shows all of us how to win big at work that matters, without losing ourselves in the process."

—William C. Taylor, Co-founder and
founding editor, *Fast Company*

"I love this book! Friedman's inspiring and refreshing *Leading the Life You Want*, through its personal and interesting stories, is a compelling case for why business leaders should embrace all aspects of life and how they can do so. This is exactly what talent in today's market is looking for."

—Laura E. Kohler, Senior Vice President,
Human Resources, Kohler Co.

"By linking the personal and professional success of six very different and highly successful individuals, Stew Friedman has given us new insight into the mechanics of living a productive and satisfying life of service. Well done!"

—Dick Couch, Captain, USNR (Retired); author, *Always
Faithful, Always Forward* and *Act of Revenge*

"In this fascinating and timely book, Professor Friedman draws on insights from the inspiring stories of six people to provide a deep analysis of the skills needed to lead the life you want and what it takes to develop these skills. This is a must-read for anyone seeking to create that elusive goal of modern lives—the purposeful integration of work and life."

—Lynda Gratton, Professor of Management Practice,
London Business School

"Stew Friedman stands out as one of the few male voices in the field. He understands better than anyone else how leadership, life, and business can fit together."

—Anne-Marie Slaughter, President and CEO,
New America Foundation

LEADING
THE LIFE
YOU WANT

LEADING THE LIFE YOU WANT

Skills for Integrating Work and Life

STEWART D. FRIEDMAN

Harvard Business Review Press

Boston, Massachusetts

Copyright 2014 Harvard Business School Publishing Corporation
All rights reserved
Printed in the United States of America

10 9 8 7 6 5 4 3 2 1

No part of this publication may be reproduced, stored in or introduced into a retrieval system, or transmitted, in any form, or by any means (electronic, mechanical, photocopying, recording, or otherwise), without the prior permission of the publisher. Requests for permission should be directed to permissions@hbsp.harvard.edu, or mailed to Permissions, Harvard Business School Publishing, 60 Harvard Way, Boston, Massachusetts 02163.

Library of Congress Cataloging-in-Publication Data

Friedman, Stewart D.
  Leading the life you want : skills for integrating work and life / Stewart D. Friedman.
    pages cm
  ISBN 978-1-4221-8941-2 (hardback)
  1. Work-life balance. 2. Work and family. I. Title.
  HD4904.25.F7537 2014

  650.1—dc23
                    2014013112

The paper used in this publication meets the requirements of the American National Standard for Permanence of Paper for Publications and Documents in Libraries and Archives Z39.48-1992.

To my students and my teachers,
especially Joel DeLuca, Richard Hackman, Bob Kahn, and Noel Tichy

Contents

PART II

Developing the Skills for Integrating Work and the Rest of Life

"Not I, nor anyone else can travel that road for you.
You must travel it by yourself.
It is not far. It is within reach."
—WALT WHITMAN

"This land was made for you and me."
—WOODY GUTHRIE

Introduction

Beyond Balance

*Between stimulus and response there is a space. In
that space is our power to choose our response. In
our response lies our growth and our freedom.*

—VIKTOR FRANKL

Out of control." That's how Sam, a divorced father of two girls
and an ambitious professional, described his life. By day he
managed an IT group for a health care conglomerate while
dreaming of starting his own company. "I feel like I can never get it
all done," Sam continued. "I'm constantly distracted. I wish I could
be under less stress and pay more attention to my daughters, especially as they're getting into their teen years, and to my mom, who's
just been diagnosed with early-stage cancer."

Sam looked down at his desk and shifted in his chair; he was in his
home office. I could see only a part of it on the computer screen (we

were videoconferencing). His sense of being overwhelmed extended to his professional life. "I'm struggling to find the right partners who can help me develop and market an app I've designed that can make it easier for people to track their personal health habits," he said, leaning forward. "I really believe that this thing can make a difference in people's lives."

It's a full life, but at that moment Sam felt not so much full as stretched thin. He continued, "When I'm at work I'm worrying about Sophie and Erin, and when I have them on the weekends I'm online taking care of loose ends at work or trying to connect with leads for funding my start-up. I just don't have enough time for it all. Yet I have this gnawing sense that I should be doing more with my life."

Sam's plight is not unique to busy managers. I often hear these sentiments, from adults young and old, whether they are executives, students, doctors, retailers, artisans, research scientists, soldiers, stay-at-home parents, teachers, or engineers—and whether they live in the United States or elsewhere. These are the chaotic, early days of the "twitch" era, in which we often feel as though we're drowning in a deluge of data and yet can't stop picking up our smartphones, checking our social media accounts, flailing in the wash of e-mails. Few of us are skilled enough psychologically to exploit the power of new communication tools, and it's increasingly difficult to maintain the boundaries that allow us to give our projects the attention they require, and our people the care they deserve.

What's more, social expectations for men and women are changing. Traditional norms are rapidly fading, leaving many people confused or disappointed (or both) about gender roles. Anne-Marie Slaughter's inquiring *Atlantic* article of June 2012 ("Why Women Still Can't Have It All") sparked a fervent national conversation. It was stoked later that year with the decision by Yahoo! CEO Marissa Mayer to revoke the work-at-home option for the tech company's employees. The fire was fanned by the book campaign of Facebook

COO Sheryl Sandberg, whose catchphrase (and book title) *Lean In* urges women not to step back from challenging careers. Women and men are hungry for help in figuring out how to navigate the turbulent modern-day waters of meaningful work, domestic responsibility, community engagement, and a satisfying inner life. No one seems to have the answers.

At the same time, economic pressures are forcing individuals, families, organizations, and communities to do more with less—or just to do less. Indeed, as I wrote last year in *Baby Bust: New Choices for Men and Women in Work and Family*, a study that compares the Wharton School's class of 1992 and the class of 2012, many young people are forsaking the opportunity to have or adopt children because they don't see how they can manage it. We remain in difficult financial times, in which large swaths of our economy have been disrupted, leaving millions displaced from their lines of work with diminished prospects for economic stability. Many of us may dream of achieving something significant in our life's work—something we can feel proud of—and yet find ourselves struggling to do so without shortchanging the people who count on us.

Perhaps you, like others, feel fragmented or discouraged. Perhaps you are looking for more purpose. You might have inklings about what to change, but you fear failure, or you fret about being selfish, or you can't stop the scramble to make ends meet, or you just don't know where to start.

The Problem with "Work/Life Balance"

For nearly thirty years, my life's work has been to help people like you find ways to bring the often warring aspects of life into greater harmony. Toward that end, my research has focused on a fundamental misconception we all have about the "costs" of success. Many people believe that to achieve great things we must make brutal sacrifices;

that to succeed in work we must focus single-mindedly, at the expense of self, family, and society. Even those who reject the idea of a zero-sum game fall prey to a kind of binary thinking revealed by the term we use to describe the ideal lifestyle: *work/life balance.*

Work/life balance is a misguided metaphor for grasping the relationship between work and the rest of life; the image of the scale forces you to think in terms of trade-offs instead of the possibilities for harmony. And the idea that "work" competes with "life" ignores the more nuanced reality of our humanity. It ignores the fact that "life" is actually the intersection and interaction of the four domains of life: work or school; home or family; community or society; and the private realm of mind, body, and spirit. Of course, you can't have it all—complete success in all the corners of your life, all at the same time. No one can. But even though it can seem impossible to bring these four domains into greater alignment, it doesn't have to be impossible. Conflict and stress aren't inevitable. Harmony is possible.

From years of studying people in many different settings, I have found that the most successful are those who can harness the passions and powers of the various parts of their lives, bringing them together to achieve what I call *four-way wins:* actions that result in life's being better in all four domains. Successful people make it their business to be conscious of what and who matter most. Their actions flow from their values. They strive to do what they can to make things better for the people who depend on them and on whom they depend, in all the different parts of their lives.

Integrating Work and the Rest of Life

Indeed, a set of discrete skills can help you find ways to integrate these four domains. You can learn these skills. And with practice you can master them. You can achieve a kind of integration that will, in turn, help you have the impact you want to have and lead a life in which you stay true to yourself, serve others, and grow as a person. This integration is the key to leading a meaningful life—the one *you* want.

To replace conflict with a sense of completeness, or integrity, doesn't require turning your whole world upside down. Instead it requires figuring out how to take incremental steps that are under your control and that move you in the direction you want to go, while bringing others along with you. Doing this means thinking and talking about what truly inspires you, whatever in the world that might be—creating new products that improve the quality of life, teaching old folks how to dance, being recognized by your peers for your accomplishments, showing children how to read, having a reputation as a trustworthy person, solving problems or puzzles, being part of a team that takes pride in its achievements, reading about new ideas or old characters, growing vegetables, designing video games, coaching hockey, or talking about movies with your mother. In pursuing your passions, whether vocational or avocational, you can extract the special something that is unique about you and convert it into something that helps make others' lives a little better. It is not only thrilling to discover a way to do what you love and to love what you do, but it usually results in your having better market value, too.

It's not easy, especially if you're facing obstacles that loom large; and there's almost always disappointment and failure along the way. But it's a creative and rewarding process. I like to think of this creative process in musical terms. Imagine that you are a musician in a jazz quartet. You're trying to make good music. Your goal is to produce sounds that take your listener on a soul-touching journey. You have a theme, a direction you've chosen for each piece, around which the players improvise. Things happen along the way that you haven't planned or that you can't control, so you must listen and continually adjust your playing. Sometimes only the saxophone plays, and other times it's the piano and the bass, or the drums and the saxophone, or only the drums. You're trying to bring them together, rhythm and melody, over a period of time to produce something uniquely beautiful and valuable. (In your case, the period of time is your entire life.)

When you start—or maybe even a long time after you start—your band fails to gel. The parts don't sync, the instruments clash, and individuals fail to meld into a whole. But you work with what you have, combining disciplined structure, practice, increasing competence, concentrated effort, dedicated commitment, and trial and error. You refine your skill so that you can produce the sound you hear inside your head, the melodies that stir your soul. Each instrument has its limits. Each has a specific contribution to make to the whole. For a jazz quartet to produce great music, discipline is as important as improvisation and serendipity. It's not magic, even if the result is often magical.

Foundations

This book describes, illustrates, and teaches the specific skills you need to pursue four-way wins. Why these skills? Why not others? It's because the skills presented in this book are the ones that have proven to be the most effective in my three decades of teaching, research, and practice helping individuals—at all levels, in different stages of life, and across various spheres—integrate work and the rest of life.

In the 1980s I began asking the question, What does it take to bring together the different parts of life in mutually enriching ways? We launched the Work/Life Integration Project at the Wharton School, and in collaboration with leading scholars, practitioners, and policy makers, I initiated surveys and interviews, action research, and case studies in a wide variety of settings to find the answers. In a series of books and articles, I've shared the results of my studies and tried to make these ideas available to the wider public. In 1998, with Jessica DeGroot and Perry Christensen, I edited a collection of learning activities, written for educators, to teach what we were starting to discover about the skills for integrating work and the rest of life; it was called *Integrating Work and Life: The Wharton Resource Guide*. My book *Work and Family—Allies or Enemies?* was written in 2000 with Jeffrey Greenhaus and based on large-scale survey research. It offered new ideas for actions that individuals could take to produce greater harmony among the different parts of life. With Sharon Lobel in 2005 I wrote an article, "The Happy Workaholic: A Role Model for Employees," that described the practical lessons we uncovered in field research on senior executives who lead flexible and engaging work environments and the skills they use to do so. And in *Baby Bust*, mentioned earlier, using twenty-year longitudinal data comparing two generations of Wharton students, I explored the values and aspirations of millennials (those born between 1980 and 2000) and the skills they need to reshape our culture, our organizations, our communities, and our families.

Being Real, Being Whole, Being Innovative

The most important part of the foundation for the skills in this book is Total Leadership, a program I developed at Ford Motor Company that later evolved into a course at Wharton. Total Leadership is a set of principles for achieving four-way wins and a sequence of exercises that flow from the principles. The idea of the Total Leadership program is to enhance your capacity to be a leader in all parts of life, and for you to transform yourself from feeling unfocused, fragmented, and stagnant to feeling inspired, connected with others, and excited about the future.

It starts with three principles: be real, be whole, and be innovative. To *be real* is to act with authenticity by clarifying what's important to you. It's about exploring your answer to this basic question: What matters most to me in my life? To *be whole* is to act with integrity by recognizing how the different parts of your life affect each other. This involves identifying who matters most to you at work, at home, and in the community; understanding what you need from each other; and seeing whether and how these needs mesh or don't mesh. All this examination allows you to *be innovative*. You act with creativity by experimenting with how things get done in ways that are good for you and for the people around you. You learn how to take small steps aimed at scoring four-way wins: improved performance at work, at home, in the community, and for your private self (mind, body, and spirit).

Since 2001, thousands of people have taken the program, at Wharton or elsewhere, at in-person workshops as well as online, including on a customized social learning site built especially for this course as well as in a MOOC (massive open online course) on Coursera.org, where over 54,000 students are enrolled as of this writing. In 2008, my book *Total Leadership: Be a Better Leader, Have a Richer Life*, attempted to put this program on the page. Tens of thousands of readers, in numerous languages (including Chinese, Japanese, Korean, Polish, Portuguese, and Russian), have used the book to help them lead more fulfilling lives. I often hear from former students and other Total Leadership alumni that they are sharing the ideas and exercises with their colleagues, family members, and friends. I came to see that this approach is equally effective for people who may or may not be MBA candidates, and who may or may not aspire to run companies, governments, or public service organizations. This approach can also help anyone who is feeling frazzled by the often-competing demands of work and the other parts of life. It can help people who have found success in their professional lives but feel a nagging sense that they have failed to develop their spiritual selves. This approach—because it is entirely customized by each person who tries it—can help the many women and men who are disappointed that "having it all" is much harder than they thought when they were younger, as well as those, just starting out, who seem to have already concluded that they'll have to settle for success in only one part of their lives.

My research has shown that there are ways for everyone—from the managers of sales teams, to executives in government agencies, to computer engineers, to florists, to coaches—to achieve professional success without always having to sacrifice the things that matter in their personal lives. Indeed, we've found that the opposite is true: sustainable professional success *results from* meaningful investments in the rest of life.

Skills for Integrating Work and the Rest of Life

The *Total Leadership* book (and the Wharton course that shares its name) presents a structured program—step-by-step instruction, a process for setting goals and tracking progress, a series of exercises to complete in stages—to help you successfully pursue four-way wins. In contrast, this book drills down into specific skills for being real, being whole, and being innovative that you can learn and practice at any time. You can dip in and out of the process, focusing only on the skills you need most at any one time or in any specific situation. It's not necessary for you to have read or done any of the exercises in *Total Leadership* (but the book is now available in paperback if you're interested). You can start to produce greater harmony between work and the rest of your life with this book, assessing yourself on the skills and building them through specific exercises. You can learn and practice the skills either singly, or in small bunches, or all together.

The first step is to do a self-assessment in the next section to determine which skills most need your attention. Then you can choose to strengthen those that are weakest or build on those you've already mastered. As you read the description of each skill, think about how it plays out in your life. Which ones are your strengths, and which ones are weaknesses? If I were to ask people who know you well, what would they say about whether each skill is true of you? And how might things be different if you practiced each of these skills in your everyday life?

As you review these skills—don't score yourself yet—you might wonder whether they are easy for me to describe but difficult for you to develop. Let me ask you to take a leap of faith: don't worry too much about that right now; instead, try to approach them with curiosity and an open mind.

Skills for Being Real

The first of the three Total Leadership principles is to be real—to act with authenticity by clarifying what's important to you. This is the foundation—your values and your vision of the future you want to create.

KNOW WHAT MATTERS.

You know how important each of the different aspects of your life is to you. Your high self-awareness enables you to understand and clearly describe the value of each of the roles you play—worker, spouse, parent, sibling, son or daughter, friend, or citizen. You are also able to see the bigger picture, in which all your different roles in life contribute to your vision of the future.

EMBODY VALUES CONSISTENTLY.

You are able to be yourself wherever you are, wherever you go. You act in ways that are consistent with your core values. You have taken the time to get comfortable in your own skin. This confidence allows you to be yourself wherever you are. Rather than conform to external pressures, you rely on your internal compass to guide your words and deeds. Rather than bend to social pressures, you make choices that match your values, and you are not afraid to share your opinions.

ALIGN ACTIONS WITH VALUES.

You make choices about how to spend your time and energy in ways that match what you really care about. This skill allows you to think about your goals so that you have a clear understanding of them, making it easier for you to prioritize. You understand how what you do each day fits with your values, so you are able to persevere when things get rough. You also know when and how to say no. You do not let feelings of guilt force you to take on things that are not true to what you stand for.

CONVEY VALUES WITH STORIES.

You tell stories about the key people and events that have shaped your values in a way that binds you to others. You can pinpoint episodes in your life that have shaped your values. You allow others to gain insight into the person you are and where you've been by sharing your stories. You display both confidence and vulnerability by opening yourself up. This lays the foundation for building relationships based on mutual appreciation and trust.

ENVISION YOUR LEGACY.

You have a vision for where you are headed and the legacy you want to leave. You know not only where you've been, but also where you're going. You can paint a vivid picture of the life you want to lead, visualizing yourself in ten and even twenty years. Not only do you have a vision of the future, but you also have ideas that excite you about how to achieve that vision, even if you don't have all of the details figured out.

HOLD YOURSELF ACCOUNTABLE.

You hold yourself accountable for doing what is most important to you in your life. You don't let weeks or months pass by without reflecting on what matters. You routinely evaluate whether you are living according to your values. If you notice that you are doing things that are not important to you, you adjust your actions so that they line up better with your values. At the very least, you are willing to try to take steps to ensure that you are pursuing a life that matches what matters most.

Skills for Being Whole

The second Total Leadership principle is to be whole—to act with integrity (the Latin root is *integer,* which means whole or complete) by respecting all the different parts that constitute the whole person, ensuring that you and the people who inhabit these realms are clear about what you need from each other and are willing to provide it.

CLARIFY EXPECTATIONS.

You communicate with people important to you about expectations you have of each other, and you make sure these expectations are clear. You are willing to express your needs, values, and goals to those you care about. You are willing to set aside time for these conversations and are able to broach topics that may feel uncomfortable at first. You are an active listener who is also willing to hear constructive feedback, ask clarifying questions, and work to resolve disagreements.

HELP OTHERS.

You look for opportunities to help many different people. You are generous and caring in key relationships in your life. Whether these relationships are with colleagues, neighbors, friends, or family, you see that it's fun and fruitful to help other people. You view relationships as a means for enriching your own life *and* the lives of others.

BUILD SUPPORTIVE NETWORKS.

You are able to convince people to support you in your goals. You are able to tap into your personal and professional networks for support of what's important. With your enthusiasm and passion—and your reputation for going out of your way to connect people—you convince others to support you. You do not need to manipulate others to gain their support; it is offered freely because others share your vision of the future and want to help you realize it.

APPLY ALL YOUR RESOURCES.

You use skills and contacts from different parts of your life to help meet any need or goal. When pursuing your goals, you are able to think creatively about the resources you have developed in the various domains of your life. You do not force your relationships into rigidly defined categories or roles. Instead, you draw on assets—other people, your own talents, what you have learned—from different parts of your life to get things done.

MANAGE BOUNDARIES INTELLIGENTLY.

You are able to delineate and maintain boundaries between the different parts of your life. You not only know when to merge the different aspects of your life, but you also know when to segment, or separate, them. You are able to decide when it is beneficial to create boundaries that allow for concentration on a single goal or responsibility. Despite the 24/7 connectivity we all have to work, family, and other relationships through technology, you are able to turn your attention to one thing at a time when you need to do so, rather than try to accomplish everything at once.

WEAVE DISPARATE STRANDS.

You are able to weave together the pieces of your life so that it has coherence. You view the different aspects of your life as interconnected in a way that is mutually enriching. You see how your different roles complement each other. You have a sense that all aspects of your life are integral parts of who you are; they all fit together as one. You understand how the various parts you play enable you to realize your vision.

Skills for Being Innovative

The third principle is to be innovative—to act with creativity and courage in continually experimenting with how things get done, bringing others along with you as you progress toward goals that matter.

FOCUS ON RESULTS.

You focus on the results of your efforts to accomplish goals and are flexible about the means for achieving them. You keep your eyes on the prize. When evaluating your progress, you don't count the hours you've logged but instead look to whether or not you are producing a positive outcome. You judge yourself and others by your accomplishments and emphasize quality instead of quantity of effort.

RESOLVE CONFLICTS AMONG DOMAINS.

You seek creative solutions to conflicts rather than sacrifice one part of life for another. You realize that the different aspects of your life are not competing with one another, that it's not a zero-sum game. You don't accept the notion that engaging in one area of your life must always require sacrifices in the others. Instead, you look for ways to create win-win solutions that meet multiple goals.

CHALLENGE THE STATUS QUO.

You challenge traditional assumptions about how things are done, experimenting to make things better whenever possible. You are not constrained by conventions about how others think things should be done. Rather than follow the pack, you are willing to think and act like a rogue. You are not overly concerned about how others will perceive you. Instead, you are willing to step out on a limb to find a creative solution to the challenges you face.

SEE NEW WAYS OF DOING THINGS.

You are willing to question old habits and innovate in managing life's demands. You do not allow long-standing routines to dictate how you live your life. You are willing to try new approaches to see whether there are opportunities for greater performance in, and cohesiveness between, the different aspects of your life. You are willing to question your behaviors and to experiment with creative solutions for managing day-to-day as well as long-term goals.

EMBRACE CHANGE COURAGEOUSLY.

You look forward to change—seeing it as an opportunity—rather than fear it. You embrace opportunities for personal development. Rather than follow a strictly defined path, you realize that life takes unexpected twists and turns. You are confident that you will be able not only to survive the unexpected but also to thrive in new circumstances.

CREATE CULTURES OF INNOVATION.

You look for opportunities to encourage others to learn new ways of doing things. You encourage innovation wherever you go. Leading by example, you empower others to think creatively. You display both confidence and humility as you share with others your successes as

well as the obstacles you face. Your enthusiasm for learning is contagious, and your courage inspires others to seek out new opportunities.

————————

Although we've not gotten into specific examples of how these skills
are applied—that's a big part of what the rest of the book is about—
reading these basic descriptions should give you an initial understanding of these skills. Now let me ask you to review them again,
this time assessing yourself on each one. Rate yourself by writing
next to each skill a number from 1 to 5, using the scale shown, that
best describes whether you agree or disagree that the skill is a particular strength of yours. You can do this online using a tool developed
in partnership with Qualtrics at www.qualtrics.com/totalleadership.

1 = Strongly Disagree
2 = Disagree
3 = Neutral
4 = Agree
5 = Strongly Agree

If your total score is greater than 85, then I recommend you return
this book, although it still might be fun for you to learn more about the
people profiled here, who exemplify these skills (see the next section
for more detail on the profiles). And please get in touch with me so that
I can discover how you've mastered and applied these skills in your life.

If, on the other hand, you're like most of us—with a score between
35 and 85—then you have room to improve. And improve you can.
This may seem like a lot to absorb, and some of these skills may be
more obvious to you than others. In the chapters that follow, I flesh out
these skills for being real, being whole, and being innovative, describing and analyzing how six remarkable men and women exemplify
them in their lives. You will learn how these skills have allowed these

people, each in his or her own way, to mature over time into leaders of significance, to make their mark, and to find meaning in their lives.

Profiles of People Who Exemplify These Skills

To help you learn the skills and see them in action, the book starts, in Part I, with the stories of six extraordinary people: Tom Tierney, Sheryl Sandberg, Eric Greitens, Michelle Obama, Julie Foudy, and Bruce Springsteen (see "Six Models" for an introduction to these six people and the reasons they were chosen for this book). These individuals have found ways to integrate work and the rest of life, to achieve four-way wins, and to bring different areas of their lives into greater harmony. Taken together, the six exemplars illustrate what each skill looks like in action.

These profiles are based on extensive research into public information available—biographies, articles, books, and recorded interviews—as well as my own observations and interviews with the subject or individuals close to the subject. My goal is not to tell their entire life stories or provide complete pictures of them but rather to highlight key episodes in their lives that personify these skills. In this way, we can learn from their example how to apply the skills in our own lives.

Six Models

Each of these six models is a complicated mix of drives and desires, wants and weaknesses, confidence and self-scrutiny—just like you and me. And all of them are evolving. Let me introduce them and the skills they exemplify so you can begin to explore what you can learn from their lives, as led so far.

Tom Tierney

Envision Your Legacy, Weave Disparate
Strands, See New Ways of Doing Things

Tom Tierney is the chairman and co-founder of The Bridgespan Group, former CEO of the powerhouse global consulting firm Bain & Company, and co-author of the philanthropy guide *Give Smart*. Throughout his accomplished career, Tierney has sought creative ways of fitting together the domains of his life, including learning from his children about what really matters. He has built organizations that encourage personal growth by, for example, rewarding results and not face time and by motivating people with an inspiring vision of contribution to a greater good.

Sheryl Sandberg

Convey Values with Stories, Build Supportive
Networks, Resolve Conflicts among Domains

As COO of Facebook, Sheryl Sandberg has redefined what it means to be a leader. Especially now, following the launch of her book-cum-social movement, *Lean In*, she is a powerful advocate for new models for women's advancement in society, ideas she conveys with the confidence of a seasoned storyteller. Her candor about the challenges she faces in resolving conflicts among different parts of her life—as an executive, a catalyst for social change, a friend, a wife, a sister, and a mother—and about the nontraditional means she employs for doing so, make her a persuasive, if not controversial, role model.

Eric Greitens

Hold Yourself Accountable, Apply All Your
Resources, Focus on Results

Former Navy SEAL Eric Greitens, humanitarian, author, and founder of a nonprofit organization, has experienced many lifetimes' worth of adventure. He graduated from Duke, was both a Rhodes Scholar and a Truman scholar, and attended Oxford. After completing his

PhD, Greitens forsook high-paying career opportunities for a chance to become a Navy SEAL, enduring a stint of military training often referred to as the hardest in the world. For his service in Iraq he was awarded a Purple Heart, and—after a difficult search for a meaningful next step to take—he went on to found The Mission Continues, an organization that helps heal wounded war veterans by guiding them to be of service in their communities.

Michelle Obama

Align Actions with Values, Manage Boundaries
Intelligently, Embrace Change Courageously

Michelle Obama, the current First Lady of the United States and the first African American woman in this position, stepped carefully into the role. The self-described Mom-in-Chief explains that she considers her daughters to be her first priority, even if this stance rankles those who would have her do more in seeking broader political and cultural change. In making sure her own children were receiving the most nutritious food possible, she began to advocate for better nutrition through the national initiative Let's Move! Her policies have won national acclaim.

Julie Foudy

Know What Matters, Help Others, Challenge the Status Quo

Julie Foudy is a soccer champion who, in 1991, as a member of the US national team, won the first Women's World Cup. She was part of the iconic US soccer team that garnered Olympic gold in 1996, silver in 2000, and gold again in 2004. But Foudy is in this book because of what she has done beyond the soccer field. She has led an array of organizations that promote athletics for young people, empower young women, and advocate for social causes. Foudy's success is an outgrowth of her passion for soccer, her insistence on pursuing the most fruitful expression of her talents, and her ability to fuse all the important parts of her life—her soccer teams, her family, and her advocacy for worthy causes.

Bruce Springsteen

Embody Values Consistently, Clarify Expectations,
Create Cultures of Innovation

Although it may seem counterintuitive to think of a rock-and-roll hero as an exemplary leader, Bruce Springsteen is the real deal. Springsteen has said that he creates music "to make people happy, feel less lonely, but also [to be] a conduit for a dialogue about the events of the day, the issues that impact people's lives, personal and social and political and religious."[1] With his hard-won clarity of purpose, derived from years of painful self-scrutiny, it follows naturally that he makes clear what he expects from the people around him, whether members of his band or members of his family. He's called "The Boss" for a reason.

Learning from Their Example

Why did I decide to profile these six people as models for how to integrate work and the rest of life? As someone known as "the work/life balance guy," I get push-back almost everywhere I go, especially from high achievers. "Stew, it's nice to try to balance it all," they say to me, "but in the real world, c'mon: how can you have a substantial impact without making major sacrifices in your personal and family life?" I wanted to provide an answer to those who kept asking me for examples of people who have achieved great things and who are, in the common parlance, "balanced."

I set out to find familiar figures, role models (though certainly not universally liked) who have practiced, wittingly or unwittingly, the skills for integrating work and life, and who could help teach us all how we can cultivate these skills. The skills they've developed would enable any of us to be leaders living our lives on our own terms.

I began by generating a list of people who have demonstrated what it means to be real, to be whole, and to be innovative. I drew on biographies composed by my students, conversations with friends and colleagues, and my own research.[2] I culled the list many times to arrive, finally, at six men and women from different sectors (business, public service, and sports and entertainment).

There is no way, of course, that these few can be fully representative. I chose them as illustrative models. You don't have to identify with them to learn from their examples. You might even be tempted to shrug them off, because it's not easy to relate to people who have all the money in the world, beautiful and supportive spouses, bosses who really care about them, or supersized native talents. But their stories will open you up to new ways of thinking and acting. I'm sure you can think of others, and I hope you do; finding your own models will deepen your grasp of the skills in this book and of their practical value to you.

In each of their stories I found naturally occurring illustrations of people who did great things by discovering—usually through trial and error—ways to integrate the different parts of their lives so that they reinforced and enhanced each other. This book describes highlights of their life stories to show that even though they seem on the surface to be unusually talented, or just lucky, they are actually flawed people who have been engaged in a lifelong quest to align aspects of their lives through specific behaviors. Each chapter tells selected events of a life and analyzes how one person applied specific skills to carve a unique path. My analysis of each case will show you how to use these stories as guides. The first challenge for you in reading this book is to be curious about how their choices help you consider those you face. The second challenge is to start to practice the skills that have enabled them to lead the lives they truly want.

Still, you might be asking, Does it really make sense to try to learn leadership and life lessons from such extraordinary human beings?

These are not everyday people. But if you think their success derives only from great luck, think again. Not one of them was born into a life of high privilege. They have strived to achieve their own kind of greatness and, in one way or another, to make themselves into the people they are now. Each has suffered disappointment (half of them are on second marriages), frustration, doubt, and loss. They're human, after all. I imagine you will see possibilities for yourself in all of them.

These narratives show how accomplishment in a career is achievable not at the expense of the rest of your life, but because of commitments at home, in the community, and to your interior life. Each of these people is imperfect, more like you and me than you might imagine. Each has had a significant impact on the world beyond family, work, and the private self. And each strives to lead a meaningful life. All have made choices that integrate the different parts of their lives. This, in turn, results in both professional success and a full life that inspires them and enhances the lives of others.

Skeptics take heed. The lives of these sterling men and women in business (Tom Tierney and Sheryl Sandberg), in public service (Eric Greitens and Michelle Obama), and in sports and entertainment (Julie Foudy and Bruce Springsteen) defy the myth of the zero-sum game, in which success in your career means failure in the rest of your life, and vice versa. All of them, like the rest of us, have struggled, and their examples will help you see how you can cultivate a life in which values, actions, social contributions, and personal growth exist in harmony, like a great piece of jazz music. This is a life in which disparate pieces fall into place, not every day—that's the impossible myth of "work/life balance"—but over the course of time. Like these six, you can attain significant achievement in a way that fits the person you are. Indeed you must, because, as these leaders prove, your own way is the only way that will work for you.

How to Use This Book

Leading the Life You Want offers a new way of thinking as well as new practices that you can use now. Its purpose is to help you develop the skills you need to lead a life that you define as successful. In Part I, you'll look at how each of the six models has found a very personal way to pursue four-way wins—to integrate the different domains in mutually enriching ways—over the course of their lives. You'll see how, knowingly or intuitively, they learned, practiced, and applied discrete skills to achieve harmony in their complicated lives.

Even though each of their lives is different from yours, you will find ways to apply the lessons to your situation. These examples will help you muster the courage to initiate significant change because it's good for you as well as for the people around you. You can pick and choose which stories are of greatest interest, and you can read them in whatever order makes sense for you.

As you prepare to read about these great leaders, keep your baseline self-assessment at the ready as a point of reference. Take notes on how you see these skills in action in the lives of the people profiled here. As you read, write down your ideas about questions that arise, such as these:

- What is Tom Tierney's method for focusing on his legacy?

- How does Sheryl Sandberg's commitment to creating connections in the service of women's advancement help her company?

- When does Eric Greitens hold himself accountable for achieving meaningful results?

- Why does Michelle Obama manage the boundaries among her different roles?

TABLE I-1

Skills for integrating work and the rest of life illustrated by six models

Total Leadership principles	Tom Tierney	Sheryl Sandberg	Eric Greitens	Michelle Obama	Julie Foudy	Bruce Springsteen
Be real *Act with authenticity*	Envision your legacy.	Convey values with stories.	Hold yourself accountable.	Align actions with values.	Know what matters.	Embody values consistently.
Be whole *Act with integrity*	Weave disparate strands.	Build supportive networks.	Apply all your resources.	Manage boundaries intelligently.	Help others.	Clarify expectations.
Be innovative *Act with creativity*	See new ways of doing things.	Resolve conflicts among domains.	Focus on results.	Embrace change courageously.	Challenge the status quo.	Create cultures of innovation.

- How did Julie Foudy figure out what was important to her?

- What does Bruce Springsteen do to encourage innovation?

Then, Part II drills down into those skills, giving you simple ways to develop them yourself. You'll find concrete, actionable ideas—curated from the applied research in organizational psychology and related fields—for what you can do now to practice these skills. You don't need tons of money, the best boss, the most supportive spouse, or the greatest talent to apply these skills and thereby live with a richer sense of significance, strengthened resilience, and a more hopeful outlook on the future. It may not be possible to have it all—indeed, it surely is not—but with this set of skills it is possible to have more of it.

These skills may be useful, too, if you want to show others how they can act in ways that make things better not only for them personally but also for their families, their communities, *and* their work.

You can decide which skills to focus on first, based on your own analysis of the skills you most want to develop. Use table I-1 to locate where in the book each skill is illustrated by our models.

Leading the life you want is a craft. As with music or writing or dance, or any athletic endeavor, you can always get better at it. Some of us start with greater natural assets than others—a strong body, a gift for creative thinking, a conscientious personality, or mathematical ability. Some of us are helped by genetic endowment and by what we have learned from parents, role models, and mentors. But this capacity can be learned by any individual. In fact, it must be.

As you'll see next, in Part I, it is the drive to take what they have and use it to enrich the world around them that has given our six models the will to compose, just as an author does, their own stories. Let's see how they have exploited the power of getting the different parts of their lives humming together.

Models for Integrating Work and the Rest of Life

1

Tom Tierney

Envision Your Legacy,
Weave Disparate Strands,
See New Ways of Doing Things

It's still dark outside when Tom Tierney rises in his home outside Boston on a December morning. He dresses quietly, so as not to wake his wife, Karen, and goes to the kichen to brew some coffee. At fifty-nine, Tierney is trim and retains a certain boyishness, helped by the rimless glasses, a full head of hair, and boundless energy. He carries a mug and the fresh pot into his office and closes the door. It's 5:15 a.m., time to begin the ritual of writing what he calls his "annual review."

The term reflects Tierney's lifetime in business: the Harvard MBA, two decades at the consulting firm Bain & Company (including eight years as chief executive), and fourteen years as cofounder and guiding spirit of the nonprofit Bridgespan. But he doesn't write this personal document with the notion that it should be legible for anybody else. "It's just for me," he told me in a long interview a few years ago.[1] "I ask how I spent my time. And I ask how I'm doing. And then I ask, 'Where am I going with all this? How can I be better? What are my priorities for the next year? Five years? Ten years?'" The annual review is more than a career assessment; it might include personal goals or thoughts about how his two sons are doing. The ritual reflects the qualities that Tierney is known for: discipline, self-reflection, an ability to think big and creatively, and a dedication to personal development, his own and others'.

As he works, he goes back through journal entries that he's written on cross-country flights and in other spare moments. Tierney, who has been journaling for decades, believes the practice helps him record meaningful data. "I keep track of every single travel day, of every day that I'm home after seven, and of how many nights I'm away and what's causing that." But it also helps him think through bigger life questions, track his progess toward long-term goals, and capture ideas and dreams about what might be.

In an entry from 1988, for instance, Tierney—who was then running the San Francisco office of Bain & Company—wrote about what he called a "Make a Difference Company." The idea percolated in Tierney's mind and kept surfacing in his journal until 1999, when Bridgespan was born, initially as a start-up incubated within Bain.

The Bridgespan Group is most easily described as a nonprofit version of Bain Consulting—an organization that provides services such as strategic consulting and leadership development to philanthropists, foundations, and nonprofit organizations. Now in its second decade, Bridgespan helps many nonprofit clients and is what Duke University's Joel Fleishman (a Tierney coauthor) calls "the gold standard in nonprofit consulting."[2] That category hardly existed at its founding, but today the Bill & Melinda Gates Foundation (a Bridgespan client) and hundreds of other ventures in social entrepreneurialism have joined Bridgespan in chipping away at the notion that standard practices from the for-profit world—let alone successful business leaders—have no place in philanthropy and the social sector.

When Tierney left his job as Worldwide Managing Director at Bain & Company in 2000 for Bridgespan it was, he said, "not a natural act." Yet Tierney has always believed that the notion of a person's predetermined track is "hogwash." Instead, he said, "You're on your own track."[3]

Building His Own Track

Tom Tierney was born in San Francisco, the older of two boys. His father had gone to college thanks to the GI Bill and worked at a Colgate-Palmolive factory that manufactured toothpaste. His mother, nominally a stay-at-home mom, volunteered for a long time as president of Sunny Hills Junior Auxiliary, helping troubled high school girls for as many as forty hours a week.[4] Tierney's family was solidly working class. "I remember being aware of the fact that we didn't have a new car and other families did," Tierney said. When he asked about this, his father told him, "It's not what you have in life that matters, it's who you are. And who you are in life is dependent not on what you say, but what you do."

College didn't initially appeal to Tierney; he dreamed of joining the Peace Corps. But his parents felt strongly about it, so strongly that the elder Tierney filled out much of his son's college application forms.[5] Tom Tierney was accepted at the University of California at Davis, where he arrived as a freshman in the fall of 1972, planning to major in engineering. But some early science classes didn't bode well. He recalls seeing the results of an exam for a chemistry class, when the long list of grades was posted on a wall, with the best scores at the top. He found his name near the bottom. "I don't want to be here," he thought. "I don't know why I am here. This is hard. I'm not smart enough. I don't know how to work any harder. Do I drop out?"

Walking home that day along a bike path, he heard someone whistling behind him. When he turned to look, he saw a fellow student in a wheelchair. "If he can whistle," Tierney thought, "I can whistle." Tierney stayed in school, although he switched his major to economics, graduating with honors. Unsure of the next step, he kept his job driving a bus, a job he'd had all through college.[6] It was a great job, he's told many audiences since. But he itched to travel. He had crossed the California border only twice: bound once for Reno, Nevada, and once for Tijuana. So after bumping into a friend whose father worked for Bechtel, he applied for a job at the global engineering firm.

"When the guy gave me the job," Tierney recalled decades later, "he said, 'We're going to send you to Algeria.' And I must have had this funny look, because he said, 'You don't know where that is, do you?' I said, 'Sir, I don't, but I'm sure it's not in California.'"[7] Less than two weeks later, Tierney landed in the northern African country as the newest field engineer at the construction site of one of the world's largest natural gas plants.[8] The assignment allowed him to acquire project-management skills, and his two years there, he says, gave him "ten years of experience." During vacations, he traveled throughout North, West, and East Africa, as well as to Europe and the Mediterranean. The period, as he put it to the authors of a Harvard Business School case, taught him "a lot about people and a lot about life."[9]

But when Bechtel offered Tierney a three-year contact to build facilities at a new natural gas site in the Sahara, he was ready for a change. He applied to business school, earning a spot at Harvard. "I was the only Algerian application that year," he told my Wharton class, explaining how he got in. "And I aced the TOEFL exam."[10]

Tierney, who had wanted to go to Stanford Business School but didn't get in, felt hesitant about going to an Ivy League institution. But his mother, who had never been to college or to New England, told him, "If you can get into Harvard, you should go to Harvard." So he did. Harvard Business School felt more foreign to Tierney than Algeria. "I understood construction, I understood blue collar stuff, I was very, very comfortable swearing," he recalled in a 2012 business school talk. "And [I] end up in Cambridge, which was different. Quite a bit different. I had to wear a coat, and some people called me Mister Tierney. It was bizarre."[11]

Growing Up at Bain

Tierney says that he initially "struggled through business school," although he did well enough to land a job at Bain after graduating with distinction in 1980, in the top 10 percent of his class. But the feeling of being a social misfit followed him to Bain. People who worked closely with the budding executive admired his integrity and discipline. They recognized his value to the firm. But in the eyes of some partners, Tierney didn't look like an executive, nor did he act like one. At his first review, he was told that of the twenty-five associates hired in his year, the partners had ranked him twenty-fifth. He told me that the partner reviewing him said, "I know you're rough. I just don't know if there is a diamond in there."

But Tierney took heart. There had been no criticism of his work, only of superficial things like his appearance, his lack of polish, his behavior. Tierney, who has since described Bain as his "finishing school," knew that he could learn to be an executive. And with dedicated effort and coaching, he did, becoming a partner in three years—a record.

Although Tierney was thrilled to make partner, the transition was no easier than his initial entry into the firm or into HBS. "You would expect a partner to be a paragon of wisdom and experience; I was twenty-nine years old. You would expect a partner to be polished and smooth like a Wall Street lawyer or investment banker; I was anything but," he said in the HBS case. It was a job he had to grow into. He began taking sales training classes and hired a clothing consultant. He was told in no uncertain terms to get rid of his white socks. Not a natural rainmaker, he left the client schmoozing to other partners and gravitated toward work that played to his strengths, becoming what he describes as the "unofficial chief operating officer" of the San Francisco office. He began managing professional development and helped institute a new performance-review system.

As a manager, Tierney encouraged employees not to work all the time or let their vacation days languish. "You want to have people there for years and years and years," he said to me, reflecting on his philosophy. "You want them to be productive. You want them not to burn out. You don't want people to turn into little piles of dust. They have to be fulfilled on multiple dimensions."[12]

This was a period of personal growth for Tierney as well. He had fallen in love with Karen McGee, a television executive, and, in 1984, the couple married. In 1987—the same year their first son, Colin, was born—Tierney, then thirty-three, was promoted to head of the one-hundred-person San Francisco office. Although he prided himself on his project-management skills, not all of his colleagues appreciated them, and one day a young partner came to his office, uninvited, to give him feedback. "You're a steamroller," she told Tierney. "You're rolling over people. You're being too controlling."[13] That young partner was Meg Whitman, current CEO of Hewlett-Packard.

She was right, Tierney realized after thinking about her comments for a couple of days. He loosened his management style, focusing not on what the members of his team were doing but on what he could do to help them succeed. John Donahoe, current CEO of eBay, also worked in the San Francisco office at the time; like most consultants, he spent most of his week on the road visiting clients. Donahoe reached a critical juncture at Bain, he told me recently, when his wife earned a prestigious year-long clerkship that would have made it impossible for her to take the couple's children to school. He went to Tierney to explain that he could no longer travel and would have to resign. "You're an idiot. You don't need to quit," Tierney said to him. "We'll get you a local client."[14] There weren't any local clients, Donahoe pointed out, but Tierney promised to find one—and within two weeks, he had. Donahoe stayed at Bain, working part-time that year, and went on to succeed Tierney as head of the San Francisco office.

If the first few months as head of the office had tested Tierney's leadership skills, they also tested his ability to live the kind of life he valued: being with his wife and sons, giving back to the community, and carving out quiet moments for himself. Time, Tierney says, is a scarce resource. "The job will not say, 'You are doing too much work, you need to cut back,'" he said. "A three-year-old will not tell you, 'I need a bigger share of your time.'"[15]

To ensure that he was spending his days wisely, Tierney created what he calls "magnets": commitments that he took as seriously as a partner meeting. One magnet was exercise; Tierney set out time exclusively for himself every morning for a workout. His wife and sons represented a second magnet, and, to protect his time with them, Tierney decided that he would not go into the office on weekends. "Over the course of my career, I maybe went into the office on a weekend ten to fifteen times," he told me. That doesn't mean he never did any work on weekends. He might read something or answer e-mails, but any work had to fit around his family's weekend activities, from Little League and soccer games to Boy Scout camping trips.

Tierney also began exploring avenues for community service. He started volunteering for the United Way of the Bay Area, an effort that led to Bain's first pro bono client. Tierney eventually joined the nonprofit's board, the first of several on which he would serve.

The Struggle to Rebuild

In his thirties, everything appeared to be falling into place for Tierney. He was happily married. He loved fatherhood, once telling me (while struggling to hold back tears) that raising a family "opens up what's important."[16] He had succeeded at Bain far beyond the partners' early expectations, and Bain itself was expanding rapidly. By the early 1980s, Bain had about forty vice presidents as well as offices in Boston, San Francisco, London, Tokyo, and Munich. But not everything was as it seemed. In the mid-1980s, Bain's seven directors—who together owned the firm—had created an employee stock plan that would distribute shares, giving a greater number of employees an ownership stake. The directors sold 30 percent of the company's shares to the newly created stock trust, which bought the shares through bank loans that would be paid with cash from Bain's revenues. But Bain's growth slumped along with the rest of the economy in the late 1980s, and the company didn't react quickly enough. Accustomed to fast growth, Bain, in Tierney's words, "had an accelerator but no brake."[17] Soon the company's liabilities—including rent, salaries, and debt related to the stock plan—threatened the firm's future. Only the small group of directors knew exactly how bad things were.

In 1990, Tierney learned the truth. "It was devastating," he recalled. "My first thoughts were, 'I'm wiped out. I have a mortgage to pay on my house. I have a three-year-old child. My wife has quit her job to be a full-time mom. I head an office of one hundred professionals whose future is now in jeopardy.'"[18]

For several weeks, Tierney grappled with whether to stay or go. "Sometime during the weeks of indecision, the issue stopped being about money or my job; seeing this through became an issue of values, integrity, and reputation," he recalled. "I decided that no matter what, I would do my part to help Bain succeed."[19] He vowed to stay with the company until it was on stronger footing and then leave.

Mitt Romney, then head of Bain's sister company, Bain Capital, stepped in as interim CEO to help get the consulting firm back on its feet. By the fall of 1991, the financial restructuring was essentially complete and Romney was itching to return to Bain Capital. But first the consulting firm needed a new leader. Romney, among others, wanted that leader to be Tierney. This posed yet another moment of soul-searching for Tierney. "Faced with a choice like that, what do you do? Me, I pray. And I talk to my wife. We talked and talked and talked."[20] Eventually he agreed to become president and chief operating officer of the company for a trial year.

During that year, Tierney officially lived in San Francisco, but he spent 220 nights on the road, tending to Bain's offices around the world. "I killed myself traveling. At some points I felt like I was running for office," he said. "At other points, I felt like I was just bailing out a leaky boat as fast as I could just to keep it afloat."[21] One day that June, Tierney arrived home from a two-week business trip, to be greeted by his wife Karen and an ultimatum: "You're gone all the time. We've got a five year-old son. This isn't going to work. Something's got to change."[22] The partners in Boston wanted a change, too. They needed the head of the firm back in Boston. So, for professional and personal reasons, the Tierneys moved east.

The company was still in decline, and, in contrast to his role in the San Francisco office, where he knew everyone well, Tierney was now running a global organization and herding partners, most of whom didn't know him personally and some of whom hadn't voted for him to take the helm. Tierney had to learn how to "exert influence as opposed to control" and how to manage "by remote control," as he told me.[23] It was a challenging time.

But the firm was on sounder financial footing, and, as the economy picked up, so did Bain's fortunes. The firm grew at 30 percent a year from 1992 through 1998, a year in which Bain raked in more than $500 million in revenues.[24] Tierney oversaw a global expansion, adding fourteen offices around the world, and instituted an internal training program to ensure that "Bainees" at every level were continuing to learn.

Still, that business success took a toll on Tierney's family, which now included a second son, Braden. "I don't know anybody who, later in their career, says, 'I wish I'd spent five percent more time at work and five percent less time with my family,'" said Tierney in 2008. "I don't think I've ever heard that sentence. Kids make that trade-off starker. There's a cost to it. If I'm not there, I'm just not there. I can't say, 'I'll make it up to you when you're forty.'"[25] Tierney tried to be as present as possible for his family. "He's taken more red-eyes than your average person," Karen, his wife, told me. And when he had to leave, "we could always count on a little love note left on the kitchen counter."[26]

Looking back at that period, Tierney described it as "extremely stressful and not always healthy" and admits he doesn't know how much longer he could have sustained it.[27] "My moment came in the mid-nineties," Tierney told John Kobara, when "a very, very thoughtful person asked me, 'What if you had ten years to live? Would you keep doing what you're doing?'" That person was John Gardner, who, as secretary of health in the Johnson administration, helped create Medicare and later went on to found Common Cause. Gardner's question stuck with Tierney, who kept asking himself, "What is my life about? What's my legacy?" "He's on my short list of heroes," said Tierney of Gardner, adding that Gardner's questions "gave me courage to follow my path."[28]

Crossing the Bridge

In October 1999, Tierney sat down to record a voice mail to Bain's two hundred partners around the world. He told them that he would not seek a third term as CEO and, moreover, that he was going half-time to give more of himself to Bridgespan. He had co-written the business plan for the nonprofit while at Bain. In fact, the company had supported his effort, bringing his Bridgespan cofounder, Jeff Bradach, on to the payroll in the early months and giving the fledgling team office space.

Soon after Tierney sent the voice mail, two partners came into his Boston office, closed the door, and asked him if he was OK. "They honestly thought I'd received bad news from the doctor," he told me recently. "To leave this company that was growing thirty-five percent per year, with twenty-two hundred people in twenty-plus countries? It was going well—I had all these perks." To join a start-up charity with three other people for no pay struck the partners as irrational.

Next, he received a call from a headhunter in Silicon Valley, who told him, "I can get you a job. I guarantee you two hundred million dollars in two years."[29] Tierney was, by his own admission, "really messed up."[30] He asked his wife whether he was being stupid. Her response was direct, even if extreme, to make the point: "Listen, if we need to live in a trailer, we'll live in a trailer. We've got to do what's right."[31]

"It was messy," Tierney said to me in retrospect. "I struggled. But eventually you come back to who you are as a human being, and you come back to that question: How do you define success?"[32]

For Tierney the idea that service was important had been planted early by his parents. His father had served in World War II. His mother had volunteered. "I am sure that one of the reasons that I was attracted to consulting is that it is a helping profession," he said to me, reflecting on the impact of his parents. "And one of the reasons that I was attracted to general management was that it felt to me that my mission as an executive was to create an environment where other people could succeed."[33] For Tierney, Bridgespan offered an opportunity to use his specific skills to serve a broader community.

The organization was formally launched in September 2000. Within nine months of its founding, Bridgespan raised $7 million in financing, hired twenty-seven employees, and expanded to a West Coast office.[34] Jeff Bradach served as Bridgespan's CEO, overseeing day-to-day operations while Tierney served as its chairman. "It was clear to me that for Jeff to succeed as CEO, I could *not* be in his neighborhood," Tierney told me, explaining why he continued to work for two-plus years from his Bain office, two blocks away, while supporting Bridgespan's launch. "I could help with strategy, I could do fund-raising, and I could work with clients."[35]

The Edna McConnell Clark Foundation was Bridgespan's first client. For decades, the foundation had worked to improve the lives of people in low-income communities through grants to organizations that fought poverty, improved schools, and strengthened communities in the United States and the developing world. To ensure that its funding was making an impact, Bridgespan helped the foundation narrow the scope of its work and develop tools to measure the results of its grantees. Today, Bridgespan's clients include the Bill & Melinda Gates Foundation, the Salvation Army, the YMCA, and hundreds more. To help nonprofits that can't afford to pay for its services, Bridgespan also makes case studies of its work freely available. Indeed, a central tenet of its social mission is to generate and distribute useful knowledge throughout the social sector— through articles, books, an award-winning Web site, speeches, and conferences.

Bringing It All Together

On a late January day in 2012, Tierney took the stage at the Georgia Tech School of Management as part of the school's Impact Speaker Series.[36] "Hi everybody," he greeted the audience, as he dropped his printed speech onto the lecturn—pages he wouldn't touch until ten minutes into his talk. "My name's Tom, and I want to be useful to you," he said as he removed his jacket and hung it on a chair.

Tierney's talk began with a subject that the student audience might not necessarily have been thinking about, as he admitted to them. "'Philanthropy?' you might say," he said, scratching his head. "'I don't have any money. I have debts.'" Then, without stopping, he launched into his stump speech about service and the role it's played in his life, drawing the throughline from his childhood values to the choice he made to walk away from a million-dollar paycheck to work for free for a nonprofit.

Tierney's story—and the lesson he wanted his listeners to take away—was that a fulfilling life does not consist of three separate serial phases in which you learn, then you earn, and then you serve. "The fact is," he said in a 2008 interview, "you ought to be learning continuously. You earn, but you earn in different ways and different amounts." He then added a rhetorical question: "Why does serving wait until you're sixty-five or seventy?"[37]

Tierney is especially troubled by the idea of service as an afterthought—something you do after you retire. "That serving bit was just as important to me, and I wasn't going to just leave it for the dessert at dinner. I wanted it as part of the main course," he said.[38]

But he doesn't merely want people to give their money away earlier; he wants them to give their money in a way that is smarter, that has more impact, and that, to use a term from the business world, gives donors a higher ROI (return on investment). Some philanthropists see giving as an end in itself, and they don't focus on the results of their gifts, he said. But the nonprofit world also lacks what Tierney calls market feedback. "If you own a restaurant and put something on the menu, you're going to know in short order whether your customers like it or not," he said.[39] Philanthropy lacks such immediate, tangible feedback. As a result, Tierney says, it tends to underperform.

Tierney has been talking about these issues a lot lately, alongside Joel Fleishman, professor of law at Duke University, whom Tierney affectionately describes as his "Jewish godfather." Fleishman helped fund Bridgespan when he was at Atlantic Philanthropies, and, more recently, the two coauthored a book called *Give Smart*. "We believe that all philanthropy is deeply personal," they wrote. "By asking the right questions . . . you will be far more likely to achieve the change you want to bring about in the world."[40]

Fleishman says Tierney has "an unbelievable knack" for conveying these lessons in simple language and commonsense analogies.[41] The notion that nonprofits should have as little overhead as possible still dominates the philanthropic world. In one of their joint speeches, Fleishman recalls, Tierney said, "It's like deciding to fly on the airline with the least maintenance." This made the concept easy to grasp.

In all of his talks, Tierney questions this conventional wisdom, arguing that there is bad overhead (say, paying for swank office space) and good overhead (such as investing in technology to track results). Tierney counsels philanthropists not to place restrictions on how their donation can be spent (Sheryl Sandberg, for one, heeded this sage advice). Tierney urges them to focus instead on results, asking grantees to agree to certain performance milestones.

"I hope that every philanthropist asks him- or herself, on a regular basis, 'How can I double my impact with the time, money, and influence at my disposal?'" he once told a reporter. "If every philanthropist does that . . . and as a result, we boost the results achieved by philanthropy by ten percent, can you imagine?" He continued, "That's like adding hundreds of billions of dollars of new philanthropy—smarter philanthropy—that achieves better results for our communities and our country. That would be a legacy to be proud of."[42]

The Skills Tom Tierney Exemplifies

Examining his life philosophy in his journal, Tierney once wrote, "Those that succeed build lives first and résumés second. When they stare in the mirror, they don't see just a professional; they see a parent, a spouse, a friend, and a member of the community."[43] Tierney knows that a leader plays many roles in life, and he seems to revel in the complex task of finding creative ways to make them work well together. He has traveled a winding path from inconsistent student to California bus driver, engineer in the Algerian desert to Harvard MBA, consultant to high-flying CEO, author to full-time charitable volunteer. He's been a perpetual traveler, a devoted father, and a significant mentor to people who are great leaders in their own right.

All along his remarkable journey, Tierney's deep-seated values, on which he regularly and critically reflects, guide him like a lodestar. The disciplined creativity he applies to his commitments large and small enables him to learn as he joyfully serves others, with stellar results. He has faced obstacles and made mistakes, fallen down and gotten up again. At every juncture, he has adopted the same approach, asking others and himself, "Am I getting better?"[44] Then he has taken the steps necessary to answer positively. He contributes his boundless energy and keen intellect to the people and things that matter to him by envisioning his legacy, weaving the domains of his life together coherently, and seeing new ways of doing things. Although Tierney is an exemplar of numerous other skills, let's dig further into these three. Then, in Part II, I give you concrete suggestions for ways you can make them part of your repertoire.

Be Real: Envision Your Legacy

Tom Tierney has a vision for where he is headed, what kind of legacy he wants to leave, and how to pursue what is most important in life. Tierney knows not only where he's been but also where he's going. He can paint a vivid picture of the life he wants to lead, visualizing himself in five, ten, and even twenty years. Not only does he have a compelling image of an achievable future, but also he has a sense of how to achieve that vision. Although he may not have all the details figured out, he understands the values that will guide him on the path to realizing his dreams.

A leader living the life he wants needs to form an optimistic and yet realistic picture of the world he wants to create. Tierney's dedication to journaling—and the practical knowledge that emerges from his rigorous self-examination—demonstrates how he goes about envisioning a future that makes sense to him, a future that is congruent with the person he wants to be and how he wants to be remembered.

Tierney's focus on his own evolution is displayed in the decisions he's made. For example, in 1990, during the crisis at Bain, he resolved to stay because he knew that his departure would be a devastating signal of indifference to the long-term interests of the firm. Some years later, after Bain found its footing and then some, at the peak of Tierney's powers as CEO, he chose to leave in the prime of his career and launch a small nonprofit start-up—not a standard move in the eyes of many in the elite world of top-tier consulting firms.

Why did he do it? The new venture allowed him to apply his mastery to help causes closer to his core values. And as Bridgespan spread its wings—as he multiplied his impact by enabling others to help those in need—Tierney saw yet greater opportunity to use his energy, talent, and networks. He dreamed of doing even greater good by reimagining the world of philanthropy. Today, by teaching wealthy people who want to help others the lessons he's learned from his own experience about how to focus on and create a future that matters, his impact as a leader of positive social change ripples outward.

Be Whole: Weave Disparate Strands

Tom Tierney weaves together the pieces of his life so that it has coherence. He views all the aspects of his life as interconnected and mutually enriching. He understands how different roles complement each other. He has a sense that all aspects of his life are integral parts of the person he is, and integral to his efforts.

Tierney's life illustrates ways to harness the different domains of life into a coherent whole. One example is his ongoing pursuit of opportunities to seek work that gives credence to his core value of producing social good. Another is the way he ensures that the most precious people in his life—his wife and children—are lodged deeply in his consciousness and receive his attention. And a third is the way he invests in developing the capacity of others to fit together the domains of *their* lives.

From volunteering for the United Way early in his career to serving on numerous nonprofit boards and founding Bridgespan, Tierney has sought the chance to serve society through his work. Throughout his professional life he has moved ever closer to achieving simultaneous four-way wins: actions that benefit work, home, community, and self, all at once. As a guest at the one-year anniversary celebration of the publication of *Give Smart*, I saw this play out as family, friends, colleagues, philanthropists, beneficiaries of charity, and others were all together in the same place to advance a common cause.

Interpersonal presence comes in two forms: physical and psychological. It's possible to be physically present with others while being psychologically absent. Of course, both forms of presence matter when it comes to demonstrating love and to making one's family a real and ongoing part of one's life. Tierney realized early, through hard lessons, that he had to be vigilant about protecting the time for his family, so he commited to being physically absent from his office on weekends. With few exceptions, he found ways to ensure that he was home and that, after hours, work matters were secondary to his family's activities, from sports to Boy Scouts. Indeed, he shepherded both of his sons to Eagle Scout, the highest rank. And even when yet another red-eye flight wouldn't get him home, or when he determined that he just had to travel, he stayed in touch and maintained a psychological presence through messages that let Karen, Colin, and Braden know that he was thinking of them.

And Tierney hasn't just taken up the task of weaving his own domains together; he's helped others do the same. He knows, from a business perspective, that it's not a good idea to burn people out. Finding John Donahoe a local client so that he wouldn't have to travel is a good example of a creative solution Tierney found to a dilemma faced by one of his key people. He also devotes time to teaching MBA students the lessons of his own experience, guiding them to integrate the pieces in ways that work for them. Recently, he's been honored to serve in the Class of 1951 Chair for the Study of Leadership at West Point, where he teaches seminars on life and leadership. For leaders living the lives they want, it's all of piece.

Be Innovative: See New Ways of Doing Things

Tom Tierney is willing to question old habits and to innovate in managing life's demands. He does not allow long-standing routines to dictate how he lives his life. He is willing to explore opportunities for greater performance in, and cohesiveness between, the different aspects of his life. He is willing to question his behaviors and to experiment with solutions for managing day-to-day as well as long-term needs.

Tierney shows how to try new things to get closer to your aspirations. He says that predetermined tracks are bunk and that you've got to chop through the weeds to make your own path. Tierney is an avid learner and a true student of his own life. He continually feeds his curiosity by observing people and the world around him.

This openness, coupled with a fearless quest for knowledge about himself, was certainly there when he landed in northern Africa on a quickly conceived adventure and then entered an even stranger country at Harvard Business School. Tierney's openness to change blossomed later, when he learned how to look the part of a business professional, then how to be a partner, and then how to be a very effective executive. He learned from negative feedback. After Meg Whitman told him he was a steamroller, he drew a picture of a steamroller on his calendar every day and, at the end of each day, crossed off the picture if he had not steamrolled anyone that day.[45]

And now, in the world of philanthopy, he continues to scour the world for best practices and has created a video interview series that shares them.[46] He rejected the traditional assumption of trade-offs implied by the "learn-earn-serve" model of personal development and has shown how it's good for you to *always* be learning, earning, and serving, even if in different measures along the way. By persistently rejecting traditional ways of doing things, Tierney has demonstrated what being innovative truly means.

When I asked people who know Tom Tierney well to describe him, the word I heard most often was *disciplined*. He has dedicated serious attention to asking himself, "How do I define real success in my life?" After he answers this question, he acts on what he says. Perhaps this is why in the world of philanthropy he finds himself, once again, to be the beating heart of an enterprise devoted to using available resources to make things better for others.

With his penchant for tracking almost everything he cares about, Tierney knows exactly where he stands in pursuit of his most critical goals. He reflects on his failures and his successes and then looks at the day ahead, and the next day, and the next week, and the next month, and the next year, to see whether he's on target. Then he adjusts accordingly, even if it means walking away from positions with great power and income.

Tierney, whose father taught him to believe in the little guy, preaches the ideology that employees are people first, with lives that matter. And he applies that to his own life, putting his family first. This commitment to his life beyond work didn't detract from his career success; to the contrary, it fortified his capacity as a business executive and inspired others, animating his achievements at work and in society. The four domains of his life all win.

I refer to Tierney as a visionary consultant. But a more apt appellation might be something like great student, because his avid thirst for useful knowledge has made it possible for him to evolve, to continually become the person he wants to become, while never forgetting his purpose: to serve, something all of us are capable of doing better.

2

Sheryl Sandberg

Convey Values with Stories,
Build Supportive Networks,
Resolve Conflicts among Domains

I can't code. I'm not very technical," acknowledged Sheryl Sandberg, COO of Facebook and, at the time, the lone woman on the company's board of directors. She was addressing a tech-savvy audience gathered at the Grace Hopper Celebration of Women in Computing conference. "For my fortieth birthday, my husband gave me a lifetime of tech support, no complaining. The no complaining part was actually important because he had been providing tech support already—but there was a *lot* of complaining [on his part]," she said, smiling broadly.[1]

Clouds had pressed down on Portland, Oregon, as Sandberg arrived to deliver the keynote, even as the forecast—"clouds today, sunshine tomorrow"—promised a brighter future. And so did Sandberg, who had come not to talk up her company or opine on the future of social media but to encourage the women in the audience to think differently about their work, their personal lives, and, more generally, the growing importance of technical skills. The forty-two-year-old leader owned the stage, walking slowly as she spoke. Her voice commanded respect, even as she admitted her own deficiency, using her hands to reiterate the point. "I would be better at my job if I were more technical."

The speech was classic Sandberg, an inspiring mix of stories and statistics, ranging from the dearth of women in corporate leadership to the oppression of girls around the world, delivered in a sometimes humorous, always humble tone. As a business leader, Sandberg has been described as "tough" and "fearless." But her manner is warm, open, friendly—even enthusiastic.

It was a speech she gave regularly after Facebook CEO Mark Zuckerberg convinced her to become the company's chief operating officer in 2008. Even before becoming a celebrated author and household name in 2013 with her book, *Lean In*, Sandberg was much more than merely a COO; she was the public face of the company, and the one responsible for many tasks that would be handled by a CEO if that CEO weren't a publicity-averse twenty-seven-year-old who preferred coding and corporate strategy to management. Hiring, firing, and the nitty-gritty of operations, growth, and revenue were skills Sandberg had honed in her previous job as vice president for global online sales and operations at Google.

Although the jury may still be out on the future of Facebook, Sandberg is credited with helping Zuckerberg transform the popular networking site into a real business. In 2008, the year Sandberg arrived, Facebook had 70 million users but not much revenue. As of this writing, it is worth more than $100 billion, counts more than 1.2 billion monthly active users, and earned more than $1 billion in net income on $6.9 billion in revenue over the past twelve months. As Charlie Rose pointed out, "If Facebook was a country it would be the third largest in the world."[2]

Few would have predicted such success for the social media company. "There was this open question," Sandberg told the *New Yorker*'s Ken Auletta in 2011. "Could we make money, ever?"[3] The engineers were more interested in building a cool site than developing a business plan, and Zuckerberg and the rest of the executive team were wary of advertising, especially after the launch of Beacon, a controversial feature that shared users' purchases with their Facebook friends.

After she was hired, Sandberg set up a weekly meeting with senior executives to address the issue of profitability, and she laid out two paths: charge users, or sell ads. Soon she had Facebook's leaders agreeing that advertising, delivered in a subtle way that didn't violate individual privacy, was the way forward.

But Sandberg didn't just make Facebook profitable. She cemented her image as a leader whom people want to work for. She spent her first two weeks at Facebook introducing herself to all of the existing employees. As Auletta observed, her "office" is a desk pushed together with the desks of Zuckerberg and three other executives in an open space. Anyone can walk up and talk to her.

Simultaneously demanding and nurturing, Sandberg believes in bringing her whole self to work. That means, for one thing, standing up for her values. In the male-dominated culture of Facebook, Sandberg isn't afraid to be an outspoken voice for women and the issues they often face in the workplace. She established a Women's Leadership Day that would encourage Facebook's female executives to talk about challenges they face as they try climb the corporate ladder and to share solutions.[4] *Lean In* is filled with practical advice for women—drawing on illustrations from her life and backed up by current social science—for how to succeed at the highest levels by not taking a back seat. Instead, she writes, women should courageously speak up, speak out, and insist on being heard.

As an executive, bringing her whole self to work also means acknowledging that both she and her employees have lives outside of Facebook's offices and that the two domains need not be in perennial conflict. She once stopped a promising young female recruit from walking out the door by saying, "If you're not taking this job because you want to have a baby soon, let's talk."[5]

And it means sharing the lessons of her experience. At the performance review of a female executive who was being told that she needed to be more assertive, Sandberg opened up: "I don't know what you're feeling, but I can imagine what it might be. Let me tell you about when I was younger . . ." The COO proceeded to talk about her own struggles with confidence and the solutions she had uncovered after years of trial and error.[6]

In Beta

Sandberg was born August 28, 1969, a birthday she shared with her maternal grandmother and role model, whom she calls Grandma Roz. She was "not the typical doting Jewish grandmother," Sandberg wrote in a Facebook status update. Born in 1917 to a very poor family, the young Grandma Roz scrubbed floors in the boarding house where she lived to help earn money. Decades later, in the 1970s, she saved her family financially when the family business was struggling. In between, she graduated from Berkeley, raised three children, lived through breast cancer, and became an active fund-raiser for causes fighting the disease. "In another era, when girls had more opportunity, I can only imagine what she would have accomplished," added Sandberg in her status update. Nevertheless, her grandmother was a huge part of the encouragement Sandberg got early on, fostering her belief that she could do anything she wanted to do.

Sandberg's childhood was normal in many ways: her parents—an ophthalmologist and a stay-at-home-mom—were comfortably middle

class. Sandberg and her two siblings went to public schools in sub-
urban North Miami Beach. She studied hard but felt uncomfortable
when she was voted "Most Likely to Succeed" in twelfth grade. In
fact, she writes in *Lean In,* she convinced the editor of the yearbook,
who happened to be her friend, to give the title to someone else.

In 1972, at the request of the rabbi at her family's synagogue,
her parents, Joel and Adele Sandberg, helped found the South
Florida Conference on Soviet Jewry. The family home became a
virtual hotel for newly emigrated Soviet Jews. Sandberg's mother
often supplied travelers with white chocolate bars disguised as
soap to smuggle to Russian dissidents so that they could then sell
them on the black market to raise funds. Sandberg credits her
childhood for her strong sense of the importance of the rights
and privileges of freedom and democracy, her belief that she was
lucky to have been born in the United States, and her feeling
that she owed something back to the world.[7] Indeed, when I said
to Adele Sandberg that she must be very proud of her daughter,
the elder Sandberg replied, "People tell me that all the time—
how proud I must be—but what I really care about is what I told
Sheryl growing up: 'It doesn't matter what you do, I just want you
to be a mensch.'"[8] That Sheryl Sandberg internalized this idea
of embodying the Yiddish word for a good person, someone who
does the right thing, became evident in her young adult years. Her
grandmother's ideal continues to guide her professional and philanthropic decisions.

Sandberg was the oldest sibling, the "mother's helper," as her
mother has described her. What's more, she demonstrated a maturity
and competence unusual for her age. One day, while in junior high,
she came home from school and announced, "Mom, we have a problem. You're not ready to let me grow up."[9] Her industriousness and
perhaps even her innate ability to lead are evident in one of her early
jobs: in college, she taught aerobics.

Sandberg entered Harvard as a freshman in 1987 and, in part because she thought she would go into public service, majored in economics. When she earned the top score in her Public Sector Economics class on her midterm and then repeated the feat on the final, she won the attention of the professor, Larry Summers, who was later to become US Treasury secretary and president of Harvard University. When Sandberg and a fellow student founded the group Women in Economics and Government, Summers signed on as faculty adviser. Later, Summers volunteered to serve as Sandberg's senior thesis adviser, helping her tackle a project on how economic inequality contributes to spousal abuse.[10]

Sandberg graduated Phi Beta Kappa in 1991 and planned to stay at Harvard for law school. But when Summers became chief economist at the World Bank that year and asked her to join him as a research assistant, she took the job. Part of her work included traveling around India for a project to curb leprosy. "There's nothing like working on something like that to really make you think about what you're doing with your time . . . and what you have to give back," she said of her time in the subcontinent.[11]

After two years at the World Bank, Sandberg returned to Harvard, this time to the business school. After graduating in 1995, she, like many recent MBAs, took a consulting job. But when Summers called again in 1996 after he had become the deputy secretary of the Treasury, she jumped at the chance to return to public service as his chief of staff.

A Time of Change

Although Sandberg looks back on her time in Washington as formative—years early in her professional career that taught her to think systematically about problems—she left politics after the Democrats lost the 2000 presidential election.

She needed a change, both personally and professionally. Her first, brief marriage had ended. In the documentary film *Makers*, she describes the painful event as "a very public failure."[12] She was leaving politics but still wanted to do something that would make an impact. Growing up, she had never imagined working for a company. But during her time at the World Bank, she had seen the impact technology could have on people's lives. So she headed to Silicon Valley. "If you think about what changes our lives, the great things that have changed lives over the course of history, there are political movements and there's technology, and technology is driving a lot of change now," she has said. "For me, I decided that working in technology was a great way to have impact."[13]

In 2001, Sandberg joined Google as the business-unit general manager of the three-hundred-person start-up. It was there that Sandberg first made her mark as a business leader. She is widely considered to have been one of the driving forces behind Google's turn to profitability, building and managing the company's online sales channels. First, she made AdWords a money-maker for the company. (When she joined Google, there were only four employees working on AdWords, the program that sells the small text ads that appear next to related search results.) Sandberg volunteered to oversee the project's sales and operations. As AdWords began to generate revenue, she focused on a second business innovation: AdSense, a program in which Google places advertisements on external websites in return for a small percentage of the revenues. Sandberg was also a key player in the development of Google.org, the company's billion-dollar philanthropy effort.[14]

When she arrived at Google, Sandberg started creating divisions. A colleague from the time told Jessi Hempel, in *CNNMoney*, "We were a ten-person team and we were thinking, 'Why are you going to hire [more people for] that?' And she said, 'Trust me, you need to think not about now, but where are we going to be in five steps and ten steps.'" Sandberg has a remarkable ability to "look around corners," as Google's David Fischer terms it. "While the rest of us are planning three quarters ahead, she was thinking about how we jump ahead a number of years."[15]

While others praised her and her visible leadership achievements, Sandberg says she was often in turmoil on the inside. For years she felt like a fraud, explaining away her successes, saying, for example, that she had gotten into Harvard because her parents had helped with the application essay, that she had scored a job at the World Bank because she had taken a class with the right professor, and so on. Then one day in 2005, Sandberg, just shy of seven months pregnant, was sitting in her office at Google when the phone rang. It was a doctoral student working on a research project on how women "do it all." Sandberg suggested someone who actually had a child might be a better interview subject, but the caller was adamant, saying that the baby was only two months away and suggesting that the parents-to-be had certainly worked out all the details—"who's going to pick up the kid when he's sick, who's going to leave work early," and so on.

"Two minutes into this," she confessed in a recent public speech, "I'm crying, not subtly, tears pouring down my face."[16] Even with all her skills—and, as a well-paid executive, with the resources to hire help—Sandberg feared taking on her new role as a mother. How would she do it all?

Working Mother with a 50/50 Partner at Home

Sandberg and her husband, David Goldberg, a fellow Harvard undergrad and longtime friend before they fell in love and married in 2004, have two children: a seven-year-old son and a four-year-old daughter. And Sandberg's career has shown no signs of slowing. After having children, Sandberg steadily climbed *Fortune* magazine's list of the "50 Most Powerful Women in Business," and that was before she wrote a number 1 *New York Times* best seller and founded a social movement alongside it. This isn't to say that motherhood hasn't changed Sandberg's approach to her work or her commitment to making the world a better place. Rather, it has forced her to focus in new ways on her priorities in each realm of her life.

After the birth of her first child, Sandberg writes in *Lean In*, she shifted her standard 7:00 to 7:00 daily time-in-the-workplace schedule to 9:00 to 5:30, working online at home early in the morning and in the evening. She also didn't shrink from finding ways to meet certain needs; for example, she would pump breast milk during conference calls. Sandberg learned to ruthlessly prioritize to get everything done. Now she urges her colleagues to do the same. "If there are five projects you want to do, you need to pick the three most important."[17] At Facebook, Sandberg told *Bloomberg Businessweek* in 2011, she established a "nongoal" list—projects that might be good ideas but that the company doesn't tackle right away.[18]

The new schedule, unusual in the hard-driving, fast-paced world of start-ups, allowed Sandberg to spend time with her husband, now CEO of SurveyMonkey, and her young children—something that has remained very important to her. Every morning she or her husband drives the kids to school. Every evening, at least one parent is home to eat dinner with the kids. And weekends are strictly family time. They have a 50/50 deal at home.

I asked Sandberg how she knew, before she married Goldberg, that it would work this way with him. "First of all, I was older," she said. "I had a really good sense of who I was. I had gotten married before, when I didn't know who I was. By the time Dave and I were together we were fully formed adults. We had very explicit conversations about it."[19]

How exactly do they manage this shared care model? "Google Calendar," she told me. "I'm on it. My husband's on it. My sister's on it. We know who's got carpool duty because we put it into Google Calendar." The couple's 50/50 arrangement isn't always an equal split every day. "In the middle of our IPO or my book launch, it was not 50/50 my way," she said. "But over time it's 50/50. We really do divide and conquer. He does some stuff, I do some stuff. It goes back and forth."

And they make time for their marriage. "When I was growing up, my parents had this thing on the refrigerator that listed five keys to raising happy children. The first one was to pay more attention to your marriage than you do to your children." She explained, "Dave and I try to take a trip alone each year, even if it's two days for our anniversary. We try to have things that we do just together. But, like all of us, we could do more."

Even though Sandberg adopted family-friendly hours years ago, she has said it's not until recently that she was "brave enough to talk about it publicly." Indeed, she felt anxious about it, worried that her colleagues would think she was slacking off.

Despite the time that she does spend with her children, Sandberg has struggled to create harmony between the domains of her work and her family. Her son will say, "Mommy, put down the BlackBerry. Put that down. Talk to *me*" far more often than she'd like. "This is hard," she said in a 2011 TED Talk. "I feel guilty sometimes. I know no women, whether they're at home or they're in the workforce, who don't feel that sometimes."[20]

The two chapters in her book about making your partner a real partner and the myth of having it all are not only a well-documented argument for how and why gender ideologies must change, but they also list examples of how she and her husband have learned to focus on the things that matter, accept less than perfection on the things that don't, and be creative when being pulled in different directions.

Building a solid foundation for sharing domestic responsibilities involved, for example, her husband conjuring a way to move his new company's headquarters from Portland to San Francisco to be more available at home. When she once neglected to dress her son for school in green on St. Patrick's Day, Goldberg didn't chastise her for the slip; instead, he convinced her that it would help their son learn that he doesn't have to be like others.[21] By admitting that she is learning how to adjust—in both the mundane and in the grand scheme—Sandberg's creative problem solving serves as inspiration to the millions who now look up to her as a big sister, one who can tell them how it is and how it can be.

Women of Silicon Valley

Sandberg is quick to talk to friends and colleagues about the challenges working women face and the ways she has managed them. She does this not only in performance reviews and job interviews but also at the monthly Women of Silicon Valley gatherings she hosts at her home in Menlo Park. Sandberg invites an eclectic group of women, professional contacts as well as personal friends, to connect and learn from each other.

These gatherings began, she told me, when journalist Andrea Mitchell came to give a book talk at Google.

> I knew her from DC, so I said to her, "What are you doing afterwards?" She was taking the red-eye. And I said, "I'd love to have you over for dinner. Could I invite my book club and we could talk about your book?" And she said, "Sure." And then I realized, wow, I have Andrea Mitchell coming to my house to talk about her book! I shouldn't just invite the ten women in my book club. So, I invited some more friends, and we sat in my living room. There were probably twenty of us. She talked to us about her life and about the challenges she faced. I realized

how infrequently I was ever in a room with that many women talking about women. It worked.

So I started inviting more guests like Andrea Mitchell—friends, colleagues from work, women I met. I continue to do these dinners roughly once a month or so. A woman who left her job and started a company told me that every single person who helped her form her company, her first client, her first partners, she met at these dinners. If you're a woman in the working world—almost industry independent, certainly in tech—you've never been in a conference room that's with all women. Certainly not regularly. You don't realize that until it happens, but there is a natural bond. Women really need to work together. For any group that's been historically discriminated against, the prospect of working together can be very complicated.[22]

As her guests meet, Sandberg's children might scamper through the room and serve themselves from the buffet. Then they all sit down to hear from the evening's featured speaker, whether boldface names such as PepsiCo CEO Indra Nooyi, Harlem Children's Zone founder Geoffrey Canada, or lesser-known speakers whose causes Sandberg wants to support, such as Somaly Mam, a Cambodian activist who was sold into slavery as a child and now runs a foundation that fights human trafficking. Inspired by Mam's talk, Sandberg asked her guests who would help organize a fund-raiser. Every hand went up, and the subsequent event raised more than $1 million for the foundation.[23]

Mam is only one beneficiary of Sandberg's philanthropy. After working at the World Bank, where she focused on ridding India of leprosy, and the US Treasury department, where she worked on African relief efforts, Sandberg has formulated a vision of what types of aid most help those in need. Her experiences as an executive at Google and Facebook have shown her the most effective ways of delivering that ideal aid.

In philanthropy, as in business, Sandberg aims to ruthlessly prioritize.[24] So, for instance, Sandberg tries to target her philanthropy outside her own local neighborhood, on children who need food and water. Sandberg also looks for systemic solutions to problems. Feeding a child will do no good if the child dies of drinking contaminated water, so she aids projects that tackle the "big stuff," projects that develop the infrastructure that will pull entire countries out of poverty.[25]

Finally, Sandberg wants the charities she supports to be strong institutions. "What we call core competence," she explained in 2010 at the Jewish Federation's Business Leadership Council, "what we call management excellence, what we call organizational capacity in the for-profit world, we call administrative overhead in our non-profits and tell them to minimize it."[26] This approach hinders many organizations, she believes. So Sandberg says she writes unrestricted checks to charities, allowing them to spend the money on what they need in order to be effective.

Speaking Out

If Sandberg is aware of how challenging it is to work hard and have a full life, she's also aware of how many women decide they can't, convinced that if they want to have a family, they need to shift their careers into a lower gear. The result, she believes, is that not enough women reach the top of the corporate world. (This belief forms the focus of Lean In.)

Sandberg often tells the story of being at a private equity office in New York to pitch a deal in a long, three-hour meeting. Two hours in, there was an obligatory break. As Sandberg stood up from the conference table, the partner running the meeting quickly apologized and admitted he didn't know the location of the women's restroom. Aghast, Sandberg asked whether she was the first woman to have pitched him a deal. "Maybe," the partner replied, "or maybe you're the only one who had to go to the bathroom."[27]

She refers to a "stalled revolution" and speaks passionately about the resulting disadvantages at conferences such as TEDWomen, the World Economic Forum in Davos, Switzerland, commencements, and *Lean In* events. In all of these contexts, Sandberg uses stories from her own life to illustrate her belief that women should be more confident and ambitious in the workplace. She repeats these exhortations:

Take a seat at the table. (Assume that you belong.)

Keep your hand up. (Men keep their hands up when they have urgent questions.)

Don't leave until you leave. (Stay engaged even as you're anticipating time off.)

These are lessons she wants to teach others, but also ones she needs to remind herself. "I am insecure. I worry that I don't put my hand up," she revealed in a 2013 interview with Tamala Edwards in front of hundreds gathered at a Philadelphia hotel ballroom. "When I was at Google . . . I was offered a really great job, and I didn't take it. I didn't take it because I loved my current job. But I also didn't take it because I wanted a second child, and I didn't think I could go through a pregnancy with a new job."[28]

Sandberg knows that she was lucky to get a second chance at an exciting new job, which came just after she returned to Google from her second maternity leave. She also knows that, had the offer not come, she might have felt that she'd passed on a great opportunity—a personal realization that drives her management style and is the core message of her book: be pragmatic, and pursue all your dreams.

Even though Sandberg is a naturally gifted storyteller, she was not willing, until recently, to share formative episodes in public because they were embarassing to her. Her husband critiqued the first draft of, *Lean In*, noting that it was "ninety percent research and ten percent little things about me."[29] He warned her that readers might find it "like eating your Wheaties." The most honest and personal things in that book were added at the very end, she told me, but she came to see that it had to be personal for her manifesto to get the message across. "Talking about my divorce; that got added in late. The truth is if I want to make the point that we need to encourage leadership in girls, there's no point I can say that makes that more real than my own story. I can tell my own story much more authentically than I can tell anyone else's story. I'm not telling stories because I want to tell stories. I'm telling these stories because I think they make really important points."

When asked by Edwards in Philadelphia whether she ever gets scared, Sandberg's reply was an emphatic "Yes, on Jon Stewart's show last night!" She then went on to say, in a more serious tone, that she often worries about whether she's a bad mother. Her response to this anxiety is to talk with her husband and find solutions with him. "Open conversation gets us there."

Sandberg also uses the world stage to talk about the traditionally unspoken link between professional success and the demands of family life, demands that still fall disproportionally on women's shoulders. "This might seem counterintuitive," she told Barnard's graduating seniors in 2011. "But the most important career decision you're going to make is whether or not you have a life partner and who that partner is."[30] She told me how she encourages young women on college campuses to take this seriously: "You won't believe me now," she tells them, "but I promise the sexiest thing in the world ten years from now is going to be a man who does the laundry."

The Skills Sheryl Sandberg Exemplifies

Sheryl Sandberg is not only a deeply engaged COO in an important company but also a person striving to live a life in which seemingly disparate parts are integrated in mutually beneficial ways. With her massive wealth, finding four-way wins might seem like a piece of cake. It's easy to have it all when you have billions of dollars, right?

But Sandberg's rise to prominence hasn't been easy. She has worked hard on her skills—sometimes intuitively, sometimes consciously, as when she used a coach to help her manage her growing team at Google or when she realized that her book should become personal. At the same time, she has grown into a role model for achieving success on one's own terms. In Sandberg we see a woman with a thoroughly modern way of acting with authenticity, integrity, and creativity.

Be Real: Convey Values with Stories

Sheryl Sandberg tells stories of the key events that have shaped her, and tells them in a way that brings her closer to others. Sandberg can pinpoint events in her life that have played a meaningful role in the development of her values. She allows others to gain insight into her authentic self by sharing her stories. She displays both confidence and vulnerability by opening herself up to others. This lays the foundation for building relationships based on mutual honesty, appreciation, and trust.

Telling powerful stories is part of clarifying what's important. We articulate our values and, in doing so, commit to them. Sandberg's high-profile life is full of engaging storytelling, especially when she recounts episodes that have made her want to advocate for gender equality. Sandberg encourages men and women to think through their own positions on hiring, promotion, and the politics of everyday life in organizations.[31]

Sandberg also gives specific advice for how to deal with obstacles, such as salary negotiations. She has learned how to be open about her own insecurities and her tendency to yield too quickly. With self-deprecating humor, she describes how her views on women and work have evolved as a result of her personal experience.

In telling stories in which she is the protagonist, Sandberg becomes more accessible to others, for listeners can see themselves in her stories. This identification makes it easier both to trust and to follow her as a leader. The story of the forgotten women's restroom creates a closer bond with her audience, while also making the case for change in the norms of gender equality. When one person is willing to reveal an awkward moment in which she felt slighted, even degraded, a dialogue is sparked.

The humor gets Sandberg's audiences engaged. It has the ring of truth, and so it gives her the opportunity to describe how, despite her own rise to the top of the corporate world, she has experienced the problems of inequality. She gets it. Although it might seem paradoxical, it is this vulnerability that enables Sandberg to capture attention and argue for change.

Beyond the numbers gap, Sandberg is intent on calling attention to the chronic confidence gap that underlies women's failures to achieve what men have. She has seen this gap in her own life, and, to help close it both for herself and for others, she uses stories, such as one about herself and two other students attending a college course in European intellectual history. Her roommate read the course materials in the original Greek and Latin and sat in rapt attention at lectures. Sandberg read the books in English and attended most lectures. Sandberg's younger brother, however, who was also in the course, read only one of the twelve assigned books and dipped in and out of lectures. After the final exam, the three were chatting about how well they thought they had done. It was a striking conversation. Sandberg's roommate felt horrible about the exam, concerned that she hadn't "drawn out the main point of the Hegelian dialectic." Sandberg's brother confidently predicted, "I got the top grade in the class."[32]

The story gets laughs, but it reveals a leadership skill that Sandberg is using knowingly: it recounts an experience to which others can relate and allows her to point to a crucial disparity between men and women in professional settings. In telling the story, Sandberg is talking about the common confidence gap. She tells this story to help make her case for the reasons attitudes and behaviors have to change. It works, because it is an authentic expression of interest in a cause that is personally meaningful and socially relevant. It conveys values through a story.

As with the first-wave feminists who came before her (and whom she is quick to praise), in Sandberg's life the personal has become the political. She could have quietly retained her high-powered position as Facebook's COO, but instead she is using her power and visibility to champion a cause for all women (and men). By revealing personal vignettes in *Lean In*, Sandberg brings people closer to her and shows them how to take their own specific actions, to insist on their own advancement. She challenges them as she challenges herself by asking, "What would you do if you weren't afraid?"

Many people can see in Sandberg's stories their own struggles, so they themselves are inspired to try to change things. This is the final result of this skill: influencing other people to act in accordance with their own values and beliefs as they pursue dreams of their own.

Be Whole: Build Supportive Networks

Sheryl Sandberg is able to convince people to support her in reaching important goals. Sandberg's career and her life outside work testify to the many ways in which she has tapped into her personal and professional networks. With her passion—and her reputation as someone who goes out of her way to connect people—she convinces others to dedicate time and energy to support her. And the support comes, because others trust her, share her vision of the future, and want to help her realize it.

When she arrived at Facebook, as a nontechie in a senior executive role at a technology company, Sandberg had to make it easy for people to approach her so that she could understand their needs and respect what was on their minds. That's essential for building support. The physical arrangement of her office—open for ready access—was a good start. And spending the first couple of weeks personally introducing herself to employees was smart, too.

Let's fast-forward and see what we can learn about supportive networks from the launch of *Lean In*. Any great leader must seek help. The pursuit of change almost always meets resistance. People are most effective in building support when they are asking for help to make things better not for themselves but for others. You are more likely to get support from others when they see that what you're trying to do is to provide help, as opposed to trying to build your own wealth and reputation. Sandberg is now garnering global support for the *Lean In* movement in part because it's intended to help other women succeed.

Further, the people Sandberg has asked for help are often those whom *she* has helped. She had helped the Women of Silicon Valley group before she asked it to support Somaly Mam. Those women had benefited from being invited to attend gatherings at her home, where Sandberg has fostered mutually supportive relationships across all spheres of her life. On realizing that she could extend the invitation to meet with Andrea Mitchell beyond her small book group, she grew the Women of Silicon Valley gatherings into a community for the exchange of advice, including sharing practical ideas for boosting self-confidence. Sandberg's friends, tech executives, venture capitalists, other mothers, book club friends, former colleagues, and family members (such as her sister) form fruitful connections.[33] In her supportive networks, all participants—including Sandberg, who enhances her own value by serving as the linchpin—gain fresh ideas, business leads, contacts, and new friendships.

Be Innovative: Resolve Conflicts among Domains

Sheryl Sandberg seeks creative solutions to conflicts to meet goals in different parts of life rather than sacrifice one part for another. She realizes that the different aspects of her life are not competing with one another all the time; her life does not have to feel like a zero-sum game. She does not accept the notion that engaging in one area of her life must always require sacrifices in the others. Instead, she looks for ways to create win-win solutions that meet multiple goals.

When Sandberg first decided to speak publicly about her life as a professional woman and to reach out to audiences of other working women, she was told that women in business don't talk about being women, and that doing so would derail her career.[34] Conventional wisdom held that talking about herself as a woman and mother (and sharing her awareness of her inner struggles) would undermine her authority in the corporate world. But she believed that the chance to encourage and teach others outweighed the personal risks. So she tried it, turning the apparent conflict into an opportunity.[35] Her personal journey, especially the ways she has dealt with many moments of doubt and guilt, became an inspiration for others. Her reputation as a powerful leader was crystallized. But more important, she developed her skill in resolving conflict among the different parts of her life by turning her personal struggle into a source of knowledge and motivation for having an impact on the wider world.

Sandberg's stories breathe life into many women's dreams of achievement. In both small and large settings, Sandberg encourages other women to challenge stereotypes and experiment with new models for integrating the different parts of their lives, as she has done. She pushes them to think past what they were taught as girls about the timetables of their roles as mothers and business professionals, and she shows, through her example, how to become a woman who actually does have lots of it all. Harmony between work and the rest of life, she says, *is* possible. This is not just a philosophical argument on her part. Sandberg prescribes specific strategies, creative solutions she has culled from her own experiences.

Sandberg has become an expert at resolving conflicts among the roles she plays in her life, especially by sharing domestic responsibilities with her husband, working with him to arrive over the long haul at an equitable distribution. And now she has ample resources available to help manage home and kids. But even though she has ample resources available to help manage home and kids, she still faces disappointments. In the end, Sandberg shows that there are no perfect solutions to meeting all of life's demands. Even those with all the wealth in the world, great intelligence, and loads of social support must make difficult choices in certain moments. To be innovative is to be on the lookout for new ways to get things done that make sense to you, and those who matter most to you, not every minute of every day, but over the course of a life.

The question Sheryl Sandberg asks young women around the world is this: What would you do if you weren't afraid? She has grappled with that question and, overcoming her doubts, mustered the will to do something about it. Her revealing, instructive book has become a powerful example of a four-way win, producing value for her work, family, community, and self.

She is a new breed of executive, one who meets the competing demands of running a supercharged global company, *and* rears children, *and* contributes to society through philanthropy, *and* advances the cause of gender equality, *and* nurtures a successful dual-career marriage, *and* stays connected to a wide array of friends, *and* remains present as a child and a sister. For Sandberg, it's not yielding to either/or; instead, it's searching for both/and. She has struggled, she has adapted, and she has felt intense guilt, but she is actively pursuing four-way wins over the long run.

Her professional success has not so much come at the expense of the other parts of her life, as it has derived *from her commitments to family,* as she's learned how to teach businesspeople around the world what she's learned about striving to enact a 50/50 marriage; *from her service to society,* as she's applied insights gained from her time in government to her work at both Google and Facebook; and *from developing herself personally,* as she's learning from coaches and mentors and thus enhancing her capacity as a business leader. Her conscience compels her to think about being a good person and living a good life, one that creates value for others and is founded on the ideals forged in the smithy of her experience.

Sandberg was developing these skills long before her meteoric professional rise. No matter where you come from, and no matter where you are on the arc of your life, Sandberg offers a model for how to shape your life by using stories that teach, building networks that provide support, and continually seeking ways to resolve tensions among the different parts of life. Coaches, mentors, friends, and family can help you too develop the kinds of skills Sandberg illustrates, in ways that fit the particulars of your life, thereby increasing the likelihood of your leading life as you want.

3

Eric Greitens

Hold Yourself Accountable,
Apply All Your Resources,
Focus on Results

Eric Greitens knew that he would awake to chaos—blanks firing at 550 rounds per minute, artillery simulators exploding, sirens blaring. It was the beginning of Hell Week: seven days and nights of almost continuously stressful training. Greitens had told the six men in his boat crew to sleep fully dressed, with their boots on. Their plan was to crawl under the side of the tent and run, and run they did—right past a group of instructors shooting another crew with a fire hose as they did push-ups.

"Drop down!" yelled the instructors, but Greitens and his men kept running, taking advantage of the chaos to run off the beach and hide behind a Dumpster while the other trainees were herded into a concrete compound, known as the grinder, for a session of push-ups and flutter-kicks. After ten minutes or so, knowing that the instructors would soon realize that his team was missing, Greitens led his men in.[1]

"We couldn't avoid 99 percent of the pain that was going to come our way, but we'd avoided a little," Greitens later wrote, in *The Heart and the Fist*, of that moment in August 2001. And he knew that the little bit they'd avoided had made a difference as he and his crew ran from the grinder and toward the water, their hundred-pound inflatable boat bouncing on their heads. Greitens could hear the exhausted men on the other teams griping to each other. "We're off to a good start, but the whole week's not going to be like this," he told his men. "Listen, though, to the other boat crews tearing into each other. We're gonna stay positive, stay together, and have fun with this."

In the middle of the third night, after their first, too-brief nap, the men were awakened; herded, half-asleep, into shoulder-deep water; and told to run south. Looking around, Greitens saw pain in their faces. "I can't remember if I started to sing or yell for our class or shout defiance at the instructors, but I remember booming at the top of my lungs," he recalled. His classmates joined in, and soon they were shouting with joy.

Greitens still wears the cropped hair of his military days, although he is no longer on active duty. The thirty-eight-year-old former SEAL and his wife, Sheena, live in his hometown of St. Louis, Missouri. From there he runs The Mission Continues (TMC), a nonprofit he created in 2007 to help veterans find ways to serve in their communities. The organization has funded more than six hundred fellowships, giving veterans the opportunity to work with service groups such as the Boys & Girls Clubs of America and Habitat for Humanity, or to volunteer for a local hospital. Greitens's efforts have also helped change the way people think about veterans. As Chris Marvin, the very first Fellow (and a former MBA student of mine who is now head of an organization that works with TMC), told me, the perception is not "kitty cats that need to be petted and loved" but competent workers looking for a new way to serve.[2]

Greitens believes deeply in the power and sense of purpose that can come from helping others. He had witnessed it in his years working in refugee camps in Rwanda and in the homes run by Mother Teresa's Missionaries of Charity, and he had experienced it as a military officer. At the beginning of the six-month training to become a SEAL, Greitens had been warned that although the program was hard for everyone, the instructors tried to make it even harder for the officers, who were expected to be at the front of every timed swim and run. But Greitens would come to believe that it was, in fact, easier for the officers, who were trained to focus on their men. "I had no place for my own pain, my own misery, my own self-pity," he recalled in his book.[3] Yet the healing and uplifting power of service remains, he says, undervalued.

A Leader of Three

Greitens is the oldest of three boys. His mother, Becky, was a special education teacher. Rob, his father, was an accountant at the Department of Agriculture, although Greitens told me in a recent interview that fatherhood was his dad's true vocation.[4] The elder Greitens had lost his father at age six; he coached the boys' soccer and Little League teams and refused to work late.

Eric Greitens was the natural leader of the rambunctious trio. "We were always organizing games together, and if they got out of line I'd knock 'em," he admitted after I probed about his "sibling leadership style." If things got out of hand, his parents would step in, but only to ask them to find a way to play together.

As a child, Greitens loved tales of adventure and was drawn to the *Choose Your Own Adventure* books with their promise that he, as reader, could control what happened in the story. Growing up, he worried that he had been born in the wrong time. "I sat in the public library and read stories of people discovering ancient cities and settling wild frontiers. I read about warriors and explorers and statesmen, but I'd look up from the book and stare out of the window onto the green, freshly mowed grass," he remembers in his book.[5] "It seemed that all the corners of the earth had been explored, all the great battles fought."

Greitens's parents, their son said, impressed on him the importance of being a good person, treating people with respect, being a team player. But they didn't hover over him, helping him with his science project or wringing their hands when he came home with a B minus in handwriting. Barb Osburg, Greitens' eleventh-grade English teacher, remembered him as friendly, attentive and thoughtful. "He was a good listener to other students," she told me, "which is rare."

Osburg also remembered Greitens as a doer, organizing the first-ever Martin Luther King celebration at his high school and calling the St. Louis mayor, who was running for reelection on an education platform, with an offer to put together an advisory board of students from across the city and county.[6]

The Education of a Humanitarian

One September evening in 1993, early in his sophomore year at Duke, Eric Greitens drove from the manicured campus to E. D. Mickle Gym in a run-down area of Durham, North Carolina. He had recently returned from a summer in China, his first trip abroad. In Beijing he had taught English, and many of his students had been involved in the democracy movement that culminated in the violence in Tiananmen Square in 1989. After China, student life at Duke felt "even emptier than before," he later recalled.[7] He hankered for experiences beyond the cloistered walls of the classroom, and, inspired in part by his grandfather's tales of boxing in Depression-era Chicago, Greitens decided to take up the sport. It was a way, he says, of testing himself.

Inside the gym, without a clue where to start, he did a few sets of push-ups and sit-ups. When a short, muscled man asked him to spar, he declined. "Man, how you gonna learn to box if you don't spar?" the man pressed. Greitens borrowed some gear from the equipment closet, stepped into the ring, and was pummeled. "The beating was comic," Greitens recalled.[8]

When he returned the following day, men chuckled. Undeterred, he came back again the next day, and the next. Soon he began training with a coach named Earl Blair and with Derrick Humphrey, a professional boxer.

Blair thought of himself as more than a boxing coach. With Blair, Greitens wrote, "every action was invested with significance. How we hung the heavy bag, God's mercy, the way a man should wrap his hands, the virtue of humility." Blair taught Greitens the value of preparation, of training hard and working through the pain. He also taught him about honor and respect.

Although the gym felt worlds away from Duke, Greitens began to see connections between the two. Greitens majored in philosophy, studying thinkers like Aristotle, who said that you know what the good thing is by seeing what the good man does. "Then I would ask Blair, 'How do I throw a punch? How do I throw a hook? How do I do an upper cut?'" Greitens told an audience at Harvard's Kennedy School years later. "And he would just say, 'Watch Derrick. Do as he does.'"[9]

In the summer of 1994, between his sophomore and junior years, with the war and ethnic violence devastating the former Yugoslavia, Greitens volunteered to work in Croatia with the project Unaccompanied Children in Exile. He was motivated in part by the post-Holocaust mantra his Jewish mother had passed down: "Never again."

On the train from Vienna to Zagreb, Greitens was approached by a Bosnian woman who asked, "Why isn't America doing anything to stop the ethnic cleansing? To stop the rapes? To stop the murders?" The questions would haunt him.

Inspired by one of his Chinese students, who had photographed demonstrations in Tiananmen Square, Greitens began to document the lives of refugees he met. He wanted the world to see not only the toll that war took on a human level but also the resilience of the survivors—for example, the Bosnian man whose brothers were killed and whose wife was dragged from the house and raped, but who considered himself lucky that his wife and children were still alive. Greitens saw that those who had the most psychological difficulties in the camps were the older teenagers and young adults, who brooded over their dashed dreams and uncertain futures. They lacked the sense of purpose that steadied those who were caring for children younger than themselves.

Back in Durham, a local church invited Greitens to speak. The congregation had read about the genocide but wanted to hear from someone who had been there. He clicked through his slides, telling the refugees' stories and answering questions. Congregants asked, "How did they wash their clothes?" "What happened to the little girl's family?" And then, "What can we do?" He answered, "We can donate money and clothing, and we can volunteer. But in the end these acts of kindness are done after people have been killed, their homes burned, their lives destroyed . . . If we really care about these people, we have to be willing to protect them from harm," he later wrote in his book.[10]

Greitens studied Milton, art history, and religion. He traced conceptions of morality and the good life from the Greeks through St. Thomas Aquinas to Martin Luther King Jr. And he continued to travel, spending one summer working for the UN High Commission for Refugees in Rwanda, and the next working with street children in Bolivia. Greitens remembered meeting a group of Rwandan women who had survived genocide. By taking their photographs, he "wanted to capture their portraits, to share what I saw with others . . . Few Americans had seen this: Strong people. Survivors. Solid. Steadfast . . . These women had suffered more than I could have ever imagined, and they still were willing to welcome me, to talk with me. After all the betrayal they had lived through, all the hardship, they were still willing to trust a stranger. If people can live through genocide and retain compassion, if they can take strength from pain, if they are able, still, to laugh, then certainly we can learn something from them."[11]

The pattern continued at Oxford, where Greitens spent four years on a Rhodes Scholarship. He dropped in on lectures on everything from the history of science to modern art. And he continued to study humanitarian work, researching past crises and traveling into the field to understand what made the best organizations effective and what form of aid people in war-torn regions really needed. He visited the Gaza Strip and a home in Varanasi, India, run by Mother Teresa's organization. He traveled from an orphanage in Albania to Cambodia to Mexico, seeking to learn from different models.

By the time he finished his dissertation, he had become an advocate for using power when necessary to defend the weak. "The great dividing line between words and results was courageous action."[12] It was a position that he argued in papers and presented at conferences. At the same time, he began to ask himself, Am I just going to talk about it, or am I going to live by my belief that the world needs warriors as well as humanitarians?

Learning to Serve

Greitens arrived at the Navy's Officer Candidate School (OCS) in Pensacola, Florida, on January 20, 2001, with a red duffel bag, a copy of the *11 General Orders of the Sentry*, and copious doubts. The constant yelling of the drill instructors, the hours spent folding clothes for inspection, the jogging in formation while singing silly songs—*this* was how the Navy trained its leaders?[13] Then a young member of his class struggled during an early workout session.

"Gritchens, get over here!" he recalled his staff sergeant yelling (and getting his name wrong, to boot). "Wong here just became your personal project. You are going to live in the same room, and you will teach Wong in every spare moment so that Wong *will* pass the final physical fitness test."

Greitens soon became the "PT body" in charge of physical training for his class. Older than many of his fellow trainees and in better shape—and seasoned both in the boxing ring and in volatile regions overseas—he didn't rattle easily. Fear didn't paralyze him. So OCS was relatively easy, and Greitens welcomed the small opportunity to lead others in his class. He would also, eventually, come to recognize that the drill instructors' attention to detail—not to mention their constant screaming—served an important purpose.

Thirteen weeks later, Greitens arrived in Coronado, California, ready to join Basic Underwater Demolition/SEALs training class 237. If Greitens hadn't felt challenged at officer training school, he was now, in one of the most difficult military training programs in the world. Over the course of six months, candidates must complete progressively harder runs on the beach, colder swims in the bone-chilling ocean, and more fearsome tests such as fifteen-foot dives to tie knots at the bottom of the training pool, sometimes with wrists and ankles bound. If a trainee fails a single test, he is out—period, end of story. Roughly 10 percent of students graduate with their original class. In his book, Greitens referred to the "vicious beauty" of the training and quoted the Jedi master from *Star Wars*, Yoda: "Do, or do not."

If the physical challenge of SEALs training was hard, the mental challenge was greater. Although Greitens found it brutal, he thrived on the challenge, pushing himself as he had in the boxing ring, this time in the service of his country.

In his first brief deployment to Afghanistan in 2003, and then as the commander of a special operations boat in Southeast Asia, Greitens began to apply skills that he had learned in SEAL training, as well as those he developed earlier. In the Philippines, the US forces were hunting the terrorist group Abu Sayyaf.[14] Greitens soon realized that his boat, though fast and powerful, was conspicuous and couldn't enter shallow waters. To collect the best intelligence, his team needed to get close to the coastline and blend in. Remembering that Cambodian fishermen used small skiffs to fish at night, Greitens convinced his team to buy two of the small, shallow, brightly painted boats. Then they outfitted them with weapons and communications equipment. The Americans pieced together enough intelligence to locate an Abu Sayyaf compound on one of the local islands.

Greitens was also sent to Manda Bay, a coastal outpost in northern Kenya, to replace a commander who had damaged relations with local leaders and the Kenyan army chief on whose base the US operation was seated. Here was another instance in which he would use his background in another field to inform his actions.

As the convoy driving him to the base passed through a small village, someone said that the villagers hated the United States. "When I looked at the villagers looking at us, I didn't see terrorist sympathizers. I saw angry parents. We had our windows rolled up, sunglasses on, rifles in our hands, and we were driving dangerously fast through a village filled with goats and children." Greitens and his fellow soldiers rebuilt basic human connections, the importance of which he had learned in his experience as a relief worker. He invited the Kenyan captain to dinner. He drank tea with the mayor of the nearest city. And, training for a marathon, he took long runs, accompanied sometimes by local children and more frequently by Daniel, one of the Kenyan guards at the base. All of these interactions were pleasant, even enjoyable. Yet the intelligence reports on the Horn of Africa showed that overall, the relations between the US military and local Kenyans were poor. "Real, valuable intelligence only came from real people," he later wrote. And so, against the advice of an adviser who warned that it could be a "career-ender" if things went badly, Greitens took his men to buy fruit in the "bad" village. He made his men take off their sunglasses and shake hands with the locals. They bought fruit and chatted.[15]

"I Got Your Back, Sir"

By spring 2007, Greitens was on his third deployment, serving in Iraq. He went to sleep on what he expected to be his last night in Fallujah and awoke to the whomp of mortar landing on the other side of the wall from his bed. Although he has no memory of the truck bomb that followed, he does remember the burning in his eyes, throat, and lungs following the explosion. He and his comrades stumbled out of the room and rushed to the roof to defend their barracks. He heard his friend Travis Manion utter the words that are military standard for indicating that you are ready to protect: "I got your back, sir."

Days later, Greitens hopped out of a helicopter—the last leg of his last trip on his last day in Iraq—and headed to the barracks. When he reached his bunk, he opened his chest pocket and took out a St. Christopher medal, a Buddhist prayer scroll, a Jewish hamsa, and a couple of other religious good-luck tokens, all gifts from different friends. He said a generic "Thank you, God" and, the next day, flew home.

One month later, Greitens was living in Washington, DC, a self-described "unemployed sailor" groping for the next thing. There he learned of the death of Travis Manion.

In school, all the way through his PhD, Greitens had known what he needed to do, what hurdles to jump. In the military, he followed orders. Now there was no clear path, no direction. Barb Osburg told me that he felt "the barrenness of omission" at that time, but then "he started thinking of his compatriots."[16] One day Greitens went to visit the wounded vets at Bethesda Naval Hospital with his old college friend and fellow Navy veteran Ken Harbaugh. He was struck: even those who had lost limbs or eyesight longed to return to their units.[17]

"I knew from my experience working with Bosnian refugees and Rwandan survivors that those who found a way to serve others were able to rebuild their own sense of purpose, despite all they had lost." In a recent conversation with me, Harbaugh recalled the visit he and Greitens made: "One man grabbed my hand and said, 'I lost my legs, but I didn't lose my desire to serve and my pride in being an American.'"[18]

Inspired, and themselves also eager to continue to serve, Greitens and Harbaugh founded The Mission Continues. The idea was to fund fellowships that granted wounded veterans opportunities to be of use at home, in their own communities.

It wasn't easy at first. Greitens initially funded the organization with his $3,500 combat pay, the disability checks of two friends (Harbaugh and Kaj Larsen), and another friend's $10,000 stake.[19] At the time, Greitens was living in an apartment furnished with a blow-up bed, a toaster oven, and an alarm clock. He thought he would have to fund the first fellowships with his credit card.[20]

But he believed in the project, and he persisted. "Eric's fund-raising goals, or the number of Fellows that he aimed to put through the program, were always orders of magnitude over what we expected at board meetings," Harbaugh explained to me. "He's not afraid to state his goals to his friends or a wider circle."[21] This is a conscious and deliberate way of holding himself accountable.

To keep himself focused, Greitens also borrowed the military concept of "commander's intent." The Center for Army Lessons Learned defines the commander's intent as "a clear and concise expression of the purpose of the operation and the desired military end state that supports mission command, provides focus to the staff, and helps subordinate and supporting commanders act to achieve the commander's desired result without further order, even when the operation does not unfold as planned."[22] In his Harvard Kennedy School Center for Public Leadership speech, Greitens said this idea was one of the best lessons he was able to translate from his military service to social entrepreneurship. "As a leader you need to be able to articulate your commander's intent and then hand it to your subordinates so that they can understand it and then use all of their own creativity, intelligence, energy to actually meet your intent." He explained how this concept applies to his work in nonprofits: "When as an entrepreneur you're able to articulate that intent and then you hire somebody . . . what starts to happen [is] you're able to not only bring your energy, you're able to bring in all of the energy, passion, intelligence, and creativity of all of these people, and it can all be directed in the right way because you've been able to articulate the intent."[23]

Spencer Kympton, a former Blackhawk pilot and TMC's chief operating officer, told me that Greitens tracks his progress on a one-page document, asking himself questions like, How many donors did I reach out to this week? Am I any closer to landing a story with one of the ten media outlets on my wish list?[24]

Funders and partner organizations initially had trouble grasping the innovative concept underlying TMC, which sees veterans as valuable, not pitiable, and does not treat them with kid gloves.[25] But the clear impact of the program on Fellows, and Greitens' ability to tell their stories, eventually brought around partners and funders, including the Goldman Sachs Foundation, the Ford Foundation, and The Home Depot. Tim Smith, the organization's first Fellow in St. Louis, had served in the infantry, losing many friends during a bloody deployment in Iraq and returning home with post-traumatic stress disorder (PTSD). "When I first met Tim, he was working the midnight shift at the post office," Greitens told me. He set up a fellowship for Smith at a local hospital, where the former infantryman helped others with PTSD. Smith, who has since earned a master's degree in social work, worked full-time at the VA, and then started his own business, Patriot Commercial Cleaning, which employs other veterans in St. Louis. A June 2013 *Time* magazine cover story about The Mission Continues described how Greitens holds TMC Fellows to a high standard. Whiners don't get a lot of sympathy. Joe Klein quoted him: "'People understand the tremendous sacrifices that veterans have made—and they instinctively want to do something for them,' he says. 'And that sometimes leads people to give veterans an excuse: Oh, you didn't show up for work on time. It must be that you have posttraumatic stress disorder. Oh, you're disabled. Don't even try. Or, you're being a bad partner to your husband or wife, or a bad father or mother. It must be that you lost a bunch of friends. We simply do not accept those excuses.'"[26]

The fact that TMC simultaneously helps veterans find a new way to serve and helps communities find leaders made it appealing to Hollywood's J. J. Abrams. "My favorite ideas are the ones that solve multiple problems," the creator of *Lost* and the director of *Mission Impossible* and recent *Star Trek* movies told me. After meeting some American troops during a promotional event several years ago, Abrams looked for a way to stay engaged. He and his wife looked at myriad veteran-related projects and set up a meeting with Greitens. "He spoke with such clarity and passion and truth that it was an inspiration," recalled Abrams, who has given the organization more than money. He dedicated *Star Trek: Into Darkness* to post-9/11 veterans and asked Greitens and several fellows to do cameos. Abrams added that the actors, who had gotten to know Greitens during the production, talked inspiringly about TMC during their publicity events.[27]

TMC's growth and success aren't the only changes in Greitens's life since he was sleeping on a mattress in an empty apartment. While visiting Harvard in 2010, Greitens met a graduate student named Sheena Chestnut. From his first cup of hot chocolate with Sheena, he told me, she seemed to know how he thought. The two married in 2011. For him it was the second time. His first marriage had ended in divorce and was another source of hard-won wisdom about failure and the stuff of resilience. These days, Greitens rises early to practice Tae Kwon Do and then returns home to eat breakfast with Sheena in the charming old Lafayette Square neighborhood of St. Louis—at least when they are both in town and she's not traveling to Asia for her research on international security.

On a sunny May afternoon in 2012, Greitens looked out over the rows of graduating seniors and their families at Tufts University. Flashing a broad smile, Greitens told the graduates that they faced "the very real danger of going home to live in your parents' basements." Eschewing the usual mix of idealism and advice, Greitens issued a challenge, just as he does daily to the TMC Fellows. "I would like to ask something of you," he began. "Look forward with confidence, knowing that you will go on to use all of your talents and abilities, all of your creativity and energy, to find a way to be of service to others."[28]

The Skills Eric Greitens Exemplifies

Eric Greitens is the youngest of the six great leaders portrayed in this book. He heaps credit for his accomplishments on family, secondary school, college, the boxing ring, graduate school, and humanitarian endeavors—as well as on his role models in the military and in the nonprofit world. But Greitens has brought to this training a relentless quest for new knowledge about the best ways to apply his innate talents in the service of helping others.

Greitens has used his knowledge about the psychology of resilience—learned in war-torn and poverty-stricken places around the world, as well as from his own education—to start an organization that provides effective service-as-healing opportunities for fellow veterans. The success of The Mission Continues, along with its growing number of supporters, is testimony to his leadership skills. Like the other subjects of this book, Greitens embodies all of the skills, but he is an especially good exemplar of these three: choosing to hold himself accountable (being real), applying all his resources from all parts of his life (being whole), and focusing on results (being innovative).

Be Real: Hold Yourself Accountable

Eric Greitens holds himself accountable for doing what is most important to him in his life. Greitens regularly reflects on his values and evaluates whether he is living according to them. If he notices that he is doing things that do not really matter, he adjusts his actions. He is committed to taking steps to ensure that he is pursuing a life that matches what he believes in.

Even as a boy, Greitens relished the idea of taking control of his destiny; he loved tales of adventurous men, seeing in them a chance to define his own ending. His parents encouraged their eldest son to be mindful of his own family's history and his place in its future. (His mother's "Never again!" resounded in his early consciousness.) And in school this idea was reinforced, as when one high school mentor, after taking him to a homeless shelter for a night, told the young Greitens that he could do something about it.[29] These early lessons taught him to know his values and act on them.

On his visit to China, in the company of everyday people who had spoken truth to power, he came to see that anyone could make history. On a humanitarian expedition in Bosnia, after a woman asked why the victims of horrific crimes were suffering in a war as the world watched, he began to question whether merely providing relief was a noble enough service to humanity. Truly caring for others, he realized, meant providing more than just charity. He saw that what he calls "courageous action"—protection with force—was a necessary complement to sending food and medicine in the real world of violent political strife. Without a fist, he observed, all the heart in the world ultimately didn't matter. He took responsibility, holding himself accountable, by understanding what needed to be done and then acting on this realization. Forsaking more comfortable career paths, he signed up to become a Navy SEAL. "I could keep talking or I could live my beliefs," he wrote.

He had many opportunities to demonstrate accountability in the military. On his first deployment as an officer, for example, when he discovered drug use among his men, he saw it not as a small mistake but as a violation of the SEAL code, and so he took appropriate action. Holding himself to a high standard, he didn't let his subordinates get away with their transgression; he documented the case for firing them and then implemented that decision. (After the men were thrown out of the military, he faced antagonism from some SEALs and wondered whether he could have done more to help them.[30] Again, he held himself accountable.)

And after he arrived home from his military service, when Greitens saw wounded fellow veterans in need of opportunities, he envisioned a way to make that happen. TMC was a cause connected to the values he had absorbed from military tradition and his own war-time experience. He saw himself as a link in the unbroken chain of an honorable fight for freedom. His awareness of having a role in a majestic historical narrative—if those before him served nobly, so should he—motivated Greitens to step up. TMC's founding shows Greitens's skill in holding himself accountable for acting on his values, for seeing what had to be done, and, despite being daunted, actually doing it. It wasn't about money or fame; it was about doing something meaningful.

Be Whole: Apply All Your Resources

Eric Greitens uses skills and contacts from different parts of his life to help meet needs and goals in other parts of his life. When pursuing his goals, Greitens thinks creatively about skills, relationships, and ways of thinking that he has developed in the various domains of his life. He does not force his relationships into rigidly defined categories or roles. Barb Osburg, for example, is not only his former English teacher but also a lifelong mentor with whom he talked as he struggled to conceive his post-Navy life.

Greitens's story is captivating because, as film director J. J. Abrams told me, Greitens is a man in whom "form and function are one." All the human capital he has amassed is applied in his efforts to achieve current aims. For example, Greitens used the attitude and skills he had acquired as a boxer (in the domain of his private self) in his career as a military officer (his profession).

Inspired by his grandfather's stories, Greitens studied boxing with men who understood that the game was as much about physical training for technical excellence as it was about developing the psychological tools for winning combat. From boxing, Greitens learned that preparation is all, that one can and must remain calm in the face of fear, and that one should fight honorably.

It's not surprising that Greitens devoted more attention in his memoir to preparation for action than to any other subject. He learned from role models and teachers the sanctity of a careful, ritualized process of getting ready. He applied this in the Navy, too. As a commander, he built the confidence of his troops by helping them see that effort dedicated to building strength led to greatness. In the ring, he learned that he could manage fear, and that when uncontrolled it "rots the mind and impairs the body."[31] This understanding proved essential in his life as a warrior, from the rigors of Hell Week to the terrors of Afghanistan and Iraq. And he learned from his boxing mentors that victory must be won with integrity, according to a set of values that proscribes torture and treasures human dignity. This insight helped Greitens understand, when he was fighting the Taliban, what "distinguishes a warrior from a thug."

Greitens also applied knowledge and insight gleaned from his time as a humanitarian worker (his community service) to his professional life. In Rwanda's refugee camps, Bosnia's bullet-infested villages, Bolivia's violent streets, and other gut-wrenching places where he went to provide assistance to children in need, Greitens acquired insight about resilience. He also learned practical ideas for forging basic human connections between unfamiliar peoples to overcome their resistance to new ideas. He brought these assets, gained from his experience serving the global community, to his work in the military and in founding TMC.

The big idea for Greitens is that people in need are best helped to gain strength and recover from trauma by being challenged with opportunities to be of use. Wherever he went on his humanitarian ventures, he saw the truth of this existential principle, viscerally described by the Holocaust survivor and philosopher Viktor Frankl in *Man's Search for Meaning:* people feel better about themselves when they are helping other people, and despair and helplessness when they are not able to do so. Greitens put this concept to use when, for example, he got himself and his squad through Hell Week by focusing not on personal pain but on the team. And he had a vision for how to apply this insight when he visited wounded veterans after his combat experience: this was the originating concept for TMC. His skill was to transfer this idea, picked up in one part of his life, and use it to good effect in another part, just as he uses the military concept of commander's intent in his role as CEO of his organization.

But gaining support for TMC has not been easy because, despite good intentions, most of society views veterans as worthy of charity, and not as assets who could themselves provide help. Greitens's success in persuading others to believe in his innovative point of view—which seems clear and intuitively logical—springs from what he learned in a different part of his life about how to overcome resistance and get people on your side. Greitens's on-the-ground training in diverse societies taught him that relationships come first, before strategy and deals. Forging alliances and achieving goals require mutual respect and often cultural understanding. He learned this in Cambodian fishing villages and then applied it in Kenya, for example, chatting with locals to build alliances that led to valuable intelligence.

Greitens's capacity to see others as individuals deserving of dignity—ingrained in him during years in the field as an aid worker—enables him to forge connections, build trust, and augment his impact as a leader. In his humanitarian service and then in the military, he developed the ability to overcome resistance. He later applied this skill in yet another domain of his life: his new nonprofit.

Be Innovative: Focus on Results

Eric Greitens focuses on the results of his efforts and is flexible about the means for achieving them. Greitens doesn't count the hours he's logged but instead looks to whether he is producing a positive outcome. He judges himself and others by accomplishments, by results, emphasizing quality of effort instead of quantity.

From his days as a high school kid in St. Louis trying to persuade the mayor to listen to students' voices to his founding of TMC as a way to help wounded veterans heal, Eric Greitens has learned the skill of keeping the big idea in mind—the goal—while being both imaginative and practical about how to achieve it. Earl Blair taught him that he didn't need fancy gym equipment to achieve his goal of learning to box: you make do with what you have and put all your effort into it.[32] This taught Greitens to focus on the result and to be flexible about how you pursue it.

In Rwanda Greitens's aim was to help provide relief for needy children. As he explained, he had to scramble to figure out how to have a positive impact. "I was not . . . an academic researcher bedecked with degrees. I was not an anthropologist. I was not a social worker. I was not a nurse or a doctor . . . I was an expert in nothing."[33] He realized that he could use photography to tell stories. His were not the standard narratives of helplessness but images of resilience and strength. Children and their families were shown as they wrapped their arms around each other. To produce a new way of seeing these people, Greitens found in his photography a creative way to achieve the result of inspiring Americans to take notice, and take action.

Another example of his flexibility while focusing on results: to stay sane and on track for successful completion of the extreme rigors of Hell Week, he discovered inventive strategies. He started singing during one onerous exercise and energetically led his tired classmates through a rendition of the Hokey Pokey, which helped them get their minds off their immediate struggle and feel some measure of psychological control over their oppressive situation.[33] He realized in retrospect that this was part of the purpose of training: to be taught, as he later wrote, "how to adapt our tactics and take advantage of opportunities to complete our mission." This gets at the heart of this skill.

Through his education—in boxing, as a scholar, and as a warrior—Greitens constructively applied the principle of taking small steps that are under your control as you progress toward a big, compelling goal; focusing on results while being creative about the means to achieve them. He saw that his small part in the Kenyan operation was not to win a major battle but rather to make "persistent strategic progress" toward the larger goal of building strong allies. That meant connecting with people on a basic human level, such as by drinking tea with the mayor, training with Kenyan guards, and chatting with fruit vendors.[34]

The Mission Continues gives full expression to Greitens's creative powers. He saw a problem—wounded veterans in need of a sense of purpose—and produced a way for them to express their sense of purpose. To achieve this result, he drew on knowledge he'd been picking up through his observations of others and from his own life, such as when he realized—looking back on Hell Week—that the "hardest moment was also the only moment . . . when I was alone, focused on my own pain" and that service on behalf of a purpose beyond immediate needs can produce transcendence.[35] And, just as he had reframed the picture of children in need by creating pictures of them as strong, he now reframed the picture of wounded veterans by showing them to be valuable community assets.

In the military, the principle of commander's intent is taught to show officers how to make the goal clear while encouraging flexibility in its achievement. Greitens's success as head of TMC, Abrams told me, stems in part from his communicating the goal and hearing ideas from all sources for how best to advance the cause. One way that Greitens does this is with a steady stream of "yes" when he's taking in different points of view, said Abrams, which expresses an "encouragement to the person he's speaking with that is a natural by-product of being someone who's not just inquisitive and not just incredibly smart, but also so deeply optimistic." This optimism springs from Greitens's commitment to the goal of preserving human dignity and the many ways that this noble aspiration can be achieved.

———————

Eric Greitens searched his soul in his twenties and chose an uncertain future as a Navy SEAL. He acted on what he had learned from the failures to save innocents that he had observed overseas. He developed the belief that one needed to secure safety before humanitarian efforts could be effective. Out of his postwar personal doldrums, he envisioned a realistic way to ennoble veterans by enlisting them to serve here at home. Not only was this entrepreneurship, but also it was a way to hold himself accountable for acting on his beliefs.

He told me that he sees the integration of his life occurring, not in specific moments of perfect balance, but rather in phases. The strands of his life weave together over the course of time—from boxing, to humanitarian work, to military service, to providing a means for healing by his fellow veterans. For Greitens, leadership is about harmony over time, and not balance all the time. And it's in the service of producing not financial gain, but a meaningful life.

In his effort to preserve human dignity, Greitens uses whatever tools are at his disposal. He pursues his goal while dedicating himself to improving his own fitness to serve, through constant learning and training of his mind, body, and spirit. His example shows, again, that professional achievement is the result of devotion to the other parts of life—in his case, the values of his family, the needs of his community and society, and his own deeply personal beliefs. He inspires us to consider how we can learn to be more accountable for what we say we believe in, better able to work with what we have, and more attuned to our goals while finding creative ways to progress toward them.

4

Michelle Obama

Align Actions with Values,
Manage Boundaries Intelligently,
Embrace Change Courageously

On March 19, 2012, David Letterman hosted the creator of Joining Forces, a national initiative to support and honor America's service members and their families. "Ladies and gentlemen," the late-night television host told his studio audience, "please welcome the First Lady of the United States, Michelle Obama." And out she walked, greeting the host and beaming a broad smile to the audience, before nestling her nearly six-foot frame into the guest's chair.

"So, how's life in the White House?" Letterman asked.

"Trying to stay out of trouble," she replied, and the banter began. Does her husband ever complain about John Boehner (R-Ohio)? "It has never happened. He is always upbeat, particularly about Congress," she reported. Can you ever go anywhere? "I can't go *anywhere!*" she said, laughing, before telling the story of the time she successfully slipped out, incognito, to Target. "A woman actually walked up to me, right? I was in the detergent aisle, and she said, I kid you not, 'Excuse me, but I just have to ask you something. Can you reach up on that shelf and hand me that detergent?' And so I handed it to her, and the only thing she said was, 'Well, you didn't have to make it look so easy.'"

When Letterman asked for parenting advice, Obama paused, leaned in—her poise and comic timing on display—and advised him, "Sometimes you just have to be the alpha. Have you tried being the alpha?"

With the laughs out of the way, the conversation turned to the causes that Obama had come to the show to promote: Let's Move! her much-debated campaign against childhood obesity, and her military work with Joining Forces, which may not be as well known but is already making an impact, as Obama made clear. She reported convincing two thousand companies to hire more veterans and boasted that, as of August 2012, those companies had hired 125,000 veterans and committed to hiring another 250,000. She mentioned talking half of the nation's governors (at last count) into supporting laws that would make it easier for military spouses to transfer their professional licenses state to state.[1] She spoke about the struggles of military spouses, trying to raise kids and hold down a job while their partners were away—something she had some experience with during her husband's early political years. And, turning to Let's Move! she spoke about how easily takeout meals and television can creep into the daily routine of working parents and how her own children's pediatrician had called her out for it.[2]

It was a classic Michelle Obama performance: funny, honest, strategic, and yet down-to-earth, and passionate about the things that matter to her—particularly family, both hers and others'.

Michelle Obama has never been a wallflower. But it's also true that she never sought the limelight. Before she was swept onto the public stage as candidate Barack Obama's wife and campaign surrogate, she was a working mom who refused to let a dynamic career knock her family from its position of highest priority. After family came community, especially her neighborhood on Chicago's South Side. As vice president for community and external affairs at the University of Chicago's Medical School, Obama saw her job, to a large extent, as mending the long-frayed relationship between the university and the neighborhood where she had grown up and had chosen to raise her girls.

The world now knows Michelle Obama, the First Lady of the United States. Her face has graced hundreds of magazine covers. Although she hasn't always won over her biggest critics, she has maintained an approval rating most political figures can only dream of. But in 2008, Obama was still introducing herself to the American public and finding her way on the public stage. Who was this outspoken woman, who had walked away from a high-paying executive job to help her husband run for president but refused to be on the campaign trail—and away from her young daughters, Malia and Sasha—for more than one night at a time? She was a woman who spoke with conviction about community building and public service but expressed cynicism about politics; a woman who, despite that cynicism, exhibited the charisma of a born politician, whether she was rallying crowds of thousands at campaign events or making the rounds on late-night television.

Obama's previous career and her candor set her apart. As *Newsweek* noted during the campaign, "She isn't the traditional Stepford booster, smiling vacantly at her husband and sticking to a script of carefully vetted blandishments."[3] She has carved out a distinctive identity somewhere between those predecessors who were gracious hostesses or advocates for charity and those, like Eleanor

Roosevelt and Hillary Clinton, who were powerful, culture-shaping policy drivers in their own right.

Michelle Obama calls herself "Mom-in-Chief," continuing to prioritize her family while using her platform to advocate effectively for all families.[4] Her signature efforts as First Lady draw on the values instilled in her as a girl and her later experience working on the South Side, mobilizing disparate groups to work toward a common goal. They also represent an instructive, pioneering model—available for all the world to see—for managing the most common of challenges: meeting the sometimes competing demands of different parts of life.

Since moving to the White House, of course, Obama has faced an intensified challenge. On her visit to his set, David Letterman asked about her childhood and that of her daughters. "How much of those things that you remember and were meaningful to you can your kids do?" he asked. "For us, it's the values," she said. She and the president, she added, must work hard to ensure that the moment their kids walk into the residence, it feels like the South Side of Chicago. "The same values, the same rules, the same sense of responsibility. Because—of course, the *stuff* is different—there are butlers walking around. I mean, we didn't have that."[5]

Girl from the South Side

Michelle La Vaughn Robinson was born January 17, 1964, in Chicago, and grew up in a one-bedroom, one-bathroom apartment with her parents and her older brother, Craig. Her father, Fraser Robinson III, worked as a station laborer for the Chicago Water Department, earning about $5,700 a year, somewhat less than the median US household income at the time. Her mother, Marian, stayed home with the kids. Money was tight, but the family was a happy one. She was particularly close to her father, who was driven by the desire to provide a stable home for his family and a sense of hope for his children.[6]

Her parents "poured everything they had into me and Craig," Obama recalled during her speech at the Democratic National Convention in 2008. "It was the greatest gift a child could receive: never doubting for a single minute that you're loved and cherished and have a place in the world."

Around 1970, the Robinson family moved to the third-floor apartment of a brick bungalow in South Shore. It was a neighborhood in transition, as black families moved in and most of the white residents fled to the suburbs. Unlike many such neighborhoods, the remaining residents bound together to prevent the local bank and the A&P grocery store from shutting down. South Shore remained safe and stable.

Michelle Robinson was a strong student and earned a coveted spot at Whitney M. Young Magnet High School, a relatively new high school in an industrial pocket of Chicago dominated by factories, some shuttered. The thirteen-year-old had to take a bus and a train to get there, a commute that could take up to two hours, depending on the weather. Even as a teenager, Robinson was making education, highly valued in her family, a priority and taking actions to underscore that priority. She thrived, making the National Honor Society in her senior year and gaining admission to Princeton University, where Craig was a sophomore and a basketball star.

Whitney Young had drawn students of every race from every corner of Chicago and has been described as "an experiment in diversity that worked."[7] But this inclusiveness did not prepare her for the transition to Princeton in the fall of 1981. There were only ninety-four African Americans in Michelle Robinson's freshman class of eleven hundred, and she struggled to find her place among the crowd of high achievers. "I thought, there's no way I can compete with these kids," she told biographer Liza Mundy. "I'm not supposed to be here." But she would come to realize that the hardest part about

Princeton was getting in and that, she believed, her classmates from fancy prep schools weren't any smarter than she was. She found her niche socially after realizing that she and her African American peers moved less easily than others among Princeton's selective eating clubs and social organizations. "So," she says, "we created a community within a community and got involved at places like the Third World Center."[8] The center was a hub for minority students, presenting cultural and social events and offering an afterschool program, where Robinson worked in the afternoons.

At Princeton, Robinson became aware of her blackness in a way that she hadn't been in Chicago, and she grappled with the role of race in society. Despite feeling isolated as a black woman on the Ivy League campus, she began to internalize some of the thinking of her classmates, such as the drive to follow college with law school or a job in banking. Her senior thesis explored the tension she felt, analyzing the experiences of African Americans on campus and after they graduated. Did attending a predominantly white school like Princeton inevitably lead its black alumni away from the black community? she wondered. The matter of how to manage social boundaries was never far from her mind.

Robinson graduated with honors in 1985 and arrived at Harvard Law School that fall. "Princeton was a real crossroads for Michelle," her Harvard adviser, Charles Ogletree, told a biographer. "The question was whether I retain my identity given by my African American parents, or whether the education from an elite university has transformed me into something different . . . By the time she got to Harvard she had answered the question. She could be both brilliant and black."[9]

Michelle Robinson graduated in 1988 and returned to Chicago to join the blue-chip law firm Sidley Austin, where she specialized in marketing and intellectual property law. The partner who headed up the marketing group remembers her as "quite possibly the most ambitious associate I've ever seen."[10] Robinson worked hard and complained if the work wasn't challenging enough. But she kept her private life private, living in South Shore rather than downtown Chicago and rarely socializing with her coworkers.

The summer after Robinson started, the firm asked her to mentor a summer intern, a hotshot from Harvard Law named Barack Obama. After about a month, Barack asked her out, she recalled in 2011. "I thought, 'No way. This is completely tacky.'"[11] She turned him down, thinking it unprofessional to date a coworker. But he persisted, and before the end of the summer she agreed to go out for a movie and ice cream. After that, the connection between the two was obvious to any Sidley lawyer who witnessed them chatting in her office. He was courting her, and she was falling for him. The relationship continued after he returned to law school.

A few years down the partner track, Michelle Robinson began to have second thoughts about practicing law. In 1990, a close friend from college, Suzanne Alele, still in her twenties, died of cancer. Michelle's father died the following year. "If what you're doing doesn't bring you joy every single day, what's the point?" she has said. "I looked out at my neighborhood and sort of had an epiphany that I had to bring my skills to bear in the place that made me. I wanted to have a career motivated by passion and not just money."[12] She wanted to align her actions with her values.

Michelle Robinson also wanted love and a family. She married Barack Obama in the autumn of 1992; her brother Craig walked her down the aisle. Their marriage wouldn't always be easy, but it would be a partnership of equals. No one who knows the couple believes that Barack Obama would be president if he hadn't had Michelle Obama by his side.

She took a job in the office of Chicago mayor Richard Daley, eventually becoming Chicago's economic development coordinator. In 1993, she traded a job in government for one as executive director of

Public Allies, a nonprofit organization aimed at encouraging youth to work in the nonprofit sector. By all accounts, Obama liked being the boss. People who worked for her at Public Allies describe her as kind but firm. She threw herself into the organization, doing everything from raising money to licking envelopes. She expected the same dedication—and results—from her subordinates.[13]

Four years into their marriage, the Obamas posed for a photographer working on a book about couples in America. In the photograph, the couple sits on a sofa in the living room of their apartment in Hyde Park, a South Side haven that is home to more racial diversity and middle-class families than the surrounding neighborhoods, thanks to the University of Chicago campus.[14] Michelle leans back against her husband, her arm draped over his knee, looking directly toward the camera. Sunlight pours in through the windows. "There is a strong possibility that Barack will pursue a political career," she told the photographer. "I'm very wary of politics . . . When you are involved in politics, your life is an open book, and people can come in who don't necessarily have good intent. I'm pretty private, and like to surround myself with people that I trust and love."

But, she added, "it'll be interesting to see what life has to offer. In many ways, we are here for the ride, just sort of seeing what opportunities open up. And the more you experiment the easier it is to do different things." She continued, "Barack has helped me loosen up and feel comfortable with taking risks, not doing things the traditional way and sort of testing it out, because that is how he grew up."

From Springfield to the White House

In the fall of 1996, Barack Obama was elected to the Illinois State Senate, a job that required him to spend much of the week in Springfield, some two hundred miles away. Michelle Obama stayed in Chicago, soon becoming the associate dean of student services at the University of Chicago. In 1998, the Obamas' first child was born—a daughter given the Hawaiian name Malia. In 2001, their second daughter, Sasha, arrived, and Michelle was recruited to serve as a liaison between the University of Chicago hospitals and the local residents and organizations. She found the challenging position fulfilling, because the reputations of the university and its hospital system suffered in the African American community.[15]

But it was a difficult time personally for Michelle Obama, as a working woman raising two young children with a devoted but often absent husband, who spent three nights a week in Springfield. "It was hard. I was struggling with figuring out how to make this work for me," Obama told O magazine years later.[16] The period marked a low point in her marriage. Obama had never bargained for raising her girls alone, and she contemplated leaving her job to care for them full-time.

Then she rethought her situation. "I am sitting there with a new baby, angry, tired, and out of shape," she recalled to Liza Mundy. Obama needed to both carve out more time for herself and figure out a way to ease her burden on the home front that would help her marriage and her career. Asserting control of her new situation, she started rising at 4:30 to go to the gym on days when her husband was in town, both to get back in shape and to force him to take responsibility for the morning routine. She also hired a housekeeper to help with the cooking and cleaning.[17]

In 2004, her husband was elected US senator for Illinois. Michelle Obama played a small role in his campaign. She chose to keep her job and stay in the couple's South Side house after he moved to DC She wasn't willing—at that time—to uproot herself or her family for her husband's political career.

Yet on a cold February morning in Springfield, Illinois, a mere three years later, Michelle Obama climbed onto the stage with her husband, standing by his side as he announced his candidacy for president. She had come to believe that, despite her distaste for politics, her husband could achieve many of their shared goals through politics. Her quiet life on the South Side was over.

But her sense of who she was in the world remained. "There is no difference between the public Michelle and the private Michelle," attested her friend and University of Chicago law professor David Strauss.[18] Obama herself agreed: "The Michelle Obama I was last year is the same Michelle Obama I am this year. Different circumstances, same Michelle."[19] Her groundedness distinguishes her from many political wives. "Occasionally, it gives campaign people heartburn," admitted David Axelrod, the Obama campaign's chief strategist. "She's fundamentally honest—goes out there, speaks her mind, jokes. She doesn't parse her words or select them with an antenna for political correctness."[20]

Perhaps realizing the precariousness of authenticity in politics, Obama fortified the boundaries between her private life and her increasingly public one. She would campaign for her husband, but only on her own terms. And even after her husband won the election, she considered waiting until after her daughters had finished their school year before moving with him to Washington, DC, in January.[21] Even just thinking aloud about this possibility was unheard of, and it set the tone: family first. In the end, however, after making arrangements that met her children's needs, she and the girls—and her mother—all moved to the White House, as one family unit.

The First Lady was determined to bring a regular routine with them. At least five nights a week, the family eats dinner together at 6:30. She often talks of how she and President Obama struggle to maintain a "normal" life for their children under any and all circumstances. "We've always been the kind of people who go to the soccer games, shop at Target, go for bike rides, and make sure the girls get to the sleepovers," she explains. Even after becoming the First Family, "we still do that, but we usually have a lot of people watching now."[22]

Family First for the First Family

In January 2012, Michelle Obama settled into an armchair in the White House for an interview with CBS *This Morning* coanchor Gayle King. The interview began with what Obama had learned in her tenure as First Lady. "Has it been a learning curve?" King asked, throwing her a softball question for starters.

"Of course! Life is a learning curve," Obama replied.

Then King asked Obama what it had been like to leave her job, pushing back when Obama suggested that it wasn't a big deal for her. "But your career helps define who you are," King insisted.

"It doesn't for me," said Obama. "What I do in my life defines me. A career is one of the many things I do in my life. I am a mother first."[23] It is in conveying this attitude with her words and actions that she has had a powerful influence during her White House tenure. Constantly under the microscope, she knows that she is a model for young Americans; the public choices she has made about her private life are signifiers, and drivers, of cultural change.

Obama didn't dive headfirst into the First Lady job, refusing in 2008 and early 2009 to name projects she might tackle. In interview after interview she explained that the only issue she was then focused on was her children and their transition to a new city, a new school, and a new life as the president's daughters.

Only after her family had adjusted to life in the White House did she turn her focus to the East Wing. She wanted any project that she undertook as First Lady to be personally meaningful. As she told King, "I just don't get into symbolic achievements . . . I don't want this just to be PR." She added, "I'm always asking people on the ground, 'Do you feel what we're trying to do?' And until they feel it, in their own lives and in their own homes, we've got to keep working."

That is why, for instance, after initially focusing on veteran unemployment, Joining Forces had tackled the issue of license portability.

In their visits to bases over the years, Obama and Jill Biden, wife of the vice president and Michelle Obama's partner on this project, had heard countless stories about how differing state licensing requirements—for nurses, teachers, real estate brokers, and other professionals—posed a hurdle for military spouses, who move ten times as often as the average American. Obama is the initiative's best spokeswoman, saleswoman, and storyteller, and at a Governor's Association meeting in 2012, she announced their goal: that fifty states would pass legislation supporting military spouse license portability by 2014. At the time, twelve states had such laws.[24]

Obama's second initiative, for which she might be better known, is Let's Move!—her effort to end childhood obesity within a generation. Its success or failure won't be known for years, or decades, but the project offers another example of Obama's leadership style. As First Lady, Obama has powerful connections, but she wields no direct power over the millions of children in America and the local school districts that serve them lunch five days a week, not to mention the parents who control their children's afternoon activities and serve snacks and dinner.

What she can do is set specific goals for the initiative (for example, to reformulate products to improve nutrition by 2015 and to reduce the cost of fruits and vegetables) and then collaborate with government departments and use her connections, and her example, to galvanize others. By personally lobbying members of Congress, for instance, she helped pass the Hunger-Free Kids Act, which set new standards for the nutritional quality of food served in public schools. By planting a vegetable garden at the White House, she drew attention to the importance of having access to fresh vegetables. As for encouraging kids to be more active, she has, as the *New York Times* noted, "shimmied, skipped, hopscotched, hula-hooped, jumping-jacked, and potato-sack-raced her way through her tenure as First Lady, using not just her position but her body to push for more exercise and better nutrition for children."[25]

To measure their impact, Obama and her Let's Move! staff track data, such as the number of school cafeterias with salad bars (one thousand added in the first two years) or the number of children's tennis courts that the US Tennis Association has built or refurbished (three thousand).[26]

One day in the spring of 2011, Obama and her staff huddled around a computer in an East Wing office to watch a new Beyoncé video supporting the First Lady's campaign. The pop star had recorded "Move Your Body," a catchy, heart-pumping workout song (and a play on her smash hit, "Get Me Bodied"), with a related video of Beyoncé performing the song with students in a school cafeteria, disco lights flashing. The video went viral within days, watched by millions on YouTube, changing attitudes about the importance of taking care of one's health.

"A lot of what we do [in politics] is, frankly, bullshit," David Axelrod said. "That's the nature of government. It's the nature of politics. What [Michelle Obama] is doing is very real." Her work, he added, "may end up having more of an impact" than the policy initiatives of her husband.[27]

The Skills Michelle Obama Exemplifies

Life in the White House bubble is a world away from the bungalow Michelle Obama grew up in, but South Side values give her life continuity, and they guide her in both the public and the private spheres. She follows her own moral compass, often in the face of intense pressure to do otherwise, when making decisions big and small. The public initiatives that she has undertaken build on her core values, and they reflect her ability to adapt and act on these values on a vast scale, under the glare of hottest spotlight.

Michelle Obama has broken barriers and is an inspiration to millions around the world. She is a powerful model of someone who has grown to become a leader with a rewarding life that brings the four domains together in a way that works for her and the people who depend on her. Although she embodies many other skills—knowing who she is and what matters, being clear about what she expects from others, and challenging the status quo, to name a few—I focus here on what she's learned about how to align her actions with her values (being real), manage boundaries intelligently (being whole), and embrace change courageously (being innovative).

Be Real: Align Actions with Values

Michelle Obama makes choices about how she spends her time and energy—choices that match what she cares about. Obama possesses a deep understanding of achievements she thinks are important, so she carefully watches the demands on her time. She pays attention to whether her actions flow from her values, and that gives her focus, passion, and perseverance. She also knows when and how to say no. She doesn't let others' expectations—for example, about how she should act as a mother—compel her to take on responsibilities that are not personally meaningful.

The capacity to align your actions with your values is central to acting with authenticity. It's thinking through life's choices in light of what you know matters most to you, despite social pressures to do otherwise. Developing this capacity is a lifelong journey. Obama devoted her senior year in college to exploring a social issue—one that also had deep personal significance. As with having to commute two hours as a thirteen-year-old, this process deepened her awareness of the person she was and the person she wanted to be. She was grappling with how to reconcile the ethics imbued in her as a girl from the South Side of Chicago with those she would need to adopt as an adult in the wider world. Devoting her senior thesis to this topic was in itself a moment of aligning actions with values.

This steady stream of self-exploration persisted through law school and then later, when she left the law to pursue her career in a way that would give back to the community. She was, of course, well compensated, but the role of vice president for community and external affairs at the University of Chicago's Medical School allowed her to apply her talents toward positive social ends.

Obama focuses her attention on things that, after careful consideration, she knows matter to her. As she said, it is her actions, and not her position or career trajectory, that are the truest signs of her identity ("What I do in my life defines me"). Obama, like all those who have accomplished greatness in their lives, chooses for herself what is worthy of her devotion.

Be Whole: Manage Boundaries Intelligently

Obama is able to create boundaries between the different parts of her life to help her meet important needs and goals. She knows when to merge these aspects, and she knows when to separate them. She exercises this skill when deciding to create boundaries that allow for focus on a single responsibility, such as her family. She also creates boundaries for the rest of her family, respecting the shelter that they require by ensuring that they dine together as often as possible.

This commitment to maintaining boundaries has been the pattern in her adult life. At Sidley, she lived on the South Shore rather than downtown Chicago and didn't hang out much with her coworkers; they didn't even know when her father died.[28] But this doesn't mean that she is rigid in managing the boundaries. Her choices demonstrate intelligent flexibility. Remember that at first she turned down Barack Obama's romantic attentions, thinking it unprofessional to date a coworker. This shows a clear understanding of both the importance of boundaries and the possibility of managing them creatively.

Perhaps more significantly, although she was reluctant to commit her family to a White House campaign, not to mention the public demands of being the First Family, Michelle Obama adjusted. As ever, she did so in her own distinctive way; after all, her mother lives at the White House. When the children were younger, she carved out private time to work out in the morning and, at the same time, compelled her husband to take some domestic responsibilities. This was not only managing boundaries but also creating a four-way win. It made her feel better about herself, it improved family functioning, and it shaped the attitude and behavior of the man who would be president in a way that made him, for many potential voters, a more attractive candidate.

Despite the constant hum of computers and smartphones and various demands, Obama is able to turn her attention to one thing at a time rather than try to accomplish everything at once. Some people are by nature private, others social. Michelle Obama seems to be one of those introverted types, who, because of her commitment to service, must rise to many occasions of being in a highly public role. I saw this myself when I was with her at the White House Forum on Workplace Flexibility in 2010. She was attentively engaged with each person she spoke to, with sustained, relaxed, and yet unwavering eye contact. At the same time, she was clearly self-contained. It takes real leadership skill to maintain one's focus while moving flexibly from one person or task to another.

Be Innovative: Embrace Change Courageously

Obama sees change in her life as an occasion for opportunity. She looks forward to it, she doesn't fear it, and she embraces opportunities for personal growth. She realizes that her life may take unexpected twists and turns. She is confident she will be able not only to survive the unexpected but also to thrive in new opportunities.

The young Michelle Robinson's move from her local high school to Whitney Young was an early sign of her willingness to embrace the new for the sake of expanding horizons. She had to travel far and enter a new social world, going against the tradition of staying in the neighborhood. Looking back, this move might not seem like much, but for her at the time it was a big deal, requiring both courage and the support of her family.

This same motif was in evidence at Princeton, which was at first a shocking cultural change. But trusted friends and loved ones helped it become a comfortable world, a place where Michelle Robinson could grow and increase her confidence. Significantly, Michelle Obama doesn't jump right in to new challenges; she's thoughtful and careful. She is not a natural-born risk taker. As an adult she has learned, in part from her husband's model, to "loosen up and feel comfortable" with taking on new experiences.

Indeed, getting settled in the role of First Lady was not easy. She didn't even want to move into the White House when President Obama's term began in January 2009, preferring instead to stay in Chicago for her daughters to finish out their school year there. By being unafraid to acknowledge her concerns about the enormous changes, she overcame her resistance and took advantage of this remarkable opportunity to change her daily life in a way that allowed her to have a new and larger impact on the world.

Michelle Obama learned on the rough-and-tumble road of the first White House campaign trail that the public doesn't always want leaders who choose transparency over opacity. With her, she unapologetically suggested, what you see is what you get. But this doesn't mean that she's immutable. Her continual self-exploration, and the deliberate decisions that come from it, allow Obama to quite consciously act according to her values, and not according to what others want her to be. Those values keep her close to her family and to real people on the ground, to whom she listens with care. Doing so makes her effective in seeking realistic ways to better their lives. As First Lady, she helps children embrace healthy choices, ensures veterans are treated with dignity, and provides a model for young women around the world by demonstrating how to be a strong, caring mother who achieves significant goals by serving the world beyond the home.

Michelle Obama's success as a public figure and the voice of our nation's First Family is a direct consequence of her adherence to her core values and her dedication to family and community. She's open about the difficulties she has faced as a person of color, the duplicities of the political world, and the challenges of protecting her children from the vagaries of White House life. This candor, combined with her genuine commitment to advocating for those in need—not to mention her great sense of humor and humility—explains her unusual popularity. She leads the life she wants.

5

Julie Foudy

*Know What Matters,
Help Others,
Challenge the Status Quo*

One afternoon in June 2010, a dozen South African boys and girls converted a dusty, all-dirt courtyard in the middle of Soweto Township into a soccer field, using trash cans in place of nets. It happens every day, thousands of times, in every country around the world. Someone has a soccer ball, kids gather, they set up a makeshift field, they play. But there was something special about this game. Julie Foudy—retired American soccer star, member of the team that won the first Women's World Cup, athlete with two Olympic gold medals to her name—wanted to join. Someone suggested they play boys versus girls.

Foudy had traveled to South Africa to cover the World Cup for ESPN. She was dressed like a stylish TV host, even in the pickup game, wearing a blue sleeveless top, black trousers, and heels. Yet she ran comfortably up and down the impromptu pitch, calling out to other players, still the very image of a national team player, even if her dark brown mane wasn't pulled into the ponytail of her pro days. And after scoring a goal, she circled back to her teammates, one arm raised in a power fist. "Girls, two-zero!" she shouted. Reaching them, she held both hands up to do high tens with each of her protégées.[1]

These days, Foudy is most often in the public eye as a soccer commentator and feature reporter for ESPN and ABC. With her girl-next-door looks, easy manner, and experience on the field, she's a natural for the part—not to mention that, as she said in her Hall of Fame induction speech, "I've never met a microphone that I don't like."[2] She breaks down games, explaining strategy and walking less soccer-savvy viewers through plays, and she doesn't hold back her opinions, as when she ranted against the use of penalty kicks to decide games still tied after two overtimes. "I think they should play 'til they die," she once quipped.[3] But she is still best known as a soccer star in her own right.

Foudy earned a spot on the US national team in 1987, at the age of sixteen, and played for the squad for seventeen years. For thirteen of those seasons, she served as a captain, exemplifying what could have been the team motto: train hard, laugh harder. The *New York Times* once described Foudy as "the team's comic relief and its social conscience."[4] The latter label was a nod to the causes she has championed off the field, the most high profile being her support for Title IX. But as captain, she helped manage the inevitable conflicts that arise on a team through a combination of straight talk and humor. She led a squad that supported its players through marriages and divorces, births and deaths.

Through it all, Foudy kept the team focused on the goal: to win. And win it did: two World Cup trophies, three Olympic medals, hundreds of thousands of fans, and oodles of respect. By 2004, when Foudy retired, US women's soccer had been transformed from a hobby to a professional sport. Foudy's retirement after the 2004

Olympic games, alongside fellow soccer legends Mia Hamm and Joy Fawcett, marked the end of what the Associated Press called a "golden era" of US women's soccer.[5]

The First Kick

Julie Foudy grew up in Mission Viejo, California, a mostly residential town south of Los Angeles. Her parents, Jim and Judy, encouraged their children to be active, and Julie, the youngest of four, was kicking soccer balls with her older brothers as soon as she could walk. Although she enjoyed tennis and even surfing, soccer was her favorite sport, and she had mastered dribbling by the age of six. Foudy's parents made it clear: if she chose to play soccer and to set aside other activities in order to focus on the game, that was her choice to make. As long as she did well in school, they would support it. "They opened the doors for me and said, 'Walk through the ones you want to—no, *leap* through them,'" she recalled.[6]

The day she turned seven and became eligible for the local American Youth Soccer Organization team, she signed up. One of the most talented girls in the Southern California AYSO league, Foudy was assigned to play midfield. The position is physically demanding, and it requires a keen sense of strategy. Like a football quarterback or a point guard on the basketball court, a soccer midfielder watches the game as it unfolds and calls out plays. Foudy was named a league all-star and invited to join a traveling team, the Soccerettes.

As a Soccerette, Foudy thrived. She was a natural athlete, but she was also committed to improving her game, spending hours every day kicking a ball against her parent's garage. She developed the aggressive style that would make her an offensive threat over the course of her career. She was named Southern California Player of the Year for three years straight.

At thirteen, Foudy tried out for the state team run by the Olympic Development Program, an effort designed to sift out players talented enough to compete for a shot at the national team. In a matter of months, Foudy went from the California team to the West Regional team to the US "19 and under" team, landing a spot on the national team in 1987 while she was still in high school.

To play for the national team, Foudy had to devote even more time to soccer. She spent her summer vacations training and traveling for games rather than hanging out with her friends. She missed proms and even her high school graduation.[7] Foudy told me that her commitment to soccer made such decisions clear, if not always easy. On the evening of graduation, she lay in a hotel bed in Italy, where her team was for a tournament, depressed. Then her coach knocked on the door. He'd come to tell her that her hard work had earned her a spot on the starting lineup. The news erased any lingering sadness, she told biographer Matt Christopher.[8] And the truth was, she hadn't given up her friends to train with the national team. Her teammates *were* her friends.

Heavily recruited by colleges, Foudy narrowed her choices to Harvard, Stanford, Berkeley, and the University of North Carolina. UNC had an advantage. Anson Dorrance, the coach of the national team, also headed up the school's women's soccer program, and many of Foudy's national teammates played for UNC. The program was considered the top in the nation, and Dorrance offered Foudy a full scholarship.[9]

But even though soccer was important to Foudy, so was her education. She knew she wanted to attend a college with the highest academic standards. She chose Stanford, helped in her decision by the belief that she could make a big impact on the school's up-and-coming program.

Foudy majored in biology and fulfilled rigorous pre-med requirements, with the intention of going to medical school. As a Stanford Cardinal, Foudy quickly emerged as the linchpin of the team.

Christopher describes her "almost nonstop string of chatter as she encourages her teammates, calls out changes in strategy, and alerts them to what is happening around them."[10] Her never-ending talk earned her the nickname "Loudy Foudy."

Foudy was still playing for the national team, and people were starting to recognize its engine. If Foudy's teammate Mia Hamm was "the face of women's soccer" in the United States—signing lucrative deals with Nike and other commercial brands—Foudy was its voice. She was the one who set up the offense on the field and, in critical seconds before win-or-lose minutes, urged her teammates to "beat them to every ball."[11]

She had to learn how to motivate her teammates, though. "I was incredibly competitive and outspoken," she told me recently, and that could cause problems. "I would be in the middle of a game, veins popping out of my neck, and in the moment, I would lose it on a player," she admitted. On the field and in the locker room, though, she observed other styles, from the feisty leadership of the team's first captain, April Heinrichs, to the quiet, lead-by-example mode of Mia Hamm. "What I learned over the years is that you have to realize *who* you're talking to, and which style works best," she told me.[12]

Playing for the national team wasn't glamorous. The players earned no salary. They traveled by bus, stayed in cheap motels, and were given $10 a day in meal money. "We were the red-headed stepchild team," fellow player Michelle Akers recalled. "The men's team was what was going to give US soccer and this country a name, and so they got all the money and the respect."[13] But for Foudy, the national team offered a chance to work hard, fulfill a personal passion, and spend time with friends. Many players on the national team describe it as a sisterhood. As the group grew closer personally, they became stronger as a unit.

"When I first started playing soccer, there was no national team," Foudy recalled in a 2009 speech. "And then after I made the team people said, 'Well, there will never be a Women's World Cup.' And we said, 'Yes, there will be, and we are going to win the first one.'"[14] And in 1991, the team did just that, winning the first-ever Women's World Cup trophy (and beating the US men's team to a world championship) in front of more than sixty-five thousand cheering, autograph-seeking fans in Beijing. The excitement in the stadium and on the streets after the win gave Foudy the first inkling that her team could make history. The team members thought, Foudy said in the HBO documentary *Dare to Dream*, "It's going to be like this when we get home. People are now going to pay attention!"[15]

But they didn't. No media showed up at the airport to capture the champions' home coming. In *Dare to Dream*, Foudy recalled that the US Soccer Federation even considered disbanding the women's national team, thinking a new team could be assembled if and when another Women's World Cup was announced.

But the national team survived, and soon young fans began showing up at the games, asking for autographs. "My heroes and my role models were three-hundred-pound football players and eight-foot-tall basketball players," Foudy said about her childhood in the documentary. "I don't remember ever having a woman that I've pointed to and said, 'That's who I'm going to be one day.'"[16] But Foudy began to see herself as an ambassador for the sport, as someone who could inspire the next generation of female soccer players.

Activist

Foudy graduated from Stanford in the spring of 1994 and immediately faced a big decision: attend Stanford Medical School, where she had been admitted, or pursue soccer, a less certain career. With the national team on hiatus and no other team to train with over the summer, it would have been easy to retire her number 11 jersey. But Foudy wasn't ready to leave the sport she loved and abandon the growing numbers of young fans. And her longtime boyfriend, Ian

Sawyers—a British-born soccer coach whom she'd met through club circles in Southern California and who would start coaching the Cardinals the following year—supported her.

Foudy chose to pursue what was most meaningful to her. She deferred medical school for a year and moved to Sweden, where she trained with a local team, although she returned the following year to marry Sawyers and continue training with the national team.

"We always said we could really make a huge impact on soccer if people had a glimpse of what we were all about," Foudy said.[17] And she saw the 1996 Olympic games in Atlanta as an opportunity. But it was an opportunity that Foudy almost walked away from when she learned that the women's team had been offered a mere $1,000-a-month stipend, with a bonus if it won gold. Their male counterparts had been promised a bonus if they won *any* medal.[18] This struck Foudy as fundamentally unfair. As the captain and the team's most garrulous player, Foudy pushed the issue with the US Soccer Federation and found resistance. Fortuitously, Foudy met Billie Jean King.

"I would get these calls, 'Hey, King—help!'" the tennis legend recalled. "Don't play," King advised. "That's the only leverage you have."[19] It was a scary proposition for the players, who knew they might be giving up their only chance for Olympic gold. But Foudy convinced eight key players on the team to strike, and she called them daily to bolster their spirits during the tense weeks that followed.

Ultimately, the committee gave in, agreeing to give the women's team the same deal as the men's. Foudy and her team went on to win the gold. But the experience changed her. It made her step back and ask what kind of legacy she and her team wanted to leave. As she would later say, "Winning was great, really great. But more important, we wanted to leave the sport in a better state."[20] Inside the Olympic athlete, the seed of activism had been planted. Foudy told me that Billie Jean King "would always say to me, 'If you had a clean slate what would you want to do, not for you, but for the next generation coming behind you? Think about them. That's what I want you to think about.'" Foudy brought this perspective to every contract negotiation after that.

Winning at the Olympics earned the players media attention and sponsorship offers: soon, Reebok offered Foudy an endorsement deal, which she was thrilled by but hesitant to accept. She had seen reports about sporting goods companies employing child labor and felt troubled not only by the revelation but also by the apathy of fellow athletes, reported Jeff Savage in a 1999 biography.[21] Foudy wasn't about to link her name to a company that was taking advantage of children, even if that meant giving up a lucrative endorsement deal.

Reebok said that its soccer balls were manufactured without using child labor, but Foudy insisted on traveling to the factory in rural Pakistan to see for herself. Satisfied, she agreed to endorse the company. For taking her stand, she was awarded the FIFA Fair Play Award—the first American and the first woman to receive that award.

But if sponsors, not to mention the US Soccer Federation, had come around, the media hadn't. Broadcasters hadn't even aired the medal-winning game live. And when the federation announced that the next Women's World Cup would be held in arenas like Giants Stadium (now MetLife Stadium) and the Rose Bowl, sportswriters ridiculed the decision. Some even accused the federation of lying about early ticket sales.

Foudy and her team went on to win the 1999 World Cup in a sold-out Giants Stadium and to play for the San Diego Spirit, one of the eight teams in the short-lived Women's United Soccer Association, the first US professional women's soccer league.

Off the Field

In February 2002, the National Wrestling Coaches Association, the College Gymnastics Association, and the US Track and Field and

Cross Country Coaches Association, among other groups representing male athletes and alumni, filed suit against the federal government, challenging the constitutionality of Title IX.

Enacted in 1972 and officially called the Patsy T. Mink Equal
Opportunity in Education Act, Title IX transformed athletics programs across the United States. If a school received any money from
Washington, DC, it had to offer female athletes the same opportunities that it offered male athletes. Foudy has described Title IX as "one
of the most profound civil rights laws ever passed in this country."[22]
Sports programs for girls and women sprouted in response to the law,
opening a world of opportunity for female athletes, Foudy among
them. There would be no women's national soccer team without Title
IX, no World Cup trophy. And now it was under attack.

Then, in June 2002, US secretary of education Rod Paige set up
a commission to review the impact of Title IX and recommend revi-
sions. It was a move many people read as the beginning of an attack
on Title IX from within the US government. Foudy was asked to serve
on the commission and poured herself into it, building up a network
of experts to help her understand the subtleties of the legislation.
"It was clear she wasn't just taking the party line," recalled Jocelyn
Samuels, a vice president of the National Women's Law Center, who
remembered getting calls from Foudy at all hours. The combination
of frequent cross-country trips to Washington for meetings and the
high-stress challenge of learning about the law in order to defend it
was hard on Foudy. "She felt it was a defining moment for women's
athletics," said Samuels, "and that took a lot out of her."[23]

When the commission released a draft report in early 2003, suggesting that the policy be weakened, Foudy and fellow commission
member Donna de Varona, a former Olympic swimmer, released a
much-publicized minority report stating that the commission's work
had not been undertaken in an open, fair, and inclusive manner
(for instance, a critical procedural vote had been taken while Foudy

was in the bathroom). The two women also argued that the official findings did not properly address the disparity between men and women or the continuing discrimination against women and girls in athletics. The Department of Education ultimately decided not to push to change Title IX.

Foudy continued to take on causes. She has filmed public-service announcements for the American Youth Soccer Organization and antismoking campaigns. She has served as president and as a board member of the Women's Sports Foundation; on the board of Athletes for Hope, a nonprofit organization that encourages athletes to give back to their communities; and as a spokesperson for GlobalGirl Media, a nonprofit organization dedicated to empowering high school girls from underserved communities through training in media, leadership, and journalism. "When you are holding the camera and you're telling stories that people are typically not hearing," Foudy said in one GlobalGirl Media video, "you are providing insight into your community and providing leadership for all of the other young girls out there who want to do the same thing."[24]

"During an era in which most athletes stand for nothing more than their shoe company's logo, Foudy has been called this generation's Billie Jean King," wrote USA *Today* reporter Kelly Whiteside.[25]

Overtime

Foudy played her final game for the national team in December 2004. She had experienced big-time victories and crushing losses, but most of all, she and her teammates had transformed women's soccer. "We're getting paid, and these women provided it for us," said Cat Whitehill, a current player on the national team. "What my life is like now is completely due to them," agreed Whitehill's teammate Abby Wambach.[26]

Foudy hadn't achieved everything she'd wanted—most notably, a successful professional women's soccer league. But she felt upbeat as she spoke to her teammates in the pregame huddle. "Let's have a ball out there tonight, huh? Let's have fun. That's what this team has been about for eighteen years. Let's do it! Here we go!"[27]

Foudy was happy to be able to spend more time with her husband. In her national team days, and especially now that the couple had two young children—Isabel Ann and Declan—the travel had gotten hard. "I have gotten very good at saying no," she told me. "Because every trip, even though you want to do them, is a missed opportunity with your kids."

But her job as an ESPN sports commentator and soccer analyst still requires a certain amount of time on the road, something that Sawyers encourages. "To have that person in your life who tells you, 'No, this is great, you're doing what you love, and I fully support it' makes a world of difference," Foudy said to me. She works during early mornings and school hours from a home office. When she flies around the world to cover the World Cup, Sawyers is home with the kids in Southern California. "And he's a great cook," she said, adding, "My specialty is cereal."

Although she doesn't train as she did in her national team days, Foudy still runs regularly or goes mountain biking. "I exercise for my sanity," she told *Fitness* magazine. "I can't imagine not having some physical activity to de-stress." She told me that she also wants her children to play sports, though not necessarily soccer. Her attitude, like her parents', is that her children should play what they want.

In 1995, Foudy and Sawyers launched the Julie Foudy Soccer Camp and, in 2006, the Julie Foudy Sports Leadership Academy. "All these things I learned on the soccer field, they gave me confidence, taught me how to be disciplined—how to deal with loss and adversity," Foudy explained in a video interview with Soccer.com, her young kids audible in the background.[28] The six-day residential

academy teaches young girls ages twelve to eighteen how to be leaders on the field and in life. There are different styles of leadership, she
tells the girls. "It's okay to be quiet. You can still make a difference."[29]

Foudy and her family attend every academy, and there are
always other members of the women's national team and star athletes such as Billie Jean King, Robin Roberts, and Aimee Mull.
Together, these women impart lessons on leadership, volunteerism,
and social change. They show girls that they can do whatever they
set their minds to and that each girl should feel comfortable with
the person she is. "Love the skin you are in" is the watchword.
The academy is a place where girls can gain confidence and feel
empowered.

"Other than my kids and my family, I am most proud of what we
have created with our leadership academies," Foudy said in 2011.
"Sports gives you a gift in life like no other: self-confidence and perseverance, and how to deal with setbacks, how to deal with losses,
how to deal with adversity—all these things that are so vital to being
a complete human being and a successful leader in life."[30]

The Skills Julie Foudy Exemplifies

Countless others have benefited from Julie Foudy's courage to take
action and mobilize people toward goals that matter. Not content
with winning at the highest levels of her sport, inspired by the injus-
tices she encountered on her path to soccer glory, Foudy has turned
her talents to making things better for future generations of athletes
through her political action and her role as an educator.

As a result of her perseverance—and with the support of family, teammates, friends, and coaches—she has cultivated leadership
skills as an athlete and as a public advocate for gender equality and
human rights. Like the other five examples in this book, Foudy illustrates all the skills, but I focus here on what her life teaches us about

how to know what matters (being real), help others (being whole), and challenge the status quo (being innovative).

Be Real: Know What Matters

Julie Foudy knows how important each of the different aspects of her life is to her. She is able to clearly articulate the facets of her life that deserve her attention, energy, and time. Her self-awareness enables her to understand the value of each of her roles and relationships. She is also able to see the bigger picture, in which all her different roles contribute to her vision of the future.

Foudy missed her high school graduation in order to play a critical national team game in Europe. And she missed other normal activities that high school kids look forward to. What's noteworthy is the confidence she demonstrated in making conscious choices about what mattered to her. It was a method of decision making she learned early from her parents, who compelled her to make her own choices. She didn't follow the social pressures of the day, as do many teenagers. She knew her mind and her heart, and she acted accordingly.

Leadership requires identifying the parts of your life that deserve your attention. Foudy demonstrated the ability to know what matters when she took a stand against child labor, helping push a global tragedy to the front burner in the wealthy nations of the West by demanding to know whether children were being employed in the production of Reebok gear before consenting to an endorsement. She risked losing a lot of money in doing so, but she emerged as a role model for athletes with a conscience. By having the courage to act on her values, Foudy solidified her sense of purpose and her ability to create positive change.

When Foudy chose to attend Stanford University, she demonstrated a deep understanding of her life priorities. At Stanford, she saw the opportunity to contribute to a growing soccer program as well as to advance her academic aspirations. To make this choice, she had to know she cared about more than just being a great soccer player. She knew enough about her values and beliefs to make a difficult decision.

Perhaps a more profound illustration of this skill was Foudy's response to the unfairness she observed in the differential stipends for men and women players at the 1996 Olympics and in the early years with the US Women's national team. Her belief in equality fed her and her teammates' fight for gender parity. She didn't deny her feelings of righteous indignation; instead, she used them to refine her understanding of her values. "One of the big issues for me and the team in this fight for equality was to *not* be angry, but to be strong and to be fair," she told me. "It was our job to show them the light, not to reach out in anger and disgust, which are completely counterproductive and cause regression, rather than progression."[31]

Be Whole: Help Others

Foudy looks for opportunities to help many different people. Today she has a strong web of supportive relationships. Whether these relationships are with colleagues, neighbors, past teammates (to whom she often says, "You are stuck with me as my BFF for life!"), friends, or family, she sees the value in helping others. Her relationships are built on mutual trust, with a focus on mutual well-being. She views relationships as a means for enriching her own life and the lives of others.

Let's look at some of the highlights of her efforts to help people. Foudy grew up in a strongly supportive environment, and this no doubt contributed to her capacity to create beneficent communities for the next generation of girls. Her leadership academy allows her to express most directly her commitment to promoting sports as a vehicle not only for promoting youth fitness but also for building confidence and self-esteem. And in doing so she helps cultivate a new cohort of leaders, one girl at a time. As a spokesperson for

GlobalGirl Media, Foudy helped promote the organization's 2009 Kick It Up! campaign, a program in South Africa and Los Angeles to mentor and train high school girls as digital video journalists for the 2010 FIFA World Cup. Not only do all these activities serve to empower young women, but also they produce in Foudy a sense of meaning and purpose and establish her as a role model for her own children.

In devoting substantial effort to fighting the rollback of Title IX, Foudy again showed her commitment to making things fair for women and girls and to help those coming after her. Her dedication to being an informed and persuasive advocate helped shape the regulatory environment for sports. And Foudy continues to use the opportunities she has as a journalist and public figure to educate and to promote causes—such as Beyond Sport, a nonprofit group committed to using sports as a vehicle for positive social change, as well as Athletes for Hope, mentioned earlier—that provide assistance to people in need. These aren't just items on a curriculum vitae. Foudy's many roles as a spokeswoman and board member show her looking for ways to make things better by helping others. By dedicating her attention to providing resources—time, money, ideas, reputation, and contacts—for others, Foudy gives her own life a greater sense of purpose, and, at the same time, she propagates a virtuous cycle, enlarging the reservoir of support for the causes she is passionate about. It's the law of reciprocity, and it's true in cultures around the world and throughout history: people want to help people who help people. Great leaders find their own ways to follow this law wherever they go.

Be Innovative: Challenge the Status Quo

Foudy challenges traditional assumptions about how things are done, experimenting to make things better whenever possible. When making decisions about how to spend her time and energy, Foudy is not constrained by conventions. Rather than follow the pack, she is willing to be the first one to try new ways of accomplishing goals. She is not overly concerned about how others will perceive her. Instead, she is willing to step out on a limb to find a creative solution to the challenges she faces.

By traveling to Pakistan to see for herself the conditions under which Reebok products were made, Foudy confronted the traditional path taken by sponsored athletes. She demonstrated that she was not willing to take a great cash deal without first drawing attention to a human rights issue. In so doing she inspired other athletes to follow her lead.

Battling the forces that would repeal Title IX regulations designed to create parity for women's sports required investing time and energy in a cause about which Foudy felt deeply. Her actions in expressing dissent in 2003 demonstrated her willingness to challenge sexist institutional arrangements. In the face of the review commission's majority recommendation to weaken Title IX, others might have lost their cool or quit in protest. But Foudy applied the relentless tenacity she had come to know as an ingredient for success on the soccer field. On a team, she recalled, "you're sometimes going to have to make decisions that aren't popular . . . and talk to teammates who maybe aren't, you know, staying with the team's principles and foundations."[32]

Asked by an interviewer what she would change if she had a magic wand, Foudy recently said, "You find so many kids who grow up and think, 'Well, I'm not this or I'm not that, so I can't be a leader. It's not what I see in magazines. It's not what I read in history books. I don't look that way. I don't sound that way. I don't have CEO or president next to my name.' If I could, which is what we're doing with the Leadership Academy, I would open up the definition of leadership so all kids understand that yes, you do have it. It just comes in different forms. We don't all have the same type of leadership skills, so figure out what your leadership skill set is, and be true to that."[33] Foudy is using her talents and her time in the service of giving younger women the encouragement and tools they need to question cultural messages they've internalized about the limits of what is possible. She contests outmoded models.

Because she knew what mattered to her, Julie Foudy was inspiring and vivid about the dream: we will have a Women's Cup team! She had suffered the consequences of gender inequity, she had seen how she wanted women's soccer to advance, and then she stood up for the rights of women athletes—her people—in the face of injustice, with the hope of leaving the sport in a better state than it was when she started. Foudy's is an admirable life story, because she has achieved success in her professional world by reaping the benefits of harmonious integration among the disparate parts of her life. We see the pursuit of four-way wins as she strives to create value not only in her career, but also in her role as a family member, as an advocate for women's empowerment, and for her own personal growth and health.

Based on her own experience, and from what she learned about the importance of girls having a different mind-set about what they could accomplish, she committed to helping build their confidence. "Choose to matter!" is what girls gleefully chant at her training camps. And when she needed support in mustering the will to challenge long-standing traditions, she asked for it, from mentors like Billie Jean King and teachers of her own.

6

Bruce Springsteen

Embody Values Consistently,
Clarify Expectations,
Create Cultures of Innovation

Bruce Springsteen has always appeared at ease on stage. Indeed, he commands it. But on March, 15, 1999, he stood somewhat hesitantly, shifting from one leg to the other, at his induction into the Rock and Roll Hall of Fame, facing a black-tie audience and a standing ovation. He'd spoken at inductions for Roy Orbison, Bob Dylan, and others—"artists whose music was a critical part of my life," he said—and now it was his turn.[1] After failing to get the audience to sit by repeating "thank you" again and again, he cleared his throat a few times. That did the trick.

"You were scaring me a bit there," he told U2's Bono, who had introduced The Boss. "I wasn't *that* good." Then he offered a warning to the audience: "The records took two years, the shows three hours, so the speech may take a little while!"

The evening gave Springsteen a chance to credit the artists whose music had fed his creative mind, and to thank the people who had helped him along the way, starting with his mother, Adele, who sat beaming in the audience. She had once taken out a loan to buy her son a guitar for Christmas.[2] "As importantly," Springsteen noted, "she gave me a sense of work as something that was joyous, and that committed you to your world. This is yours tonight," he said, holding up the Hall of Fame statuette and looking at her. "Take it home as a small return on the investment you made in your son," he finished with a chuckle.

Of his father—who had died earlier that year but lived on as a brooding figure in the musician's early songs and as a source for much of his artistic output ever since—Springsteen was ambivalent. "What would I conceivably have written about without him? . . . If everything had gone great between us, it would have been a disaster, you know? I would have written just happy songs."

"I tried to do that in the early nineties, and it didn't work," he added, to laughs.

Springsteen thanked "the *mighty* men and women of the E Street Band," mentioning each of them, and poked fun at himself when it came to E Street's lone woman. "It went like this: 'OK, fellas, there's gonna be a woman in the band. We need someone to sing all the high parts. How complicated can it get?'" Pause. The audience, of course, knew she had become his wife and the mother of his three children. "Well, ten of the best years of my life. Evan, Jessie, Sam—three children genealogically linked to the E Street Band—tells the rest of the story."[3]

At sixty-three, Springsteen is no longer the scraggly, wide-eyed Bruuuuuuuuuuuce (as his audiences call him) who first drew a cult following with his shows around New Jersey's shore in the early 1970s. He's a more tailored and tweaked version of his earlier self; he runs on a treadmill and lifts weights with a trainer to fit into the dark skinny jeans he wears on stage and to deliver the emotionally intense and physically exhausting performances his fans have come to expect.[4]

David Remnick, writing in the *New Yorker*, recently described Springsteen's performance style as "as close as a white man of Social Security age can get to James Brown circa 1962 without risking a herniated disk. Concerts last in excess of three hours, without a break, and he is constantly dancing, screaming, imploring, mugging, kicking, wind-milling, crowd-surfing, climbing a drum riser, jumping on an amp."[5] Writer Rob Kirkpatrick reported in 2007 that Springsteen described his concerts as "part circus, part political rally, part spiritual meeting, and part dance party."[6]

After four decades in the business—and a musical repertoire that has continued to evolve, drawing on blues and Motown, country and punk, folk and rap—Springsteen can still dominate the charts. His 2012 album, *Wrecking Ball*, went straight to number 1, even if it didn't linger there. The related worldwide tour pulled in $200 million in 2012, making it the year's second-highest-grossing tour, after Madonna's.[7] Over the course of his career, Springsteen has sold more than 65 million albums in the United States and more than 120 million worldwide. He has earned, among other honors, twenty Grammy awards, two Golden Globes, and an Oscar.

You might attribute Springsteen's success to sheer musical talent: he sings; he writes songs; he plays great guitar, decent piano, and a mean harmonica. Springsteen has been lauded as our "rock laureate" for his innate ability to capture a sentiment in song—from the lonely nights of adolescent longing to the emotional scars of working-class unemployment to the grief of the nation after 9/11. Or perhaps his success is owed to his ability over the years to churn out new material, with his lyrics always speaking to the political or social issues of the day. Or to his penchant for scheduling tours around new albums and fresh artistic ideas rather than Rolling Stones–like recaps of greatest hits.

These explanations, though, miss one often-unnoticed source of Springsteen's success: his strength as a leader. He is, after all, the front man, the band leader, The Boss. It was a nickname he earned in his early performing days, as the one who collected money and distributed it to his bandmates. He didn't particularly like the nickname—why *would* an artist so aligned with the plight of the working man?—but it stuck.[8] Springsteen is a man whose passion and perfectionism transformed a ragtag group of talented Jersey Shore musicians into a world-famous band. Springsteen's obsession with artistic excellence drove him and his collaborators to be the best they could be and to deliver—really deliver—to their fans.

It's worth noting that the E Street Band members are salaried musicians. "This is not the Beatles," drummer Max Weinberg told David Remnick.[9] That doesn't just mean that the band rehearses, plays, and tours when Springsteen says it does. It means that Springsteen can compel the band to spend three months recording a single song. Or take three years to work on one album. Or spend three days testing locations to get just the right sound of Weinberg playing the snare drum. The extremely high standards of performance Springsteen expects can exhaust those around him. For *Darkness on the Edge of Town*, the band recorded some seventy songs and spent hours and hours of heavy labor in the studio before Springsteen was satisfied.[10]

With maturity, however, these standards have relaxed, even as his impact and audience continue to expand internationally. "If you don't figure out how to do it a different way, you don't have a life," he said recently. "I have learned the skill of putting that away and moving on to other things that demand your time and attention if you want them in your life." Although it might seem paradoxical, he says he's become even more productive now that he has learned how to put "boundaries on how you work, when you work, how long you work."[11]

Springsteen is a moral figure, having built a global community centered on a core set of values. As he wrote in a *New York Times* op-ed, he has tried to promote ideals of "economic justice, civil rights, a humane foreign policy, freedom and a decent life for all of our citizens."[12] Through his songs and public positions, he has helped raise awareness of problems such as AIDS, gun violence, racism, the plight of illegal immigrants, hunger, and economic inequality. He has helped raise money for food banks and hurricane relief. (In 2012, he took part in the 12-12-12 benefit concert and live album, which brought in more than $50 million after Hurricane Sandy devastated the coasts of New Jersey and New York.)

Bob Dylan was the voice of the 1960s counterculture, Bono has kept global poverty and AIDS in the public eye, and Paul McCartney promotes animal rights and warns of land mines. But few have done as much as Springsteen, for more than four decades, to implore his listeners to help others. His powerful voice was evident on a crisp January day in 2009, when he stood with Pete Seeger at the foot of the Lincoln Memorial and, backed by a red-robed gospel choir, sang Woody Guthrie's "This Land Is Your Land" at the inaugural celebration for President Barack Obama.

Backstreets: Greetings from Freehold

Springsteen was born September 23, 1949, in Freehold, New Jersey, a blue-collar town half an hour inland from the Atlantic Ocean. Most of Freehold's residents worked in nearby factories. His mother, whom Springsteen has described as Superwoman, worked as a legal secretary.[13] His father did a stint working as a prison guard and another driving a bus. If Springsteen was inspired by his mother, he was shaped by his father's difficulties in finding work. The elder Springsteen suffered from bipolar disorder, although he didn't always take the drugs prescribed for him, and he was known for terrible rages, often directed at Bruce. Life for the young Springsteen and his two younger sisters was hard. "My parents' struggles, it's *the* subject of my life," Springsteen told Remnick. "It's the thing that eats at me and always will. Those wounds stay with you, and you turn them into language and purpose."[14] His early albums are filled with stories of sons battling fathers, and the promise of escape his father saw in the open road.

If life wasn't easy at home, school offered no refuge. Whether at the St. Rose of Lima Catholic School that the young Bruce attended through eighth grade or at Freehold Regional, the integrated public high school that he later demanded his parents transfer him to, Springsteen felt socially alienated.[15] He was, he says, invisible—an outcast. "I wasn't even the class clown. I had nowhere near that much notoriety," he said in a 2005 VH1 interview.[16] It was music that gave him voice and direction—his identity. He remembered the night of September 9, 1956, when he and his mother watched Elvis on *The Ed Sullivan Show*. He turned to her and said, "I wanna be *"just . . . like . . . that."*[17] Springsteen later expanded on that moment, recently telling an audience of young musicians that he realized "that you did not have to be constrained by your upbringing, by the way you looked, or by the social context that oppressed you. You could call upon your own powers of imagination and you could create a transformative self."[18] A week after that Ed Sullivan show, Springsteen wrapped his fingers around a rented guitar, but they were too small to make music.

Seven years after his Elvis moment, Springsteen bought his first guitar—an $18 pawnshop find—and taught himself to play. Until then, he said in Dave Marsh's biography, *Two Hearts*, he "didn't have any way of getting [his] feelings out."[19] His mother then helped him upgrade to a $60 Kent electric guitar and a small amplifier. "It was an enormous investment, an enormous show of faith," he recalled. "I don't think I'd ever seen sixty dollars in one place at one time in anyone's hand."[20] Once a week, according to biographer Eric Alterman, she ventured around the corner to pay the finance company.[21]

Springsteen estimates that, as a teenager, he practiced six to eight hours every night. As he said in a 1975 *Time* magazine cover story, he began to write his own original material because, unable to tune his guitar properly, he couldn't accurately reproduce songs he heard on the radio.[22] He joined a string of bands and played local gigs.

When Springsteen's parents decided to move to California in search of a better life, the nineteen-year-old stayed in New Jersey, briefly attending Ocean County Community College and then gravitating to Asbury Park, a magical relic of a formerly grand seaside town, with a vibrant music scene. Most of the bands playing in Asbury Park at the time fell into one of two categories: surf music and retro rock. Springsteen didn't fit neatly into either slot. He wanted to forge a unique sound and experimented while playing in a series of bands, beginning with The Castilles. As he told Marsh, "You can't conform to the formula of always giving the audience what it wants, or you're killing yourself and you're killing the audience . . . Someone has to take the initiative and say, 'Let's step out of the mold. Let's try this.'"[23]

The "New Dylan"

By 1972, Springsteen was writing all of his own material rather than performing covers. One night, on the hood of a parked car, he signed a contract with a scrappy manager named Mike Appel. Appel then scored his client an audition with Columbia Records' John Hammond, who had signed Aretha Franklin, Bob Dylan, and others. Hammond initially marketed Springsteen as the latest "new Dylan."

Although Springsteen admired Dylan, he didn't want to make a solo folk album. Springsteen drew heavily on the Animals, the Beatles, doo-wop, and folk. Years later, at the South by Southwest keynote in 2012, he said that he soaked up "the beautifully, socially conscious sounds of Curtis Mayfield." From the Motown greats of the Sixties, he told the crowd of aspiring musicians at the Austin conference, he learned the craft: "How to write. How to arrange. What mattered and what didn't . . . How to lead a band. How to front a band."[24] He found his teachers on the radio and at the record store. His musical style didn't fit neatly into any established genre, but it resonated with his audiences.

Against Hammond's wishes, the 1970s-era Springsteen invited some of his old buddies from the Jersey Shore into the studio with him. Their first two albums, though praised by a few critics and radio DJs, didn't take off. But Springsteen's hyperenergetic live shows continued to earn him fans. In May 1974, Jon Landau, a struggling music producer moonlighting as a music critic for a Boston alternative weekly, saw one such show. Springsteen was opening for Bonnie Raitt at a small venue in Harvard Square. "Last Thursday," Landau famously wrote, "I saw rock and roll past flash before my eyes. And I saw something else: I saw rock and roll's future."[25]

Springsteen now had a cult following, but he needed a hit. Another commercial bust of an album would kill his contract with Columbia, if not his career. Springsteen tracked down Landau. The pressures from the record label, the band, and the fans were enormous. Springsteen, though, remained focused on the final product, and not the number of hours it took to create an album. (An average day involved fifteen hours in the studio, and there were some twenty-four-hour stints.) Springsteen had a vision of a single album that would include all his musical influences and creative ideas. He wanted to produce a flawless work of greatness that would "explode in people's homes and minds and change people's lives."[26] He agonized over details others considered trivial. After nine laborious months in the studio, Springsteen managed to complete only one song, "Born to Run."[27] To appease the label and the fans, according to Alterman, Appel slipped copies of the single to select radio DJs. The song, which critic Greil Marcus described as "the finest compression of the rock & roll thrill since the opening riffs of 'Layla,'" was a hit.[28]

It would take another six months to finish the album. "When it's ready, it'll be there," Springsteen kept saying. "I can't be pressured. I'll give 'em my best and it'll work out for the best in the end." He set a high standard. As Landau said to biographer Marsh, "The biggest thing I learned from him was the ability to concentrate on the big picture. He'd say, 'The release date is just one day. The record is forever.'"[29]

Still Searching for His Groove

The *Born to Run* album, released in August 1975, transformed Springsteen's career and his life. Its content was more mature than earlier albums, leaving behind, as Alterman puts it, Springsteen's "adolescent definitions of love and freedom."[30] The many months in the studio showed: the music was more refined, and the dense arrangements were reminiscent of the "wall of sound" production style developed by Phil Spector. The album shot to number 3 on the charts, and the tour kicked off with rave reviews. Yet Springsteen and the band still weren't making much money. This was in part because Springsteen preferred the intimacy of small theatres. But as he dug into why, when his career seemed to be taking off, the money didn't seem to be coming in, he found out just how lopsided his contract with Appel was. He had signed away the rights to his songs, and Appel was making more money than his rising star. Springsteen sued. Appel countersued, keeping Springsteen out of the studio.

The stalemate continued for two years, during which Springsteen insisted that he would walk away from the music business rather than give in. During this period he still wrote songs, and, to earn money, toured almost nonstop. He also began reading. Landau gave him books by John Steinbeck and Flannery O'Connor and suggested movies to watch. As David Remnick wrote in the *New Yorker*, "Springsteen started to think in larger terms than cars and highways;

he began to look at his own story, his family's story, in terms of class and American archetypes."[31] His music became less about personal liberation and more about the pain of socioeconomic changes, deindustrialization, and the scourge of unemployment.

In 1977, Appel and Springsteen reached a settlement, with the musician essentially buying back control and the rights to his music. It was a lesson learned the hard way: although Springsteen has collaborated with many musicians and producers over the years, from critic-turned-manager Jon Landau to Pete Seeger to his longtime friend and E Street band member Steve Van Zandt, he would never again give up creative control of his music.

Two platinum albums later, Springsteen was a bona fide star. But somehow, the fame felt empty, and depression hovered. He started seeing a psychotherapist, who helped him explore the roots of his unhappiness. Why did none of his romantic relationships last? Had he "inherited his father's depressive self-isolation"? Why was he obsessed with his childhood home, which he would drive by three or four nights a week? Springsteen grappled with his offstage life, trying to grasp the past and figure out a future in which he wouldn't feel so alone.[32]

By the end of his next tour with the E Street Band—marking the release of the blockbuster *Born in the USA* album—Springsteen was married, after a whirlwind romance, to actress Julianne Phillips. He was rich and famous. The album had shot straight to number 1 and ultimately produced seven hit singles and went platinum.

Chrysler offered several million dollars for the right to use the title track, "Born in the USA," in a car commercial.[33] The Boss declined. Next, Ronald Reagan tried to co-opt the same song during his 1984 reelection campaign. Springsteen, angered by the president trying to turn a song protesting the government's treatment of Vietnam vets into an unambivalent affirmation of America's future, protested the inappropriate use of his words and music.

On the personal side, Springsteen and Phillips moved into a $14 million house in Beverly Hills. But their marriage was filled with daily struggles and dashed expectations. He and Phillips divorced quietly in 1988.

Then he broke up the E Street Band.

Putting the Guitar Down

To Springsteen fans—the devoted followers who had charted his rise, concert after concert, who had been uplifted by his music and felt their spirits touched by his songs—the decision verged on apostasy.

"I [had] played with some of the guys since we were eighteen," Springsteen said of his decision. He added that he hadn't had a chance to go out and see what other people were going to bring to what he was doing. "There's some responsibility to step out a little bit, and it was frightening."[34]

The 90s marked a period of both personal growth and musical experimentation. Taking his foot off the gas pedal allowed him to experiment with other musicians and focus on his relationship with E Street Band backup singer Patti Scialfa and the family they began to create. The couple moved to Los Angeles, had their first son, Evan, in July 1990, and married the following year. Looking back on these years, Springsteen told Robert Wiersema in 2011, "Now I see that two of the best days of my life were the day I picked up the guitar and the day that I learned how to put it down."[35]

Therapy had helped Springsteen work through the scars of his childhood and learn how to create more space in his life for nonmusical activities. "It's not necessarily for everybody," he has said about therapy. "But I've accomplished things personally that felt simply impossible previously. It's a sign of strength, you know, to put your hand out and ask for help, whether it's a friend or a professional or whatever."[36]

Scialfa pushed Springsteen to become a more attentive father. As he explained to TV host Jon Stewart in 2012, "My argument was, 'Don't you understand, I'm thinking of a song! I have to lay another golden egg or we're all going down!'"[37] But Springsteen came to realize that he couldn't live long enough to make all of the music that was in his head and that his children wouldn't be young forever. Although he continued to make music, Springsteen began devoting more time and energy to his family life, making the move back to New Jersey before his daughter, Jessica, was born at the end of 1991. He wanted for his children "to know where they came from, who came before them, what they went through."[38]

After reuniting the E Street Band briefly for a greatest hits album in 1995, Springsteen did several acoustic records on his own before reuniting the band in 1999. To ensure that his work didn't interfere with his role as a husband and father—and to grant his three kids childhoods that were as normal as possible—Springsteen strictly separated the two spheres of his life and even insisted that his band members sign nondisclosure agreements.

Springsteen was back in his native New Jersey, married and raising his children only miles from his childhood home. He was back with the band. Then came the 9/11 terrorist attack, which hit Springsteen's local community hard. Many of the firefighters, not to mention many daily commuters, who died that day lived in Springsteen's own Monmouth County.

Obituaries in the local papers often mentioned that the victim had been a loyal Springsteen fan, and he began phoning their families to offer his condolences. To honor several first responders, he recorded new versions of his songs for their funerals. He called survivors, too, to see how he might be able to support them.[39]

These conversations led to *The Rising*, his first album of new material in seven years. He and his band worked furiously, recording the album in less than a month and releasing it in the summer of 2002.

Some songs were inspired by the heroism of the firefighters. Others reflected the stories he had heard from those who had lost a husband, mother, or sibling in the attack. The album, as a whole, aimed to heal the country's sorrow.

"It comes down to trying to make people happy," he said. Another purpose was "being a conduit for a dialogue about the events of the day, the issues that impact people's lives, personal and social and political and religious. That's how I always saw the job of our band. That was my service."[40]

Although The Boss had never been shy about expressing his opinions, he had stayed away from partisan politics. But in 2004, he endorsed Democratic presidential candidate John Kerry and revealed that he would join a group of fellow artists in a national concert tour called *Vote for Change*. Springsteen campaigned for Barack Obama in 2008.

Unlike efforts highlighting AIDS in Africa or children dying of hunger, causes nearly everyone can rally around, Springsteen's progressive political positions rankled some fans. His popularity in the American South and Midwest declined. Yet those same positions buoyed his popularity in bluer parts of the country and internationally, where he is respected for celebrating America's values even as he criticizes its moral and political failings.

On February 8, 2013, in Los Angeles, two nights before the Grammy Awards ceremony, Springsteen performed at the Recording Academy's annual MusiCares gala, a star-studded concert and auction to raise money for the nonprofit, which provides financial and medical help to musicians in need.

Springsteen, along with other big-name musicians, had signed a new Telecaster guitar that the auctioneer hoped would sell for $50,000. When the bids seemed tepid, Springsteen jumped to the stage. He threw in a one-hour guitar lesson and a ride in the sidecar of his Harley-Davidson. The bidding picked up, and Springsteen upped the ante: eight tickets to an upcoming concert and a backstage tour by

The Boss himself if the bids reached "two hundred thousand fucking dollars." Once they had, he dangled one more carrot: "And lasagna made by my mom! Stand up, mom!" The guitar sold for $250,000.[41]

After the auction ended, Springsteen walked to the podium to accept an award as the organization's Person of the Year. Springsteen lauded MusiCares, saying, "We are a brotherhood and sisterhood of magical fuck-ups, and we need you." But, he went on to suggest, musicians not only needed to be saved from their worst habits, but also they needed to be saved *for* the rest of us. "I've been a part of the miracle of music. I've seen people tired, depressed, weary, worn out. And I've seen them revived, rise from their seats and dance," he said.[42]

Musicians, he said, "are always in search of the power to sustain the best of ourselves and to seek out the best in you, our fans and our audience. We want to be great. And we want to be important in your life . . . to make you want to *move*, to *dance*, to *love*, to *make love*, to be *angry*, to *act*. When we play we want the hair to stand up on your arms, we want you to feel the glory, and we want you to be glad of being alive."

Springsteen wound up by thanking his fellow musicians for making him feel "like . . . *person* of the *year*." He chuckled before demanding, "Now give me that damn guitar!"

The Skills Bruce Springsteen Exemplifies

Leader isn't usually the first noun people would attach to Bruce Springsteen, the eldest of the people I've chosen for this book, and yet it fits. He is the executive of a high-performing organization. But more importantly, his persistent expression of hope and joy in the face of the disappointments of a cruel world—spoken not with resentment but with resilience—has inspired tens of millions of people the world over.

Throughout his career, Springsteen has sought opportunities to help others, to strengthen his broad community of fans by bringing people together in common cause. The poetry of his lyrics—with its universal themes about making our way in the world, struggling to hold on to joy, raging against injustice, and reveling in the laughter and sorrows of intimate relationships—unites listeners everywhere. The late Clarence Clemons, saxophonist in Springsteen's E Street Band, once described the astonishing sight of countless Japanese fans proudly waving American and Japanese flags that had been sewn together. "I wish some of the politicians had seen these things," Clemons remarked about that moment on tour. "Those kids didn't understand the words to 'Born in the U.S.A.,' but they understood what we were singing about. Those things Bruce sings about—attention to self and country—pertain not only to America. They pertain to everybody."[43]

When Springsteen performed before a crowd of 160,000 in East Berlin in 1988, he declared from the stage in thickly accented German, "I want to tell you I'm not here for or against any government. I came to play rock 'n' roll for you East Berliners in the hope that one day all the barriers will be torn down." Standing for his values was contagious. Again, Clemons: "He was always so straight and dedicated to what he believes. You became a believer simply by being around him."[44]

We see many skills in Bruce Springsteen's quest for greatness in his work and coherence in his life, including the way he learned the skill of managing boundaries. He offers a particularly good illustration of the skills of acting in ways that are consistent with one's values (being real), clarifying expectations (being whole), and learning continually (being innovative).

Be Real: Embody Values Consistently

Bruce Springsteen is able to be himself wherever he is, wherever he goes. He acts in ways that are consistent with his core values.

In the confusing warp of fame and wealth, many rock and roll stars forsake their values and fall prey to scandal, artistic stagnation, and even early death. Springsteen is grounded by his musical mission, his family, his community of origin and the world community of fans he's created, and his social and political views. This grounding has also allowed him to remain at heart the same down-to-earth Jersey boy he was before striking it big. From the earliest days of his career, Springsteen has performed only the songs that speak to him and played only with musicians who share his passion. No distraction, no matter how tempting—including the possibility of rapid popularity or easy money—has caused him to deviate from the mission that compels him.

The mature Springsteen is confident in his knowledge of himself, and this confidence allows him to be his authentic self wherever he goes. Rather than conform to external pressures, he relies on core values to guide his behavior. Rather than bend to social pressures, he makes choices that match what he believes in. He's not afraid to speak his mind. Being real is not only a matter of spending time and attention on the people and things that matter most. It's also about embodying your values consistently, in all the things you do, as we see with Springsteen.

He has been able to move his listeners because of his steadfastness. Rather than view him as just a guy with a guitar, legions of Springsteen fans think of him as a friend—even if they've never met him—and as a positive reflection of their own lives. One reason they relate to his music and lyrics on a deeply personal level is that he is consciously striving to be true to himself.[45] That's what the effort to consistently embody one's values yields: loyalty. People can see his striving to be himself wherever he goes. Springsteen builds relationships with his fans by devoting himself fully to the idea of his music and its power to elevate the human spirit, all the time. This faith is expressed in virtually all of his songs, as well as in the words he uses to describe his art in speeches he's given, articles he's written, and interviews he's held.

Springsteen's ability to give voice to the truth of his experience is a skill that he's refined over the course of his career. In the aftermath of 9/11, Springsteen struggled to come to terms with the horrifying attack. In a way that was even more explicit than his previous albums, in *The Rising* he produced songs to express the grief and hope he found in himself, his family, and his community. Not only was this prodigious effort a way to articulate what was important in all aspects of his life, but also it was a turning point, for it put him on a path to becoming more directly involved in politics, even if doing so risked alienating some of his fans. "It's unpatriotic at any given moment," he said in a *60 Minutes* interview in 2009, about his rising stature as a force in presidential politics, "to sit back and let things pass that are damaging to some place that you love so dearly. And that has given me so much. And that I believe in. I still feel and see us as a beacon of hope and possibility."[46]

Over time, Springsteen has grown more fervent in his appreciation of how important it is to take clear political stands that are rooted in his family, social, and spiritual domains. He tries to be the person he is, wherever he is. Staying true to his values in the different roles of his life has not only propelled him to the highest peaks of professional achievement but also has resulted in a rewarding and meaningful life beyond work.

Be Whole: Clarify Expectations

Bruce Springsteen communicates with people important to him about expectations they have of one another. He is willing to express his needs, values, and goals. He sets aside time for these conversations and is able to broach topics that may feel uncomfortable.

A successful leader must listen well, take in constructive feedback, ask clarifying questions, and work to resolve disagreements.

The skill of clarifying expectations involves both advocacy for your own point of view and inquiry about what others see and want. Stemming from his intense desire to produce great music, Springsteen has always been insistent and very clear—with his fellow musicians as well as producers, engineers, and audiences— about the sounds inside his head that he's striving to re-create. There are countless examples of his ardently expressing his artistic vision and making clear his expectations. It took days of laborious trial and error, for example, just to find the right timbre and volume for the drums on *Darkness*, but the young Springsteen (still in his twenties) wouldn't stop driving his bandmates, producers, and engineers until everyone grasped exactly the sound he was looking for. Another episode, much further down the line, occurred during a live performance of "American Skin (41 Shots)." The audience was noisily rustling during the introductory refrain, and Springsteen demanded quiet. A hush ensued. He is highly skilled in letting people know what he wants.

His high standards compel him to be unrelenting. Witness his unwillingness to publish prematurely because an album "is forever." Although his early obsessiveness and unending search for perfection have mellowed over the years, the energy that Springsteen and the E Streeters bring to the stage—still, even in their sixties—would not be possible without The Boss's making clear (through his own example), night after night after night, his expectations for excellent performance and full commitment to extraordinary service for their audiences.

Springsteen has also made clear his needs when it comes to his family. To protect his children from the pressures of public scrutiny, the nondisclosure agreements he required of his band members set limits on the scope of what he deemed acceptable behavior; he let the band know, in legal terms, that he expected them to guard his family's privacy. And as a father he has been clear about letting his children know what he believes in and why. The move from California back to New Jersey, for example, was to make his children mindful of their roots.

But communication about expectations must be a two-way street. Springsteen's capacity to hear the rumblings around him has enabled him to stay current with the culture. A great storyteller must be a great listener. Springsteen said he got the inspiration for *The Rising* a few days after the 9/11 attacks, when a stranger in a car stopped next to him, rolled down his window, and said, "We need you now."[47] Staying closely attuned to his audience's changing interests is a signal feature of Springsteen's leadership repertoire.

Listening to others—listening so that you understand what others really care about—often changes our point of view. Chris Christie, the current governor of New Jersey, boasts an encyclopedic knowledge of the entire Springsteen oeuvre. But because of Christie's conservative social views, The Boss would not speak with the governor—until, in the wake of Hurricane Sandy, Christie rose above partisanship and welcomed President Obama, and by doing so garnered federal support for New Jersey residents. Springsteen saw Christie's commitment to the people, and he changed his position: he told Christie that they were now friends and publicly complimented the governor for his principled stand.[48] These episodes point to Springsteen's skill in engaging in effective dialogue; people know what he needs from them, and he learns what they need from him.

Be Innovative: Create Cultures of Innovation

Bruce Springsteen looks for opportunities to show others how he's learning new ways of doing things and encourages them to innovate. He creates cultures of innovation wherever he goes. He sees the service his band provides as producing opportunities for people to explore the important issues of the day. Leading by example, he empowers others to be creative. He displays both confidence, which grew with time and experience, and humility, as he shares with others both his successes and the obstacles he faces. His enthusiasm for learning and his fearlessness are contagious and inspire others to embrace new opportunities.[49]

A main ingredient in Springsteen's recipe for success, personally and professionally, is his thirst for useful knowledge and his desire to change the world—to create something new that makes things better—and to change himself. As a wise old man offering advice to up-and-coming musicians, he recounted how this is exactly what he was up to, back at the start: trying desperately to create a new person from what he had been. He talked to the South by Southwest crowd in 2012 about his hunger to learn and explained how he had to step out of the mold to discover his own musical style. He was urging them to innovate, continually.

Not only has he been on a lifelong search for better ways to express his ideas in music, but Springsteen also has been on a quest to better understand his inner life. Here, too, he has used his own experience to inspire others to try new ways of growing. His own psychotherapy demonstrates his belief in the value of disciplined self-discovery. Therapy helped Springsteen work through the traumas of his childhood and learn how to appreciate nonmusical activities in his life, especially intimacy and family.[50]

Expressing insight about lessons he's learned about himself encourages others to keep learning about themselves, whether through therapy or other means. His pursuit of self-knowledge through counseling turned him into a role model, destigmatizing it and opening doors for people, especially men, who might not otherwise seek help. It wasn't easy to talk about these things publicly. But Springsteen mustered the will and the skill to do so. He compared therapy to getting a mechanic to check under the hood—an analogy sure to speak to his target audience. He shows others that there are practical means available to them—tools they can use—to heal their own scars.

Springsteen is a teacher.

Bruce Springsteen was lucky; he discovered very early that the only thing that made him feel right about his life was his guitar. He found what he was perfectly suited for and gave it everything. He devoted himself to learning his craft, remaining true to his beliefs, securing the resources he needed to build a world-class team, caring for the people who depend on him, and committing to serving his people and making them a bit happier and more informed about the joys and sorrows of the world through his music.

Ultimately, from the perspective of his life as a whole, his mega-star success as a performing artist has come as a consequence of, and not at a cost to, his deep investments in his family, his community, and his private self. His music is greatly enriched by these other parts of his life. And his music is the vehicle through which he is able to live a rewarding life beyond it. As his wife and bandmate, Patti Scialfa, said to him at the 2014 Rock and Roll Hall of Fame induction of The E Street Band, "Thanks for making the best of both worlds possible."[51]

You too can strengthen your ability to pursue four-way wins and create a greater sense of harmony in your life. In Part II, which follows, I offer practical suggestions for ways you—on your own schedule and in your own style—can develop the skills of being real, being whole, and being innovative.

PART II

Developing the Skills for Integrating Work and the Rest of Life

7

The Worst Thing
You Can Do

Don't Fail to Grow

To lead the life you want, you've got to do *something*. Each of the people profiled in this book illustrates Total Leadership principles and the skills that animate them. In the preceding chapters, I've described particular episodes that demonstrate how they are leaders who are real, whole, and innovative. In the final chapter, I reflect on some of the larger lessons to be gleaned from the totality of their lives. But, for now, let me underscore something that is probably obvious to you: none of them stands still for long. They find ways to persist, despite whatever obstacles are before them, in moving ever closer to becoming the people they want to become. They make mistakes. They sometimes make people angry. But they are always doing something to try to make things better. They are constantly refining certain skills, learning to integrate various parts of their lives in ways that make them more effective.

Although you may not have the same talents, financial resources, or benefactors, you have the same potential to enhance your capacity to lead the life you want. Your life circumstances are yours alone, of course. And you might feel highly constrained. But I am certain that you do have discretion to act and, if you're like most of the thousands I've coached over the years, you have more room than you think you have to try new things and learn new skills.

So let's explore what the skills illustrated in these stories mean for you. I'm going to provide actions you can take to enhance your skills for integrating work and the rest of life. Informed and inspired by these six people, these skills will help you lead the life you want. All you have to do in the next three chapters is keep an open mind, stretch, and adjust.

I realize this means an investment of time in an already time-starved life. But I also know, from my own work and from research done by many other social scientists, that the only way to improve your capacity to lead is to practice. Leading your own life is a kind of performance, and you are the performer. The most revered performers never stop trying to become more skilled at their craft. They practice the fundamentals with rigor. They exercise the basics, doing them regularly to keep their technique sharp. They scour the field for best practices and incorporate them into their own repertoire.

This practice involves initiative, discipline, maintenance, and persistence. It is research and development, and it does cost. But it can be fun, too. Indeed, if you remain conscious of why you're doing what you're doing, I am sure that you will feel more purposeful, connected, and optimistic. And you will be more successful in pursuing what matters. You, too, can refine the skills that Tierney, Sandberg, Greitens, Obama, Foudy, and Springsteen have learned, each in his or her own way. But, again, this takes practice. Gleaned from the best research in applied psychology and human development, the practical suggestions in the next three chapters will help you develop your own repertoire of skills. I've tried to show how you can make these activities a fruitful part of your life in the days and weeks to come.

Some of these activities will be captivating and will produce tangible benefits right away. Others might not suit your fancy or meet your needs right now. Some people like to run around a park, and others prefer to ride a bicycle; some need to eat gluten-free, and others have to avoid nuts. You don't have to do every one of these thirty-six exercises. And you'll see that some are closely related and complementary. So pick and choose, adapt and innovate. But keep in mind that each activity has a distinct purpose.

Take a few minutes to think about which skills you need to develop most. It's a good idea to go back to the assessment you did of your own skills in the Introduction to see which ones stood out as strengths you want to build on and which represented areas for improvement.

It's also useful to review your observations about Tierney, Sandberg, Greitens, Obama, Foudy, and Springsteen. Consider what it was in these cases that stood out for you; how were these figures models for ways of thinking and acting? You don't have to aspire to *be* any one of these textbook examples; you only have to learn from them. Doing these reviews should give you your own short list of skills to jump on first.

You're going to be using some muscles that might not be in very good shape. As with a novice musician, your fingers may not be as supple, your sound not as beautiful as you'd like, at least not at first. That's all right. Taking action to become a better performer—to

Developing Your Skills

Table 7-1 summarizes the exercises for developing each of the skills that bring to life the three principles of being real, being whole, and being innovative.

TABLE 7-1

Developing the skills for integrating work and the rest of life

	Know what matters	Embody values consistently	Align actions with values	Convey values with stories	Envision your legacy	Hold yourself accountable
Be real	• Ideal self • Four circles	• Conversation starter • Be your values everywhere	• Find the larger meaning • Want to want to	• Autobiography • Social media review	• Time travel • Near/far	• Buddy system • Tune-up and realignment

	Clarify expectations	Help others	Build supportive networks	Apply all your resources	Manage boundaries intelligently	Weave disparate strands
Be whole	• Stakeholder expectations • A better connection	• How can I help you? • Spread the love	• Who matters most • SOS!	• Talent transfer • Creative contacts	• Unitask and disconnect • Segment and merge	• Hidden identities • Compatible scripts and goals

	Focus on results	Resolve conflicts among domains	Challenge the status quo	See new ways of doing things	Embrace change courageously	Create cultures of innovation
Be innovative	• Scenarios • Metrics for success	• Allies not enemies • Energizing yourself	• In the lab • My problem = our problem	• Crowd-source solutions • Picture your idea web	• Worst case/best case • Challenging your beliefs	• Another perspective • Teach

become more of the person we want to become—involves learning. Learning requires mistakes and reflection on those mistakes. So prepare to do some thinking about yourself and your world. Accelerating your growth in a skill requires looking back as much as you can at what works and what doesn't. You really cannot take intelligent new action toward important goals without looking back a little.

I'm now going to switch from Stew the professor to Stew the music coach. Ready? Let's pick up our instruments!

8

Skills for Being Real

Acting with Authenticity

The first of the three Total Leadership principles is to be real—to act with authenticity by clarifying what's important to you and acting accordingly. This is the foundation. Here are suggestions for simple things that you can do to enhance these skills, no matter what your age or life situation.

Skill: Know What Matters

Trust thyself: every heart vibrates to that iron string.
—RALPH WALDO EMERSON

Over the course of their lives, remarkable leaders know what matters most. Julie Foudy demonstrates this skill in spades. You can strengthen your own ability to be real by imagining your ideal future self and analyzing how the four main roles in life intersect. As you try these activities, see what happens to your sense of yourself in all the different parts of your life. See if the activities help you pay closer attention to what really matters.

Exercise: Ideal Self

Identify the important roles you play in each area of your life—for example, a wife at home, a manager at work, a volunteer in the community, an athlete in your private time. Think about the type of person you wish to become in each role. Consider where you want your life to go.

Write down a few details that describe what that person—let's call her your future self—is doing in each part of her life. Identify the one or two main features of the specific roles that you would like to be playing as a wife (e.g., being caring and helpful to your spouse), as a professional (e.g., being respected by people in your industry), as a PTA member (e.g., being actively involved in your community), and as an athlete (e.g., being able to run five miles). Case Western Reserve University's Richard Boyatzis and other scholars in organizational behavior argue that imagining your "ideal self"—as opposed to the "ought-to-be self," the one you think others want you to be—can be a powerful guiding force for change in behavior, perceptions, and attitude.[1]

If you can find a physical object that somehow represents the image of your future self, place it where you can see it regularly, such as on your desk. (This makes it more prominent in your mind.) Now, on a scale of 1 to 10, assess your level of confidence about how attainable this image is, in light of how you see yourself now. Try to differentiate between the valid evidence available to you and self-defeating thoughts you might have. The latter kind of thinking kills motivation.

To increase your chances of moving toward your ideal self, challenge any self-defeating thoughts. Keep in mind your past accomplishments. Candidly assess what has stopped you from achieving goals, as well as your personal beliefs about your abilities. Consider relevant feedback from others about what you have achieved and what your potential is. This helps increase your sense of hopefulness, which research has shown is critical in imagining *and realizing* the ideal self.[2]

Exercise: Four Circles

Analyze all the roles that you now play in each of the four main aspects of your life: work or school, family (however you define that), community (friends, neighbors, religious or social groups), and self (mind, body, spirit). First, take 100 points, and allocate them according to how important each domain is to you now. Then take another 100 points, and allocate them according to the percentage of your attention dedicated to each domain in a typical week. How do the two match up? How closely aligned are the things you value and the things you pay attention to?

Next, think about how each role contributes to your sense of having a meaningful life. How does each role affect how you see yourself? Does one role enhance another? For example, does being a father enrich your role as a community leader, an artist, or a coworker—and vice versa?

Draw four circles representing each of the four domains, where the size of the circle corresponds to the relative importance of that part of your life. Do the circles overlap? In other words, are the values, goals, and interests you pursue in some roles common to others? The overlap among the circles should give you a hint as to how compatible the domains are with one another: the greater the overlap, the more compatible the domains. Compatibility doesn't mean that you are physically *in* different roles at the same time or in the same place. Rather, it means you are bringing the same person—with the same values, goals, and interests—to each part of your life.

Consider why your circles overlap, or not, and how this makes you feel. Compatibility among circles indicates harmony. Seeing this image of the four circles may generate fresh insights about what matters most to you—how much you are being real—as well as about how your different roles affect each other.[3] Would your circles have more overlap if you included members of your family when you volunteer at the local food bank or when you exercise? How might your circles look if you encouraged people at work to help a local community organization? How easy would it be to make small changes that would lead to greater overlap? Thinking about these questions gets to a main purpose of this exercise: to help you know more about the importance you place on each domain of your life.[4]

You can also do this exercise online at www.totalleadership.org.

Skill: Embody Values Consistently

A bird doesn't sing because it has an answer,
it sings because it has a song.

—MAYA ANGELOU

Let's explore further your ability to be yourself, from a slightly different angle. Bruce Springsteen has had to learn how to embody his values consistently, through trial and error and through frequent, often painful, reflection on the lessons of his experiences. But you don't need to be Bruce to sing your song wherever you go. Anyone can find ways of living in closer accord with his values. Let me suggest two activities that help you see who you are in your different roles that have proven fruitful. See what happens as you aim to be real by being more of yourself wherever you go. Use Springsteen as a model.

Exercise: Conversation Starter

How do you "show up" in the different parts of your life? One way to find out is to bring an object from your nonwork life (e.g., a family photo, a travel memento, or a trophy) into the workplace and put it in the open where people can see it. When your work colleagues notice, mention what this other part of your life means to you and—this part is important—how it helps you at work. If there's the chance, talk about how it indirectly helps your colleagues. You might ask them to do something similar.

Then try the reverse: bring something from work, and put it somewhere in your home where your family can see it. Use it as a conversation starter with kids or dinner guests. Tell them about what you do and who you are at work, focusing especially on what this might mean for them.

Reflect on your deviations. Do you act differently in the different parts of your life? Apply your insights. But keep in mind, of course, that no one is always consistent. We all get tempted to do something we consider bad behavior, to feign interest when we don't care, to fail to stand up for something we believe in. Situational pressures can make us stray from our values. Think of an episode when you didn't rise to the occasion. What was it exactly that caused you to cave in, to behave in a way that wasn't like the person you want to be? Imagine small steps you might take to rebuff bad influences or avoid them entirely to stay closer to the person you want to be.

Exercise: Be Your Values Everywhere

Identify one simple action toward a goal that is consistent with the values you've thought about. Be sure that the goal is reasonable, and then commit to completing this action every day for thirty days. For example, if your core value is living a healthy lifestyle so that you can be around for your children for a long time to come, then your daily action might be to walk for fifteen minutes per day for thirty days, or ninety minutes per week as part of your work or job routine.

Between knowing and doing there is, of course, a gap. So, once you are committed to your action, inform a trusted friend about your commitment and ask him to help you complete your activity daily. Making goals public increases motivation through social pressure. Write a message to yourself that reminds you about this and the reason you're doing it. Leave it on a sticky note on the last mirror you see before you leave your home. As you glance in the mirror, read that note.

After completing your attempt at such a goal each day, rate how difficult it was for you to do so, on a scale of 1 to 10. Keep track of your scores, and, after thirty days, look at the trend in your scores. Ask yourself, did it get harder or easier to complete your daily activity? Or did it remain about the same difficulty? What might you do to continue the activity after thirty days? Think of a way to reinforce your commitment. At some point during the thirty days, did you stop having to remind yourself? Habitual action—more than just thinking about it—can change neural pathways, enlisting the muscles of your mind to support the action; it's tough at first, but once those pathways are formed, you've got a new habit.[5]

Is there another values-driven action that you can add to your routine for another thirty days?

Skill: Align Actions with Values

Let us consider the way in which we spend our lives.
—HENRY DAVID THOREAU

Acting in ways that are consistent with your values, like Michelle Obama and the other five examples in Part I, is one of the most difficult skills to master. It requires committed and sustained effort: the task never ceases. As you undertake the next two activities, look for new insights about how you can take other steps—actions that are under your control now—to better fit what you do with what you care about most.

Exercise: Find the Larger Meaning

Spend a few moments thinking expansively about how a task you already do, or a responsibility you now have, contributes to the well-being of others, either directly or indirectly. Jot down your ideas; start a list that you can add to at any time. You might invite others to help you. Here are examples: identify how a work task helps better serve clients, or explore how a chore at home helps your family function. In some cases, your actions do serve a meaningful purpose, but you fail to recognize it. As another example, sometimes health care workers, researchers, and even trash collectors fail to keep in mind that their work is, in and of itself, a community service. In a nonwork example, consider how taking a few minutes at night to put away the dishes or prepare healthy lunches for the next day might enable your spouse to get more rest and give you more quality time with your kids in the morning, making family life a bit lighter and brighter.

Reflecting on the meaning of what you do helps you better appreciate the ways your actions are evidence of living your values. You'll probably come up with fresh ideas about how you can do so even more, now and in the future, by developing new, highly motivating goals that are what psychologists call "self-concordant"—that is, goals that you consider important, fun, and in accord with your core values.[6] Research has found that when we can identify how even mundane tasks hold meaning, we can put more effort into them, thus achieving our goals more quickly and feeling a greater sense of well-being. It is satisfying and energizing to act in ways that reflect core values.

You'll become more aware of how some of your daily activities are not aligned with your core values, and this awareness may help you see how to reduce or even eliminate them. To take this idea a step further, think about one thing that you could and should stop doing. What would be difficult in attempting this? What would be easy?

Exercise: Want to Want To

Here's something you might try the next time you are in a conversation with a close colleague, friend, or loved one and you sense that something is holding her back from doing something that she really wants to do. Let's say your friend tells you she doesn't want to run daily because it is just too strenuous and boring, but to become healthier she genuinely *wants* to want to run daily. Ask her to rate on a scale of 1 to 10 how much she wants to run, where, for example, 1 means "I *really* don't want to run," and 10 means "There's nothing I'd rather do than run." Then begin mining (asking increasingly deeper questions), but persist with care: ask her what she would need to focus on in order to increase her desire to run. Perhaps she could not only improve her fitness but also bring better energy to her family and display more self-confidence at work.

You're coaching now, so ask your "client" what she can do to boost her motivation. This might involve thinking differently, seeing that running might reduce her blood pressure so that she can live longer, reduce medications, and feel energetic throughout the day, with all the benefits that might obtain. And she would serve as a better role model for her kids. Continue this line of questioning; be gently relentless in your curiosity about benefits that might motivate her, even as she might resist ("Don't you get it? It's because I'm just too busy!"). Try to get your client as close as possible to a 10 rating on our "want to want to" scale.

All right, what does this have to do with your aligning your values and actions? Well, now comes the hard part: switch roles, and have your partner lead you through this same kind of inquiry with something that you do not really want to do but that you want to want to do. This exercise pushes you to grapple with the oh-so-simple-to-imagine-but-hard-to-execute   shifting   of   your awareness. It is possible to reframe, to see how what we do connects with what we care about. The philosopher William James argued that will is the ability to direct and sustain attention, and that action results from an idea that is held stable in the mind. To act in better alignment with our values, we need to master the ability to sustain focus on those values. This exercise creates a greater sense of authority and internal ownership of the goals you are pursuing. It engenders what psychologists call a "state of flow" by feeding the desire to change behaviors in ways that allow you to live your values.[7]

Skill: Convey Values with Stories

It is the storyteller who makes us what
we are, who creates history.
—CHINUA ACHEBE

Storytelling is a craft that you can learn, and management literature since the early 1980s has elevated it to an essential part of any leader's repertoire. Our six leaders are all storytellers. You saw in chapter 2 how Sheryl Sandberg's ability to be a mensch is in no small part due to her ability to connect with an audience through her stories. To strengthen your ability to convey the real stories of your life, start to think through how you can use your actual history to inspire and bring others closer to you.

Exercise: Autobiography

Identify some of the significant events in your life, from birth to today, that have shaped the person you are. List three or four episodes that taught you something about yourself. Briefly describe in writing each event, and explain how it changed or clarified what you value most.

Social scientists call such events "crucible experiences" and see them as part of a leader's "emotional journey line." These episodes provide us with insights about how we adapt in the face of adversity.[8] If possible, identify the tension in each experience, and describe how you dealt with it. It is this tension that, if we can reframe it and resolve it, leads to resilience.

Now connect the dots: How do these episodes shape your beliefs? These connections are the cornerstones of the stories you can tell about your life. Stones built on this foundation convey your own authenticity. Honestly articulating these connections allows others to understand the person you are and what you stand for, and it generates trust and even fondness in an audience.[9]

Once you've gotten the essence of your story, find a colleague at work, and, in a comfortable setting, tell it to him (best without notes). Or, if it's easier, start with a close friend or family member, and then take your show on the road.

You might try telling a version of your story to your own child or another child you know—niece, godson, neighbor. Make sure the story has an implicit point that the child can understand, while trying to avoid sermonizing. Tell your story in a way that is exciting: bring it alive with vivid sensory detail (sights, sounds, smells). Try to include a description of a struggle between dream and reality—what you or someone else wanted that was somehow thwarted—and what ultimately came to pass. Such a practice is not only utilitarian (helping you refine your own art of storytelling) but also generous. Children love to hear stories, and they are a receptive audience. But there's one more step that makes your bedtime story not only an avuncular act but also an act of leadership: study the reaction of your audience, and then think through what you might have done differently to make the story more vividly useful. This part of the exercise will turn you from a rote reciter into a real raconteur.

Exercise: Social Media Review

If you use Facebook, Twitter, or other social media to share your experiences with friends, family, or coworkers, take a few minutes to review the posts you've recently shared. What events or themes stand out? Are you posting in a way that's consistent with your values? What are you leaving out? And which posts get the most comments or retweets? This activity will help you reflect on the stories you have shared with others and what they say about you. First, it increases your awareness of how—and how much—you reveal yourself. But it also provides a chance, again, to improve your act. These narratives are more important than they might seem, even in the off-the-cuff world of social media. Our personal narratives lead to our own sense of ourselves as well as our beliefs about others and the world.

Consider asking a friend or trusted colleague to review your posts and give you feedback. If you're not active with online social media, you might glean useful insight about your own stories by asking yourself these same questions about other people's posts.

Skill: Envision Your Legacy

Some of us have great runways already built
for us. If you have one, take off!
But if you don't have one, realize it is your
responsibility to grab a shovel and build one for
yourself and for those who will follow after you.
—AMELIA EARHART

To envision your legacy means to think about what might be said in retrospect about your life. It is to flesh out an idea of the impact you'll have on the world—as Tom Tierney did when he first imagined his "Make a Difference Company"—and to consider whether choices you must make will take you closer or further from your desired future.

Exercise: Time Travel

Take fifteen minutes this week to remove yourself from your everyday hustle and bustle and imagine the life you'd like to lead. Find a quiet spot. Take a few easy, deep breaths to clear your mind, and then let it wander and see where it takes you, while guiding yourself to dream where your life will go. Consider all the different parts of your life. You might try thinking about your life at some specific time, far into the future, say fifteen years. You have worked hard and succeeded at accomplishing your life goals and have realized your dreams. You are living the life you want to live. Picture what happens in a typical day. You wake up: Whom are you with? What do you do throughout the day? What impact are you having?

Be like Tierney, and take a few minutes to write about what you imagine as your legacy as concretely and in as much detail as possible. How would you like to be remembered by your descendants? What would you like colleagues to say at your retirement dinner? If the words don't flow, draw a picture, make a sculpture, or maybe even produce a video. Studies have shown that if you can visualize yourself successfully achieving your long-term goals, producing the legacy you want to leave, you are more likely to succeed. When everyday actions are seen as part of something significant, you improve your ability to plan, reduce impulsivity, and increase perseverance. Also, you reduce anxiety about the future.[10]

Exercise: Near/Far

Think of a decision between two options that you need to make now or very soon. (It's best to do this after you've done the preceding exercise.) It could be about your work or career (e.g., going back to school versus staying in the workforce) or about some other part of your life (e.g., whether or not to marry someone you're dating). Now, for one of the options, create two columns, one labeled "near" and the other labeled "far." In the "near" column, write down how that option will bring you nearer to the life that you envision for yourself. In the "far" column, write down how making that choice will take you further from your dreams. Your alternative option will usually be the flip of your first, but if you think it might be slightly different, complete a second near/far chart for the alternative. The chart with more items in the "near" column is the choice you should probably take, right? This simple exercise is richer than a pro/con list, because it can help you understand better how current decisions lead you on the path toward the life you desire—how, in other words, to be more real.

Skill: Hold Yourself Accountable

He that is good for making excuses is
seldom good for anything else.
—BENJAMIN FRANKLIN

To be accountable means having the strength to act according to the values you hold dear. Although all of our models do this, each in his or her own way, it's hard to think of a better modern example of someone holding himself accountable than Eric Greitens. Here are two activities that can help you discover how to bolster your ability to be real by demonstrating—to others and, most of all, to yourself— what you believe in.

Exercise: Buddy System

Greitens found the motivation to get through the drills at OCS after he was compelled to take responsibility for helping one of his classmates. Having a partner can make a big difference when you're struggling to do the right thing, especially when the challenge is fraught with obstacles. If you're having difficulty holding yourself accountable for achieving an important goal, try to find someone in a similar predicament—a buddy. Then hold each other accountable. Research shows that when you make a public commitment to a goal, you're more likely to follow through with your intentions than if you don't tell anyone.[11]

The goal should be specific, measurable, and moderately challenging. It should be aligned with your core values. And it should be your choice. Psychologists have shown that individuals who set their own goals are more likely to direct their efforts toward activities that help realize the goal (and away from activities that don't). They also persist more.[12] Such an activity should stretch you somewhat, but it should be achievable in the face of life's daily demands. Examples include writing a plan for a new business you'd like to launch, embarking on an exercise program, or increasing the number of evenings you attend community events.

Share your goal and its intentions with your buddy, and ask her to do the same, setting a rough timeline. Based on what you discover from this exchange, commit to taking one specific and realistic action toward your goal—even if it seems very small or perhaps trivial—and communicate that action to people you trust. Evidence indicates that it's important to act once you make a commitment to a goal; this creates self-reinforcing positive emotions (hope, pride, joy), building your confidence about taking further action that's in line with your values.[13] Check in with your partner regularly, even if very briefly or virtually, to (a) share your thoughts about your progress and (b) ask for feedback about how to adjust to ensure further progress.

You can experiment with the addition of a carrot or a stick to augment your motivation: set up a reward (e.g., give yourself a fifteen-minute chair massage at your gym) or a punishment (e. g., donate to a cause that holds political views antagonistic to your own) associated with taking your intended action. Authorize your buddy to mete out the punishment or make the award.

Exercise: Tune-up and Realignment

We usually remember to take our cars in for maintenance, but we forget to do the same for ourselves. Use your car tune-ups as a reminder cue. Every time you take your car in for maintenance, set aside thirty minutes on that same day for a reflection and planning date with yourself. Look under the hood, kick the tires, listen to the engine, and identify the one or two adjustments you need to make to better align what you do with what you believe is most important as you—taking the analogy a bit further—travel down the road of life. The key question: What are you not doing that you could be doing to express what's important to you? It could be something simple, such as spending time with friends, reading, or literally stopping to smell the flowers.

If you don't have a car, then use some other marker—such as your birthday, the day you get your hair cut, payday (perhaps to remind yourself that you're about more than just a paycheck), or waiting in line at the grocery store—to make time to clear your mind and focus on this simple question: What am I not doing that I should be doing? Consider isolating yourself for some or all of that time; try being alone, with no online connectivity. Think of this as an investment in your personal research and development, from which you can expect to reap long-term rewards.

9

Skills for Being Whole

Acting with Integrity

The second Total Leadership principle is to be whole: to act with integrity, striving to produce a feeling of oneness ("integrity" stems from the Latin *integer*, which means whole or complete). Acting with integrity demands respecting that you are a person who plays a number of important roles and practicing the skills that enable you to do so purposefully.

Clarifying what's most important to you, the first principle, is essential. But that's only the starting point. You also must embrace, serve, and draw strength from the various people who matter to you so that the whole is greater than the sum of the parts. In this chapter I suggest activities you can do to make these skills a part of how you go about navigating the hurly-burly of every day, bringing greater coherence to it all by cultivating allies and giving projects in the different parts of your life the attention they need. At the same time, you must be smart about braiding these fibers as one.

Skill: Clarify Expectations

Any fool can know. The point is to understand.
—ALBERT EINSTEIN

Certain practices can help you strengthen your ability to listen well—to understand the interests of others—while advocating what's important to you. Bruce Springsteen is especially good at clarifying expectations. You can start by identifying who matters most to you, and then consider what you think they need from you. Then talk with them, and take mindful steps to increase the focus you put on them and the conversations you have with them.

Exercise: Stakeholder Expectations

Think of an important person in your life, someone who matters to you and who you believe has a stake in your future. Imagine how he would answer this question from you: "What are the main things you want or need from me?" Then write whatever comes to mind that he might say: attention, emotional support, material resources, information, a point of view about an important topic—anything. Write your responses in as much detail as you can. Repeat the same exercise for other important people at work or in school, in your home or family, and among your community or social circle. This exercise will help you lay the foundation for identifying what your stakeholders need from you, and vice versa.

Then think of a conversation that you would like to have with one of your close friends but that you've been avoiding (about his constant lateness), family members (about resolving a conflict on parenting), or work colleagues (about how to manage a client dispute). Before you engage in this conversation, ask another trusted friend to pretend to play that person's role in a conversation, after you provide background about your relationship. Run through scenarios of how that person might respond. How did you react in each scenario? What did you learn from the role-play that will help you prepare for the actual conversation and your ability to blend both inquiry (listening well) and advocacy (sharing your point of view)?

Then, once you've had the real conversation, reflect on what transpired and how you might do this differently with other dear friends or colleagues, and repeat the cycle. Most of us don't usually take time to practice expressing ourselves and reflecting on how we react to others. Role-playing can prepare you for meaningful and productive conversations. The result is often clarity and insight about what you can do differently to better meet others' needs, as well as support from them about how they can help you to meet yours.[1]

Exercise: A Better Connection

Identify a relationship in which communication could use improvement: in your team at work, between you and your teenage son, or with a neighbor. Think about what you could do to improve the communication by creating connections with a rich, genuine, enlivening, and mutual exchange of ideas and feelings. Research by Jane Dutton and her colleagues at the University of Michigan has shown these simple ways to create better connections.[2]

- Commit to being present, attentive, and affirming. (Put the smartphone away!)

- Communicate your desire to give your help on what matters to him.

- If you have it, express your trust in his ability to live up to your expectations.

- Create positive images of the future.

- Allow yourself to have fun with him, especially to laugh at yourself.

- Assume positive intent—that he is on your side—until proven otherwise.

Choose one, or a combination, to create a high-quality connection with someone close to you. A firm connection allows both of you to talk about what you need from each other to make the relationship stronger.

Skill: Help Others

When you concern yourself with others, you
naturally develop a sense of self-confidence.
To help others takes courage and inner strength.
—THE DALAI LAMA

It's well established that most of us feel good when we help others.[3] But it's easy to lose sight of this fundamental aspect of human nature and instead to act selfishly, to forget that relationships are a means for enriching our own lives and the lives of others. Let's learn from the example of Julie Foudy, whose efforts to help others have taken place on a public stage, and look at some concrete actions you can take to help people. To do this you must reflect on the exchange of support in an important relationship and find out how you can assist him. Then you must take action on what you discover. With these activities you can leap into the hearts and minds of others, determine what they need from you, and develop your capacity to provide for those needs.

Exercise: How Can I Help You?

Identify a goal that either directly or indirectly benefits at least one other person, if not lots of other people. It might be to serve as a board member for the homeowners association in your neck of the woods, because you want both to make your neighborhood a more desirable place to live and to feel well connected to others who live around you. Then identify the potential beneficiaries of your efforts. It might be your neighbors whose lives would be a bit better as a result of something you can do for them, or it might be people whom you don't know very well.

Once you have identified the beneficiaries, have a quick conversation with them. Let your sole focus be finding out how your efforts might help them. Be relentless in your curiosity about what they need and care about. Ask pointed questions such as, "How would your feeling about the block be better if you had this help?" Then, if it's at all feasible, commit to providing that help—in a way that is as easy for you as possible.

The main idea is to keep on the lookout for opportunities to contribute to others, while, at the same time, not being a doormat. Organizational psychologist Adam Grant and others have shown that the most successful people are those who both help others, very efficiently, *and* take the initiative to ask for help in pursuing goals that serve a collective purpose.[4]

Exercise: Spread the Love

Here's an even simpler method for enhancing your reputation as the kind of person whom people turn to for help and in turn want to help. Over the course of the next week, on your own initiative, perform one simple act of kindness each day. It doesn't have to take much out of you; help an elderly person walk across the street, donate blood, write a thank-you letter, visit someone who is sick, apologize for a transgression, or volunteer to carpool—whatever suits you. In some instances, the recipients might not even be aware of what you're doing to benefit them. Keep a daily log, and, at the end of the week, take a few minutes to reflect on how your acts of kindness affected both you and your beneficiaries. If the recipients were not aware of what you did, then imagine how they would respond if they became aware of it.

This activity provides practice in identifying the needs of others and initiating action to contribute to their well-being—an essential element in building meaningful relationships and generating virtuous cycles of compassion and mutual support.[5]

Skill: Build Supportive Networks

Walking with a friend in the dark is better
than walking alone in the light.

—HELEN KELLER

Leading the life you want requires having the encouragement and resources that come from other people: opportunities, materials, ideas, money, and someone to talk to when you're hurt or afraid of what might come next. Leadership does not happen in social isolation: it is a team sport, as Sheryl Sandberg's Women of Silicon Valley demonstrates clearly. Yet many of us fundamentally misunderstand how much others are willing to help when asked.[6] So it's a lifelong enterprise to build your networks, by both asking for and giving help. To practice cultivating support, identify how you can strengthen relationships with those in your inner circle, and—go ahead—ask for help with something you're working on.

Exercise: Who Matters Most

List the names of the three to five people (individuals or groups) who matter most to you in each domain of your life—in your work or career, in your home or family, and in the community or society. Write a sentence about why each one of these people or groups is important to your future and why it's in their interest to aid you.

Then come up with one thing (the simpler and easier, the better) that you can do to provide some kind of help for some or all of these people or groups, something that fits with the vision you're trying to create for yourself. If you can't think of anything, then find out: How can you learn about what they need that you can provide? Now, give that help (again, the less costly for you, the better)—for example, provide a professional introduction for a friend or coworker—and observe the results, both in how you feel about yourself and in how your supportive action fortifies your relationships. Research has shown that experiences that spark an individual's genuine desire to help others can strengthen social bonds.[7]

(While you're at it, you might consider those people or groups whom you help—perhaps too much, in proportion to how much they matter to your future—and brainstorm possibilities for ways you might gracefully reduce what you're giving to them. There is a limit, after all.)

Look at your list of the most important people in your life, and for each one estimate the percentage of all your communication that you engage in using (a) face-to-face, (b) virtual synchronous communication—shifting place, but not time (e.g., phone, video conferencing)—or (c) virtual asynchronous communication, shifting both place and time (e.g., e-mail, letters—you remember those, right?). Think about whether the form of communication you use for each one helps or hinders your ability to gain support for your goals. You might even ask them which media they prefer.

What ideas come to mind for ways you might use different media to bring others closer to you? Keep in mind that "virtual" shrinks physical distances and allows you to reach many people through one message, and that "in-person" is richer and gives you information through tone and body language. You might discover that you would benefit from more in-person contact with some (such as your family or clients) and less with others (such as your boss), or more videoconferencing and texting with others (the younger people in your network) and less e-mailing with still others (those from the old school).

Exercise: SOS!

Identify a specific area in your life—personal, professional, or both— where you could benefit from help. For instance, are you struggling to get to the gym in the morning? Are you having difficulty meeting a deadline? Are you feeling stuck in a dead-end job with no other options? Do you want to learn how to cook? It could be anything— large or small.

Now think of someone you know who might be able to provide support. Do you have a friend who gets to the gym regularly? Do you know someone who rarely misses deadlines? Do you know someone who is a recruiter or who has used a good recruiter in the past? Do you know someone who loves to cook? Consider this person to be your helper, and plan a time to meet with her, describe your situation, and ask for the help you are seeking. Then be sure to express genuine appreciation for her help and identify how it has made a difference, whether through a personal note, a small gift, or some sort of public acknowledgment. And be sure to take the call when others ask for help. Pay it forward. Even more fun: connect people who you believe might be able to help each other.

Skill: Apply All Your Resources

If food is poetry, is not poetry also food?
—JOYCE CAROL OATES

Eric Greitens used what he discovered about himself and the world to enhance his impact as a military leader and CEO. There are countless ways that people can take what they have gained in one part of their lives and use it to pursue a goal that matters to them in another part.

The first exercise for this skill is designed to help you become aware of how you can take advantage of what you know from one domain (as, for example, what you learn from being a good father or son) and use it to improve your effectiveness in other parts (being a good mentor at work or in your community). The possibilities, when brought to bear in your everyday life, produce a greater sense of coherence—the elegant unity of form and function that J. J. Abrams admires in Greitens. The second is intended to jump-start how you think about new ways of connecting people across all your different networks.

Exercise: Talent Transfer

Think of a skill that you've developed—maybe mentoring colleagues, organizing activities for your family, or running the church bake sale. You might even write a very short résumé for each of your different roles, highlighting such skills. Think of these talents as muscles that can be used to achieve different ends, just as a strong arm can be used to swim, throw, lift crates, or carry a sleeping child. Let's say you successfully planned your wedding—congratulations! Now use what you learned to plan a community gathering for two hundred people or a conference at work. Are you an accountant by day? Turn into a teacher at night, running a budgeting-skills class for your kid's high school. Organizational psychologists call this a "strength development approach": first identify your talents, and then apply them in new areas. This practice actually enhances the initial competency.[8] By transferring skills from one area of your life to another, you capitalize on them, further honing your strengths in other areas. You become better able to meet goals in all parts of your life.

Another way to do this is to reflect on something that makes you proud: a work accomplishment, a fruitful friendship, or your commitment to salsa dancing. What skills, as opposed to raw talent or experience, helped your success? Persistence? Listening? Practice? Next, identify an area in your life that you feel could use improvement. How might you use the skills that were instrumental in improving the first area, which you are proud of, in the second area, where you want to improve? Create a simple plan that uses those skills in this other part of your life. Suppose you're good at making strong friendships but struggle with anxiety: you might try applying your ability to forge partnerships to enlist one of your trusted friends to help you manage your anxiety.

Exercise: Creative Contacts

A basic concept in social capital theory is that you gain access to resources through your personal and professional networks and that your reputation is strengthened in your networks when you help others. This, in turn, increases the chances that others will share resources with you. Here's a simple exercise that puts these ideas into action, with an emphasis on connecting *across* domains: name three people in your life who are untapped resources. You may know these people through one domain in your life, and yet, by thinking creatively, you may see the potential to draw on their support in other areas of your life, while contributing meaningfully to their lives as well. Read through your contact lists or your church or school directory for ideas. You might, for example, think of the other parents on your child's soccer team as people who might work with you on a neighborhood cleanup or as a focus group for a new health care service your company is planning to launch. Draft a plan for enlisting their help with something that matters to you. Make sure that this plan explains how their assistance will be mutually beneficial—good for them and for you.

Skill: Manage Boundaries Intelligently

*God saw that the light was good, and he
separated the light from the darkness.*

—GENESIS

Michelle Obama's example shows the importance of carefully grappling with the demands of different roles by consciously managing the boundaries among them. As we accelerate into the frenzy of digital contact and the ubiquity of screens streaming information at us, it is harder to focus our attention on what and who matters most. This psychological skill is surely one of the most important to learn if you are to thrive in a networked world. To improve your ability to manage boundaries intelligently, and thereby integrate the various roles you play, to feel more whole, let yourself step out from time to time. Also, see how you can both segment and merge the different domains of life, depending on what you and the people around you need at a particular moment.

Exercise: Unitask and Disconnect

There's a growing body of evidence on the risks associated with so-called multitasking, so it's wise to develop an appreciation for what you can do to counteract its effects.[9] In the first part of this exercise, pick an activity that you engage in daily, such as exercising, cooking, or responding to e-mails. On two separate days, first do that same activity while multitasking—that is, while doing something else such as watching a movie or talking with a friend. On the second day, do that same activity on its own, with no distractions at all. Then ask yourself, Was the quality of the experience better in one scenario? Was one scenario more fun, more engaging, or more efficient? If others were with you, ask them whether they could tell the difference. This simple experiment will help you identify the costs and benefits associated with multitasking and will give you new ideas for how best to manage your attention.

For the second part, select a one-hour time slot in which you will not use any technology—no internet, no smartphone, no electronic connectivity. Nothing! Select this time window wisely, and consider who or what would benefit from your full and complete attention. Then, after powering down for that one hour, consider the following: Were you craving your technology or fretting about someone not being able to reach you? Why? How did this affect your experience? How did it affect others whom you were with during this time? Then consider trying longer stretches of such glorious concentration.

This exercise will give you ideas about when it is appropriate to set up useful boundaries and to focus on a few people and things. The practice will help you get accustomed to switching among the different spheres of your life. That, in turn, will make you more successful in mastering what I call the "art of interruptability"—the ability to move with grace and efficiency from one thing to another.[10]

Exercise: Segment and Merge

Some organizational psychologists have found that people vary in their preferences for either segmenting or merging.[11] The activity described here helps you understand what works for you. It also involves two complementary experiments. First, set a time to talk with people you see daily or weekly about how you might try segmenting the different parts of your life. Get them to help you imagine a boundary—for example, reserving a special time or place dedicated to one thing—that allows you to focus in a way that works for you *and* makes things demonstrably better for them.

For this exercise, try to create a separation among different roles. For example, you might try, for the next week or month, dedicating the home office for Mom's work only, agreeing that she will occupy that space from 9:00 a.m. to noon, and then again from 1:00 p.m. to 6:00 p.m. (This helps her do what she needs to do to be successful as a breadwinner for the family.) Or you might agree that smartphones will be off and stored in a kitchen drawer during family dinner time. (This boundary fosters better conversation and helps kids learn to be psychologically present by disconnecting from their wired worlds.) That's the segment part of this exercise.[12]

Then, for the merge part, think about opportunities for you to bring together two or more parts of your life. (Again, focus on time and space.) The goal is not only doubling up but also improving the quality in each sphere. You might take a child to a company-sponsored charity run, or bring a coworker to a block party in your neighborhood. Experiment with ways to measure whether this attempt to blend domains made things better not only for you but also for the people around you. Suppose you organized a park cleanup day that included your partner and some coworkers who live nearby. Did each enjoy being a greater part of your life? Ask them afterward how they felt about being there.

After you've tried a new way of separating and a new way of merging, jot down your insights about what worked and what didn't. The key questions: Did you find yourself more or less distracted? Were you more or less productive? How did other people react to you? Were they put off, or did they seem to feel closer and more trusting of you?

Skill: Weave Disparate Strands

In the sky, there is no distinction of east and west;
people create distinctions out of their own
minds and then believe them to be true.

—BUDDHA

Being able to manage boundaries is an important skill, but it's not quite the same as fitting the pieces of your life together into a coherent whole. Explore how people in the different parts of your life see you, and identify the scripts and goals that are compatible among your essential roles. Think of how well Tom Tierney invested effort to produce the fabric of his life with its interwoven strands.

Exercise: Hidden Identities

Pick a few important stakeholders—people you believe are important to your future—from different areas of your life. Ask them to describe you briefly. Does each person see you similarly? Are some stakeholders unaware of aspects of your life that are important to you? Why? This is what psychologists call a "reflected best-self" exercise. It's helpful for developing an improved understanding of your unique values and talents.[13]

It's useful to wonder about the aspects of your identity that are currently hidden from some people. Your spouse might know you are a scholar of European history, but your coworkers might not know anything beyond your vacations to major capitals on the continent. Let people know something about an aspect of your life that is opaque to them. Sharing a personal side of yourself at work can increase trust and strengthen relationships with your colleagues. Explaining a conflict at work can help a child understand the ethics you share. Discovering how people see you helps knit together the threads of your life.

Exercise: Compatible Scripts and Goals

This exercise complements the preceding one by asking you to look from the inside out rather than from the outside in. Let's start with role scripts (or *schema*, the term used by personality researchers).[14] These are the mental frameworks that inform your knowledge about the appropriate behaviors for a person in a particular role, whether husband, neighbor, lover, boss, or son.

Think about the different roles that you actually play, and briefly write your view of the script for each of these roles. For example, let's say you're a husband. How do you believe a husband should act? Next, think about whether any of your behaviors overlap across domains; for example, does acting with compassion appear under both your husband and your boss role? Identify behaviors in one role that might strengthen your impact in a different area of your life; for example, does acting with compassion in your marriage make you a better neighbor? A better coworker? Thinking through these questions helps you see how you can bring more of yourself to the different spheres of your life.

Strengthen the weave by identifying a goal and writing a short note that explains how each domain of your life—work, home, community, and self—benefits from and contributes to your achievement of that goal. This will help you see connections in your life and understand how they are affected by your pursuit of a goal. This insight, in turn, enables you to think more expansively and creatively about how to bring the domains together in a way that makes sense to you. If your goal is to be remembered as someone who made the world better, for example, jot down how your actions in each part are moving you closer toward that aim. Then note how, in turn, your feelings about how things are going in each domain are enriched by those actions. Now, what ideas pop up about what you can do to tighten the connections?

10

Skills for Being Innovative

Acting with Creativity

The third Total Leadership principle is to be innovative—to act with creativity by continually experimenting with ways to get things done. Innovation here means strengthening your ability to see and pursue more four-way wins; to create changes that are sustainable because they work not only for you but also for your family, your community, and your job or career.

Skill: Focus on Results

However beautiful the strategy, you should
occasionally look at the results.
—WINSTON CHURCHILL

To lead the life you truly want to lead, you have to believe in your cause and attend laserlike to the aim. Eric Greitens demonstrates powerfully that you must have your purpose in mind wvhile, at the same time, moving, always moving, with your feet on the ground, sidestepping boulders and seeking the best route forward. Here are two activities you might try to practice your version of this march: imagining alternative scenarios and identifying useful metrics for success.

Exercise: Scenarios

Identify a goal in any part of your life, and describe in a sentence the results you want to achieve. Be as specific as you can in describing what success will look like. Then identify three alternative courses of action available to you that would achieve the same results. For each potential path, list the following:

- Resources you will need

- People whose help you'll draw on

- How much of a stretch beyond your comfort zone this would be for you

By taking time to think through different options, you increase the flexibility of your thinking. Brainstorming about creative possibilities puts your focus on the goal, or results, rather than on one way to get there.

A variation: mess with a pattern of behavior that you already use by, just once, doing that activity at a new time or in a different place. It could be something as simple as shaving at the gym instead of at home to cut several minutes out of your daily routine, or practicing your trumpet at the office after hours rather than disturbing your neighbors at home. What fears or concerns did you have about making this change? What were the pros and cons of switching up your routine? How did it affect your results? Although it might be disruptive, practicing this form of experimentation can strengthen your ability to generate alternative means to achieving goals.

Exercise: Metrics for Success

As famed UCLA basketball coach John Wooden said, "Don't mistake activity for achievement." Think about an important goal, and write down the metrics (or measures) that you will use to judge whether you have been successful in achieving it. Metrics can be objective (something you can weigh or count, such as money you want to earn, pages you want to write, sales calls you want to make, or pounds you want to shed) or subjective (whether coworkers perceive you as less grumpy or more approachable, or how your children feel about the quality of your relationship with them).

Review your metrics and consider whether they measure results you hope to achieve, or whether instead they address the method you used or the amount of time you put in to your pursuit of the goal. Run these by a trusted friend or colleague to get another perspective. How do your metrics affect how you approach the goal? Refine them so that they measure *results*.

Reframing how you define success may enable you to adopt a more results-oriented approach—keeping your eyes on the prize—instead of one that emphasizes, and narrowly restricts your thinking about, the where, when, and how.

Skill: Resolve Conflicts among Domains

Think left and think right and think low and think high.
Oh, the things you can think up if only you try.
—DR. SEUSS

Resolving conflicts among the domains of your life requires, first and foremost, a flexible approach. This critical skill—which Sheryl

Sandberg articulates well and which undergirds her success—comes down to how you think about what's possible. Research on cognitive bias and decision making shows that we react differently to choices depending on whether the options we face are perceived as losses or as gains.[1] How we frame options, therefore, becomes an important part of being able to find creative solutions that yield benefits, rather than harm, to the different parts of our lives.

To enlarge your own cognitive capacity, which is what this is, imagine that all the things that call for your attention are nourishment. Then do what I call "four-way thinking" about yourself, your family, your work, and your community, seeking ways for your home life to energize your work life, your community involvement to extend your professional calling, your private time to feed your public time.

The following exercises are designed to help you discover new approaches that make sense for your life and your specific situation. They will help you assess the impact of one aspect of your life on others, and they will enhance your ability to find mutual enrichment in the different areas of your life.

Exercise: Allies Not Enemies

Identify a conflict that exists between two (or more) domains; for example, find a situation in which work and family are at war. Consider for a moment how you might change your behavior to satisfy your needs in both competing domains. Are there specific activities—small or large—that could change the dynamic? What action within your control might create a benefit where now there is a cost? Suppose your teenage children perceive you to be a heartless corporate tool. You might talk with one or two of your employees about how you can help them solve problems they're having beyond their jobs. Then, when the opportunity arises, you might tell your kids about your efforts. This is an example of what psychologists call *job crafting*: the process of molding your work tasks and relationships to better fit your life.[2]

Is there a different perspective, or way of thinking, that you can adopt that might eliminate tension resulting from conflict? How might you look at the situation differently so that, instead of focusing on the conflict, you imagine alternative scenarios in which the domains are useful to each other? For example, work might force you to be physically separated from your family. Now consider how it both provides you with financial resources and enhanced self-esteem—which, in turn, make you a better parent—and brings a useful service to people and makes the world a better place.

Another way to see things from the point of view of mutual gains is to imagine a couple of simple ways to improve one aspect of your life: your work, family, community, or private self. Write down ways that this change will positively affect the other three areas, especially for the people who matter most to you. Will any of these things produce demonstrable gains in all four areas, either directly or indirectly, through a kind of ripple effect (what organizational psychologists call "positive spillover")? This activity helps you see that changes in one part of life can produce benefits in other parts; it isn't always a matter of sacrificing one part for another.

The more you think in this way, the more likely it is that you will devote your attention to actions that reduce your sense of conflict between work and the rest of life. All kinds of possibilities abound: taking a yoga class with your spouse, starting a book club with friends and coworkers, painting murals on your town's walls with customers, bringing the results of new recipes to colleagues, keeping sacrosanct a weekly lunch with your kids at your place of work. Small steps matter when it comes to improving *all* the different parts of your life without having to trade one for the others. And the more you try taking small steps, whether or not you get the results you want in the short run, the more possibilities you'll be able to imagine, and move forward on, in the days to come.

Exercise: Energizing Yourself

Many people think that they don't have enough time to take care of themselves. Or they feel guilty about doing so. However, setting aside time for energizing behaviors can actually enhance the efficiency you bring to *all* the things you want to do in *all* the different parts of life—and not only for you, but also for the people who matter to you.[3]

This exercise asks you to take care of your mind, body, and spirit. First, identify a behavior that makes you feel healthy, such as eating a nutritious snack, taking a nap, walking briskly, or meditating. Now do it, even if very briefly. How did you feel after that activity, and for the rest of the day? Did taking time out for that behavior give you less energy, or more? This practice can persuade you that what might seem like a conflict—trading time working for time energizing—is actually a benefit to your mind and body as well as to your work.

Skill: Challenge the Status Quo

The philosophers have only interpreted
the world, in various ways.
The point, however, is to change it.
—KARL MARX

Challenging assumptions, as Julie Foudy did, is hard, for when you do so you encounter resistance, either from within or from without. But you can improve this skill for being innovative. The more you are able to understand what traditional assumptions are, the more effectively you can overcome them as mere sources of constraint.

Exercise: In the Lab

Just as a scientist keeps a roster of ideas for experiments, try keeping a journal or log for a few days. Record any hypotheses that occur to you for new ways of getting things done, especially if they would benefit different parts of your life and help you design the kind of life you want to lead in the future. Think of these as experiments; you are a scientist, with your life as your laboratory. Don't judge your ideas. Use this opportunity to come up with options for things you might do differently.

Now choose one such idea to implement. It could involve doing a new activity, such as getting feedback from end users of a prototype you're developing. It could also mean stopping or reducing something you're already doing, such as checking your social media accounts fifteen times a day. What assumptions about the way things are now would you have to challenge in order to move forward on these actions? Who could you talk to about your thinking? Who can help you understand your assumptions and implement the idea successfully? Perhaps you're anxious about getting feedback on that prototype. You decide to talk it over with a friend. He persuades you to see that your fear of discovering that it's all a big waste of time is misguided and that any critique of your model will give you what you need to improve it.

This might seem like a far cry from Foudy's challenging the Title IX commission, but as studies on the theory of "small wins" have shown, thinking about our assumptions and then designing incremental steps to create change can give us greater confidence to question the status quo.[4]

Exercise: My Problem = Our Problem

Think of a dilemma with which you are currently grappling. Gather a small group of people who are affected by this dilemma. Describe how you see the problem, especially how it affects them. Ask the group to come up with ideas for potential solutions, and record them, no matter how impractical they might seem. Once you have exhausted the creativity of your group, review each possible solution. First, let each person do so separately (to encourage independent thinking and reduce bias from social pressure). Then, as a group, draw on the wisdom of different viewpoints. Discuss the pros and cons of each, including the underlying assumptions about how each one might affect members of the group and others who might have a stake.

Identify the best, second-best, and third-best options. Then identify the next action you can take on your first-choice solution, with the understanding that if it fails, then you'll adjust or pursue the second or third choices. This exercise should bolster your ability to think critically and test assumptions, thereby enabling you to be more innovative as a leader.[5]

Skill: See New Ways of Doing Things

My favorite thing is to go where I've never been.

—DIANE ARBUS

You can see from Tom Tierney's example that it's possible to exercise your innovation muscles by developing the skill of seeing new ways of doing things. He foresaw the idea of what was to become Bridgespan in his early imaginings about a "Make a Difference Company." What desired future—over the long haul or in the day-to-day—can you foresee more clearly?

Exercise: Crowd-Source Solutions

Social scientists I-Shou Chen and Jui-Kuei Chen explain that not all people are creative and that some personalities in particular have difficulty becoming more creative.[6] Enlisting others in discovering creative solutions can help overcome those personality barriers. Want to become more open to fresh perspectives? Ask your most creative friends to lunch.

Before that lunch, start the process of change by taking five minutes to write about a pattern of behavior that is no longer working for you. How is it preventing you from living the life you want? (Identifying unhelpful habits is a natural starting point for change.) Contact people in your life who are related somehow to this bad habit. Describe the problem and your wish to solve it. Then ask for ideas about potential solutions, and record what you hear. Adopt the one you think wisest, drafting a plan and trying to make it happen. Stay in touch with the people who helped you think about it, at least weekly. After a month or so, review your results with them, even if the plan didn't work, to explore what happened and what you learned about trying to produce a change.

If it didn't work, or if you need more time to solve the problem, craft a revised plan of action using other ideas that you heard and drawing on what you learned from your first try. Keep innovating; not every experiment clicks. Thoughtfully trying something new can help you realize, in concrete terms, that you don't have to stay in the same rut. And it strengthens your confidence in your creative skills.

Exercise: Picture Your Idea Web

Creating visual images (some call them *mind maps*) of the connections among different strands of an idea forces you to use a range of cognitive tools. Mind maps are graphic representations that allow an individual to look at a large amount of information about a subject on one page in a holistic, nonlinear way.[7] Think of a specific goal in your life, or perhaps a problem that needs to be solved. Gather a few large pieces of blank artist's paper and various colored markers. Find a quiet spot and give yourself time to relax. Choose a word or image that represents the goal or problem, and write it down or draw it on the center of the page. (Suspend judgment about your drawing skills, and use images whenever possible.) For example, if your goal is be a valued member of a nonprofit board, then draw a picture of you in a meeting of such a group (or just a picture of the table around which you meet) in the center of the page.

Next, create different-colored branches of ideas relating to your central goal, using either an image or a few words to describe each related concept. In the example, you might draw the following branches: prestige, network connections, learning, and self-esteem. Write down any thoughts, even those that may seem obscure in the moment. Draw sub-branches from each branch to further expand on your ideas until you can't think of any more. Draw boxes around the most important information. Edit, regroup as you wish, and draw a final version on a fresh sheet of paper. Once you have completed your final version, ask yourself, What did I discover, and how is what I learned important to my values and goals? How can I actually use what I've designed in this picture?

Studies show that mind mapping encourages whole-brain thinking.[8] It enhances creativity and productivity, as well as efficiency. It allows you to make connections between ideas and to be flexible in their application. As you play with mind maps and find ways to use them, your ability to act creatively will blossom.

Skill: Embrace Change Courageously

Only those who keep changing remain akin to me.
—FRIEDRICH NIETZSCHE

Learning to try new things can be rife with trepidation and fear. To fortify your courage, follow Michelle Obama's example: weigh the worst-case result and the best-case result for an upcoming change, and challenge your beliefs about what it might mean for you as well as the people who matter most to you. These activities can help you overcome inhibitions, accomplish more, and feel better about the life you lead.

Exercise: Worst Case/Best Case

Think of an upcoming change that you are worried about; maybe it's a geographic move, a switch in jobs or companies, a child leaving home, a divorce, or surgery. Envision the worst possible outcomes that could occur. Now visualize the best possible outcomes that could occur. Which is more likely, and why? Estimate the likelihood that each one of those outcomes will happen—one in a million, 75 percent chance, somewhere in the middle?—and write down those odds for both the worst and the best possible outcomes.

Then consider the effects each outcome would have on the people around you. Further, note the one or two most critical effects of not taking any action. It boils down to this: which would be better—the status quo or change? Talk over your forecasts with a friend or two, and get their read on the outcomes you imagine.

Taking the most likely outcomes into consideration (naturally, those likely will fall somewhere between the worst and best cases), draft a simple plan for the next action step you can take to create the change. When people approach changes that will improve their lives or their impact, they sometimes spend time thinking only about the bad things that might happen. It is crucial to devote attention to imagining the best case, too. It's often more likely than the worst.

Exercise: Challenging Your Beliefs

Some research shows that an individual's beliefs about change either enhance or inhibit that change. In other words, your outlook influences your ability to make change succeed.[9] When you fear change it's useful to think about the reasons for your dread. (Apprehension is linked to your beliefs.) Write down, in detail, your beliefs. For each one, ask yourself whether it is accurate. Research it to find expert advice. Challenge your current thinking; differentiate realistic concerns from the unrealistic ones that crop up as a result of bias, ignorance, or past experiences. (Misinformation and irrational thinking can make us resist change.)[10] Can you address the realistic concerns you have as you embark on a new path? You have more control over the outcomes than you may now believe.

Poor self-esteem can make us resistant to change; confidence and resilience allow us to change and grow. Talk over your ideas with a friend, asking him to ask you (to borrow a phrase from Sheryl Sandberg), what would it be like if you weren't afraid?[11]

If fear or anxiety about change is preventing you from taking the steps necessary to achieve important goals, try exploring techniques for anxiety management. Investigate different approaches: quick breathing exercises, weekly yoga, visualization, fifteen-minute meditation, physical exercise, talking to a trusted friend about your fears, or psychological therapy. Pick an approach appropriate for you. If making the change is important enough to you, then it's probably a good idea to tackle directly the anxiety that prevents you from moving forward.

Skill: Create Cultures of Innovation

If you have an apple and I have an apple and we exchange
these apples then you and I will still each have one
apple. But if you have an idea and I have an idea and we
exchange these ideas, then each of us will have two ideas.
—GEORGE BERNARD SHAW

Anyone's mind can open more. Bruce Springsteen's life and work are a certain testament to this idea. Research shows that when you display openness to discovery you inspire others to learn, too.[12] You can demonstrate your own eagerness to learn by letting others know you want to learn from them and also by teaching. Encouraging others to pursue new knowledge about their work and their lives beyond work can enhance your own ability to be innovative.

Exercise: Another Perspective

Becoming an individual with multiple facets to his life was not easy for Bruce Springsteen. Therapy helped him wrestle with his inner demons and free up his hopes for the future. Although you may or may not benefit from having your own psychotherapist, everyone can benefit from gaining another perspective. There are countless ways of seeking it. When others see you appreciate alternative points of view, they are more likely to offer them.

At a certain point in the creation of *Born to Run*, Springsteen risked carrying his perfectionism too far by setting such extremely high standards that the album almost got canned because of delays. Only his manager's pragmatism (releasing a single while waiting for the whole album) saved Springsteen from never getting it done. On whom do you rely to rein in your excesses with a healthy dose of practicality? Whom do you talk to when there are indicators that you have gone too far in pursuing a dream by, for example, ignoring quality for the sake of timetables or by toiling on a product for so long that it loses relevance? Observe others, ask open-ended questions of them, and learn from them.

You might make what researchers call an *appreciative inquiry*. Bring together a few people who can play a role in the realization of one of your goals. At work, for example, this might include executives, middle managers, and customers. At home, it might be members of your family. Identify your goal in positive terms—to become world class in customer service or a more tight-knit, loving family. Next, ask people to share their stories about real successes within the group that reflect your goal. For example, someone might recount the time when Sue's customer e-mailed the CEO to rave about her experience in buying a car, or the time when your brother generously donated his time to a charity you started. Once you have shared your successes as a group, identify the possibilities of what could be. What is the group's vision of success, and what does that look like? Considering both your real successes and your vision for the future, write a simple purpose statement that is realistic and inspiring to you and to them. Then spend a few minutes listing ideas for ways to pursue this vision and carry out your purpose.[13]

Exercise: Teach

Think of a skill that you could teach to someone—for example, showing your octogenarian aunt how to use some new technology or teaching a coworker how to use the coffee maker. Now ask that person if she would like to learn the new skill. If the answer is yes, go for it. If no, move on and find something to teach someone else. Then ask yourself, how did you feel in your role as teacher? Simply taking opportunities to practice sharing your knowledge and skills with others will enhance your ability to cultivate a learning environment wherever you go.

Or think about something that you've accomplished recently about which you are particularly proud—finishing a major report, being admitted to a new association, or completing a big financial deal. Now, tell someone (someone you wouldn't normally tell) about how significant this was for you, emphasizing not so much the achievement as what you had to learn—and how you learned it—to get there.

How did you feel telling others about what you did, what it took, and what it means to you? Were you uncomfortable crowing, or did it feel natural? How did the other person react? Although people sometimes feel uncomfortable sharing their successes, showing with your example what's possible and sharing how you did it, as long as you're willing to take the risk of stretching yourself, creates opportunities for others to try new things.

Conclusion

Try to Be Kinder—
to Others and to Yourself

Where is the harmony, sweet harmony?
—ELVIS COSTELLO

When I began writing this book, I used the working title *Great Leaders, Good Lives.* I believed that truly great leaders found a way to harmonize the different parts of their lives and that this harmony had a synergistic effect. Harmony begot more harmony and, even more important, the achievement of meaningful goals. What ensued was not only fortune or fame but also the deeply personal rewards of a good life.

Reflecting on what I've learned from the stories in this book, I am more convinced now than before that significant achievement in the world results from consciously compassionate action, from using one's talents to make the world somehow better. It's a paradox: leading the life *you* want requires striving to help *others*. This noble pursuit of a calling is available to us all. And the new title, I hope, underscores this.

The stories I've told show six very different people discovering the person they wanted to be and finding creative ways to become that person. By choosing to do what they really care about, they have built not résumés, and not necessarily great fortunes, but lives that matter. They have had lots of help. They have been fueled by a passionate interest in making the most of their time on earth as well as by a compulsion to serve. Each one has demonstrated how accomplishment in one's career comes not at the expense of the rest of one's life, but because of one's commitments at home, in the community, and to an inner life.

Tom Tierney, Sheryl Sandberg, Eric Greitens, Michelle Obama, Julie Foudy, and Bruce Springsteen have struggled to become the people they are and to lead their lives as they wish. They have all made compromises, and yet they've stayed true to themselves. Each personifies the skills I've been encouraging you to practice. And each helps us see how we can cultivate a life in which our own values and social contributions work in harmony—not necessarily every minute of every day, but consistently over the course of time.

I'm most heartened by the possibility for growth shown in their stories. Although you and I may not achieve their renown, we can see that their accomplishments are the happy result not only of good fortune but also of a willingness to be agents in shaping their lives. The world beckons to each one of us, challenging us to ply our talents and carve our own paths. As the existential philosopher and psychiatrist Viktor Frankl discovered during his World War II concentration camp internment, it is our voluntary action, and not what we're forced to do, that determines the excellence of our character. Frankl observed that even in the most horrific and highly constrained circumstances, a life imbued with a sense of meaning is possible.

This sense of meaning is what a feeling of well-being is about. But, interestingly, contemporary psychologists and neurophysiologists identify two very different kinds of well-being. *Eudaimonic well-being* is the feeling that results from helping others. *Hedonic well-being* is the constant pursuit of immediate happiness. We need both types. Without eudaimonic well-being, hedonic behavior leads to the same gene patterns that develop in response to persistent adversity. Too much self-interest, in other words, is physically damaging. The optimal bodily state, research reveals, results from the combination of both doing good (creating meaning) and feeling good (creating happiness).[1] That blend of meaning and happiness is the good life. And the good life brings an inner serenity—a feeling of peace and contentment—in the midst of the chaotic world.

The promise of leading the life you want is this feeling of satisfaction. It begins with a belief in the dignity of other people and our ability to express compassion for them. We also have to provide value to others through our work and must be conscious of how this not only is a part of our identity but also is essential to our sense of purpose. George Saunders, a contemporary American novelist, put it well in his address to graduating college seniors in 2013. To counteract a common malady of our times—what Saunders called a "confusion in each of us, a sickness," and "selfishness"—Saunders offered a goal he called both "facile" and "hard to implement." He advised the graduates to "try to be kinder."[2]

Generosity of spirit, grace, forgiveness—the challenge is to embody these qualities as we pursue something that will reside peacefully in the world after we leave it. To do so requires creating boundaries that allow for a feeling of coherence, our own identity distinct from everything else in the world and yet very much a part of it. Harmonious connection demands meaningful separation.

We must have our heads in the clouds and our feet on the ground, dealing with reality while dreaming of a better future. We must be optimists *and* realists. And we must never quit trying to live the life we want. In the steps we take toward becoming more of, and truer to, ourselves, in the service of others, our own greatness becomes apparent. We find the will to persist, overcoming the fear that often stops people from trying, by seeing that what we're doing with our lives is not only for ourselves alone but also for others.

The ancient philosopher Lao Tzu urges us to be ever curious about ourselves and about how we can be better. He said, "Knowing others is wisdom. Knowing yourself is enlightenment." Just like the people in this book, we have to slake our thirst for learning throughout our lives. We have to put a lot of stock in preparation, and experience joy in discovery. We must go through moments of painful growth, episodes from which we observe something important about ourselves. We have to ask for help from teachers and mentors, wherever we can find them. And we must become teachers. Eventually we grow into seeing how we can serve as role models and, in so doing, extend our reach and impact.

I hope the stories and the skills they illustrate inspire you to create meaningful change in your world—change that's sustainable because it's good for you as well as for the people around you. Our broken world needs you to lead the life you want.

Look around. Once you begin to search for people who weave their work lives with the rest of their lives in mutually enriching ways, I bet you'll find many of your own exemplars to add to the ones I've presented here. They will put to rest the canard that you can't achieve greatness in work without forsaking the rest of your life.

Notes

Introduction

1. J. Levy, "Bruce Springsteen: The Rolling Stone Interview," *Rolling Stone*, November 1, 2007, http://www.rollingstone.com/music/news/bruce-springsteen-the-rolling-stone-interview-20071101.

2. Visit http://www.slideshare.net/totalleadership/presentations for examples of these student biographies.

Chapter 1

1. T. Tierney, "Tom Tierney: Staying Grounded in Who I Am," interview by S. D. Friedman, video, http://www.totalleadership.org/tltv (2008). Unless otherwise indicated, all interview quotations from Tom Tierney are from this interview.

2. Personal communication, January 23, 2013.

3. T. Tierney, "Tom Tierney in Conversation with John Kobara," interview by J. Kobara, video, http://vimeo.com/28346864 (2011).

4. Background in this paragraph is from ibid.

5. Tierney told this story in a guest lecture in my Wharton MBA class (T. Tierney, guest lecture, University of Pennsylvania, Philadelphia, video, April 10, 2008).

6. K. Morrell, A. Nanda, and P. L. Fagan, *Tom Tierney's Reflections* (Boston: Harvard Business School Publishing, 2003).

7. T. Tierney, "Tom Tierney in Conversation with John Kobara."

8. Morrell, Nanda, and Fagan, *Tom Tierney's Reflections*.

9. Ashish Nanda, Kelley Morrell, and Monica Mullick, "To Tierney's Reflections," Case 9–903–127 (Boston, Harvard Business School, 2003).

10. T. Tierney, guest lecture, University of Pennsylvania.

11. T. Tierney, "IMPACT Speaker Tom Tierney," lecture, Georgia Institute of Technology College of Management, Atlanta, video, January 25, 2012, http://www.youtube.com/watch?v=J5PoE53oa2M.

12. T. Tierney, "Tom Tierney: It's Easy to Ignore the Soul," interview by S. D. Friedman, video, http://www.totalleadership.org/tltv/ (2008).

13. T. Tierney, "Tom Tierney: You're a Steamroller," interview by S. D. Friedman, video, http://www.totalleadership.org/tltv/ (2008).

14. J. Donahoe, personal communication, February 1, 2013.

15. T. Tierney, guest lecture, University of Pennsylvania.

16. T. Tierney, "Easy to Ignore the Soul."

17. Morrell, Nanda, and Fagan, *Tom Tierney's Reflections*.

18. Ibid.

19. Ibid.

20. Ibid.

21. Ibid., 10.

22. T. Tierney, guest lecture, University of Pennsylvania.

23. T. Tierney, personal communication, January 16, 2013.
24. Morrell, Nanda, and Fagan, *Tom Tierney's Reflections*, 10.
25. T. Tierney, "Easy to Ignore the Soul."
26. Karen Tierney, personal communication, January 25, 2013.
27. Morrell, Nanda, and Fagan, *Tom Tierney's Reflections*.
28. T. Tierney, interview by J. Kobara.
29. Ibid.
30. T. Tierney, guest lecture, University of Pennsylvania.
31. T. Tierney, interview by J. Kobara.
32. T. Tierney, guest lecture, University of Pennsylvania.
33. T. Tierney, "Easy to Ignore the Soul."
34. Morrell, Nanda, and Fagan, *Tom Tierney's Reflections*.
35. T. Tierney, personal communication, January 16, 2013.
36. Quotations from this talk are from T. Tierney, "IMPACT Speaker Tom Tierney."
37. T. Tierney, "Easy to Ignore the Soul."
38. Ibid.
39. M. Nauffts, "Tom Tierney, Chairman/Co-founder, Bridgespan Group: Philanthropy That Gets Results," *Philanthropy News Digest*, May 6, 2011, http://foundationcenter.org/pnd/newsmakers/nwsmkr.jhtml?id=339200006.
40. J. Fleishman and T. Tierney, *Give Smart: Philanthropy That Gets Results* (New York: PublicAffairs, 2011), ix.
41. This and the following quote are from J. Fleishman, personal communication, January 23, 2013.
42. Nauffts, "Tom Tierney, Chairman/Co-founder, Bridgespan Group."
43. Morrell, Nanda, and Fagan, *Tom Tierney's Reflections*.
44. T. Tierney, "An Interview with Tom Tierney, co-author of *Give Smart: Philanthropy That Gets Results*," interview by R. Kanani, http://www.huffingtonpost.com/rahim-kanani/an-interview-with-tom-tie_b_862049.html (May 15, 2011).
45. T. Tierney, "Easy to Ignore the Soul."
46. To view the *Give Smart* video series, visit givesmart.org and click on the videos section.

Chapter 2

1. S. Sandberg, "Sheryl Sandberg's Keynote Address at the Grace Hopper Celebration of Women in Computing," video, November 10, 2011, http://www.livestream.com/fbtechtalks/video?clipId=pla_e6b1a965–8cc5–4ef9–9ac8c2048d612e96&utm_source=lslibrary&utm_medium=ui-thumb&time=1.
2. C. Rose, *The Charlie Rose Show*, November 7, 2011.
3. K. Auletta, "A Woman's Place: Can Sheryl Sandberg Upend Silicon Valley's Male-Dominated Culture?" *New Yorker*, July 11, 2011, http://www.newyorker.com/reporting/2011/07/11/110711fa_fact_auletta.
4. The preceding descriptions are from ibid.
5. S. Sandberg, Grace Hopper keynote.
6. Auletta, "A Woman's Place."
7. These details are from Auletta, "A Woman's Place"; K. Conley, "Sheryl Sandberg: What She Saw at the Revolution," *Vogue*, April 15, 2010, http://www.vogue.com/magazine/article/sheryl-sandberg-what-she-saw-at-the-revolution/; and S. Sandberg, "Sheryl Sandberg on Facebook's Future," interview by S. J. Adler, *Bloomberg Businessweek*, April 8, 2009, http://www.businessweek.com/stories/2009–04–08/sheryl-sandberg-on-facebooks-futurebusinessweek-business-news-stock-market-and-financial-advice.

8. Personal communication, April 4, 2013.

9. Auletta, "A Woman's Place."

10. Ibid.

11. S. Sandberg, "Sheryl Sandberg: Spotlight on Scalability," Entrepreneurial Thought Leader Lecture, audio file, April 22, 2009, http://ecorner.stanford.edu/authorMaterialInfo.html?mid=2214.

12. S. Sandberg, *Sheryl Sandberg: A public failure* [video interview clip, 2013]. Retrieved from http://www.makers.com/sheryl-sandberg/moments/public-failure.

13. S. Sandberg, personal communication, March 18, 2014.

14. Auletta, "A Woman's Place."

15. J. Hempel, "Meet Facebook's New Number Two," *CNNMoney*, April 12, 2008, http://money.cnn.com/2008/04/11/technology/facebook_sandberg.fortune/index.htm.

16. S. Sandberg, Grace Hopper keynote, 2011.

17. S. Sandberg, *Lean In: Women, Work, and the Will to Lead* (New York: Alfred A. Knopf, 2013).

18. B. Stone, "Everybody Needs a Sheryl Sandberg," *Bloomberg Businessweek*, May 12, 2011, audio file, http://www.businessweek.com/mediacenter/podcasts/cover_stories/covercast_05_12_11.htm.

19. This and the following quotations are from S. Sandberg, personal communication, August 7, 2013.

20. S. Sandberg, "Sheryl Sandberg: Why We Have Too Few Women Leaders," TED.com, December 21, 2010; http://www.ted.com/talks/sheryl_sandberg_why_we_have_too_few_women_leaders.html.

21. S. Sandberg, *Lean In.*

22. S. Sandberg, personal communication, 2013.

23. Stone, "Everybody Needs a Sheryl Sandberg."

24. She applies three principles in her business-informed approach to philanthropy: (1) focus on the most critical problems at hand; (2) find systemic solutions to problems; and (3) create core competence in the agencies you support. This formulation evolved from Sandberg's private sector experience, which drove home to her that some of the most essential members of an organization are the ones who work behind the scenes. She says that if she worked for a nonprofit, she'd be considered administrative overhead and likely discarded. But such a simplistic approach means nonprofits are not able to build the basic infrastructure needed to drive change. Because of her grasp of the ways different kinds of people make a business succeed, Sandberg provides the kind of financial support that allows charitable agencies to spend her money on direct and indirect costs, including on staffing and other administrative needs. Thus she applies to charitable initiatives some hard-won knowledge from her business experience, having learned that in any field of endeavor, an organization can have the strength to produce lasting results only if it has a strong foundation of competent, committed people.

25. S. Sandberg, "Sheryl Sandberg's Keynote at the 2010 BLC Breakfast," March 5, 2010, video, http://www.jewishfed.org/community/page/blcvideos#Sandberg.

26. Ibid.

27. S. Sandberg, "Sheryl Sandberg: Why We Have Too Few Women Leaders," video, December 21, 2010, http://www.ted.com/talks/sheryl_sandberg_why_we_have_too_few_women_leaders.html.

28. S. Sandberg, "Sheryl Sandberg: Not Heeding Own Advice," video clip, 2013, http://www.makers.com/sheryl-sandberg/moments/not-heeding-own-advice. For more information, see also Sandberg, *Lean In*, p. 97, where Sandberg discusses turning down an opportunity to become the new CEO of LinkedIn after Reid Hoffman reached out to her.

29. S. Sandberg, personal communication, 2013.

30. S. Sandberg, "Sheryl Sandberg: Barnard College Commencement," speech, Barnard College, New York, video, May 17, 2011, http://barnard.edu/headlines/facebook-executive-barnard-graduates-world-needs-you-run-it.

31. Cisco CEO John Chambers is one example of someone whose thinking was altered by the stories Sandberg tells. In an internal e-mail he said, "While I have always considered myself sensitive to and effective on gender issues in the workplace . . . [a]fter reading *Lean In* and listening to Sheryl, I realize that, while I believe I am relatively enlightened, I have not consistently walked the talk." K. Swisher, "Telling Employees He Hasn't 'Walked the Talk,' Cisco's John Chambers Leans In on Women in the Workplace Issue," *All Things D*, March 13, 2013, http://allthingsd.com/20130313/telling-employees-hes-not-walked-the-talk-ciscos-john-chambers-leans-in-on-women-in-the-workplace/.

32. S. Sandberg, "Why We Have Too Few Women Leaders."

33. Conley, "Sheryl Sandberg: What She Saw at the Revolution."

34. "Facebook's Sheryl Sandberg on What Makes Women Succeed," *CNN Money*, October 4, 2011, http://Management.fortune.cnn.com/2011/10/04/facebook-sheryl-sandberg.

35. J. Samakow, "Adele Sandberg, Sheryl Sandberg's Mom, Inspired Daughter to 'Lean In from Childhood until Today,'" *Huffington Post*, May 7, 2013, http://www.huffingtonpost.com/2013/05/07/adele-sandberg-sheryl-sandberg-mom-tribute_n_3230540.html.

Chapter 3

1. For an account of Greitens's Hell Week experience, see E. Greitens, *The Heart and the Fist: The Education of a Humanitarian, the Making of a Navy SEAL* (New York: Houghton Mifflin Harcourt Publishing, 2011).

2. Personal communication March 7, 2013.

3. Greitens, *Heart and the Fist*.

4. Unless otherwise noted, all "told me" quotations from Greitens are from personal communications with me over the years 2013–2014.

5. Greitens, *Heart and the Fist*.

6. B. Osburg, personal communication, April 18, 2013.

7. Greitens, *Heart and the Fist*.

8. Ibid.

9. E. Greitens, "Eric Greitens on *The Heart and the Fist*," Harvard Kennedy School Center for Public Leadership, video, 2012, http://www.youtube.com/watch?feature=player_embedded&v=Iql6V60d1mM. Greitens continued, "I started to see after a while that what I was learning in the classroom was actually reflected here in this very different environment in the boxing gym."

10. Greitens, *Heart and the Fist*.

11. Ibid.

12. Greitens, *Heart and the Fist*.

13. For more on Greitens's initial disappointment with OCS, see Greitens, *Heart and Fist*, 136.

14. Greitens, *Heart and the Fist*.

15. For Greitens's account of taking his men to the "bad village," see Greitens, *Heart and Fist*, 267–268.

16. Osburg, personal communication, 2013.

17. For more on this visit and the patients' determination to return to service, see Greitens, *Heart and Fist*, 288–290.

18. K. Harbaugh, personal communication, April 11, 2013.

19. Some sources give a slightly different account: "To launch the program, Greitens ponied up his lieutenant's combat pay and tax-free earnings from Iraq—a total of $3,500. Two fellow veterans chipped in about $3,000, and another friend put in $10,000." See K. Hinman, "Captain America," *Riverfront Times*, April 9, 2008, http://www.riverfronttimes.com/2008–04–09/news/navy-seal-eric-greitens-has-come-home-to-st-louis-to-help-fellow-iraq-vets/.

20. Osburg, personal communication, 2013; Greitens, *Heart and Fist*, 292.

21. Harbaugh, personal communication, 2013.

22. United States Army Combined Arms Center, Center for Army Lessons Learned, http://usacac.army.mil/cac2/call/thesaurus/toc.asp?id=33978.

23. Greitens, "Eric Greitens on *The Heart and the Fist*."

24. S. Kympton, personal communication, April 12, 2013.

25. Chris Marvin explained to me, "Everybody wants to deal with veterans with kid gloves, especially wounded veterans. They want to give them something. They want to feel this somewhat sympathetic pity or whatever it is toward the wounded veteran." For The Mission Continues, a major challenge was "just convincing nonprofits, partners that we wanted to work with, because each fellow is placed in a different nonprofit. Convincing just anybody on the street that the approach for wounded veterans should be to tell them to get off their butts and go do something to help their community provided a lot of cognitive dissonance for people. Because that's not what they were being taught by the culture." Personal communication, April 12, 2013.

26. J. Klein, "Can Service Save Us?" *Time*, June 20, 2013, http://nation.time.com/2013/06/20/can-service-save-us/.

27. J. J. Abrams, personal communication, June 10, 2013.

28. E. Greitens, "Commencement Speech," Tufts University, Medford, Massachusetts, May 20, 2012, transcript, http://now.tufts.edu/commencement-address-eric-greitens.

29. For more on Greitens' experience visiting a homeless shelter, see Greitens, *Heart and Fist*, 10–12.

30. Greitens wrote that he has an ongoing relationship with two of these young men: "They put their bad decision behind them in a positive way and they found a way to move on. They both learned—and we all were reminded—that to be a warrior is as much a question of moral character as it is a question of physical courage." For more, see Greitens, *Heart and Fist*, 246.

31. Ibid.

32. For more on Earl Blair's parking lot training, see Greitens, *Heart and Fist*, 31.

33. In his memoir (p. 196), Greitens recalls how uplifting an experience dancing the Hokey Pokey proved to be during Hell Week: "When I'd finished, the instructor turned to me. 'Mr. Greitens, that was the best damn Hell Week Hokey Pokey I've ever seen. You guys all get five minutes' rest.' We sat down next to our boats. We were too tired to joke now, almost too tired to breathe deeply, but as the guys in my crew leaned against the side of our boat and fell immediately asleep, I sat in the sand, very proud of myself. I was not the fastest runner, not the fastest swimmer, not the fastest man on the obstacle course, but at least for the moment, I was the world's greatest living Hokey Pokey Warrior."

34. And it meant paying close attention and listening to how others were feeling—such as complaints about the frustration caused by a forklift stranded by the United States on a Kenyan beach—and creatively figuring out solutions, which in the forklift case meant slicing through thick layers of military bureaucracy. For more on the stranded forklift, its deleterious effect on local relations, and Greitens's push for a solution, see *Heart and Fist*, 261–263.

35. Greitens, *Heart and the Fist*.

Chapter 4

1. M. Obama, "Remarks by the First Lady at Joining Forces Veterans Hiring Event," Mayport Naval Station, Mayport, Florida, August 22, 2012, transcript, http://www.whitehouse.gov/the-press-office/2012/08/22/remarks-first-lady-joining-forces-veterans-hiring-event.

2. M. Obama, interview by David Letterman, *Late Show with David Letterman*, CBS, March 19, 2012.

3. R. Wolfe, "Barack's Rock," *Newsweek*, February 16, 2008, http://www.thedailybeast.com/newsweek/2008/02/16/barack-s-rock.html.

4. For Obama's self-described role as "Mom-in-Chief," see L. Rogak, *Michelle Obama: In Her Own Words* (New York: PublicAffairs, 2009), viii.

5. M. Obama, *Late Show with David Letterman*, 2012.

6. L. Mundy, *Michelle: A Biography* (New York Simon & Schuster Paperbacks, 2008); and L. Collins, "The Other Obama: Michelle Obama and the Politics of Candor," *New Yorker*, March 10, 2008, http://www.newyorker.com/reporting/2008/03/10/080310fa_fact_collins?currentPage=all.

7. For L. Mundy's judgment of the school's effectiveness based on her research, see Mundy, *Michelle: A Biography*, p. 54.

8. Rogak, *Michelle Obama: In Her Own Words*.

9. For the description by Charles Ogletree, Obama's faculty mentor at Harvard, see D. Remnick, *The Bridge: The Life and Rise of Barack Obama* (New York: Random House Digital, 2011), 204.

10. For a description of Obama's time at the firm by Quincy White, see Mundy, *Michelle: A Biography*, 102.

11. "Michelle Obama," Biography.com, 2011, http://www.biography.com/people/michelle-obama-307592.

12. Mundy, *Michelle: A Biography*, 116.

13. For a characterization of Obama by Julian Posada (deputy director at Public Allies), see Mundy, *Michelle: A Biography*, 131.

14. To view the May 1996 photo and read about it, see M. Cook, "A Couple in Chicago," *New Yorker*, January 19, 2009, http://www.newyorker.com/reporting/2009/01/19/090119fa_fact_cook#ixzz2BeuCKwGy.

15. See Mundy, *Michelle: A Biography*, 157.

16. H. Yeager, "The Heart and Mind of Michelle Obama," *O Magazine*, November 2007, http://www.oprah.com/world/The-Heart-and-Mind-of-Michelle-Obama/1.

17. Mundy, *Michelle: A Biography*, 158.

18. For a description of Obama by University of Chicago law professor David Strauss, see Wolfe, *"Who Is Michelle Obama?"*

19. Rogak, *Michelle Obama: In Her Own Words*, 141.

20. Collins, "The Other Obama."

21. J. Kantor, *The Obamas* (New York: Penguin Group, 2012), 12.

22. Rogak, *Michelle Obama: In Her Own Words*, 56.

23. M. Obama, interview by G. King, "Mrs. Obama 'Confident' in Her Husband's Campaign," *CBS This Morning*, video, January 11, 2012, http://www.youtube.com/watch?v=M8MF9vT0VAM.

24. M. Obama and J. Biden, "Remarks by the First Lady and Dr. Biden Discussing Military Spouse Employment at National Governors Association Annual Meeting," February 27, 2012, transcript, http://www.whitehouse.gov/the-press-office/2012/02/27/remarks-first-lady-and-dr-biden-discussing-military-spouse-employment-na.

25. J. Kantor, "First Lady Strives for Caring Image above Partisan Fray," *New York Times*, September 3, 2012, http://www.nytimes.com/2012/09/04/us/politics/michelle-obamas-role-in-presidents-re-election-bid.html?pagewanted=all&_r=0.

26. "Let's Move! Two Years of Healthy Changes for Our Nation's Kids," blog post, February 3, 2012, http://www.letsmove.gov/blog/2012/02/03/ let%E2%80%99s-move-two-years-healthy-changes-our-nation%E2%80%99s-kids.

27. Kantor, *The Obamas*, 454.

28. Mundy, *Michelle: A Biography*, 104.

Chapter 5

1. "ESPN's Julie Foudy Scores One for the Girls," video, June 28, 2010, http:// espn.go.com/high-school/girls-soccer/video/clip?id=6571465.

2. J. Foudy, "Julie Foudy Hall of Fame Induction Speech," Oneonta, New York, video, August 26, 2007, http://www.youtube.com/watch?v=RdDjP9Uq9PA.

3. M. Christopher, *On the Field with . . . Julie Foudy* (New York Little, Brown Young Readers, 2000).

4. J. Longman, "Women's World Cup: Foudy Is the U.S. Team's Renaissance Midfielder," *New York Times*, June 16, 1999, http://www.nytimes.com/1999/06/16/ sports/women-s-world-cup-foudy-is-the-us-team-s-renaissance-midfielder.html.

5. Associated Press, "Retiring Trio Major Players in Golden Era of U.S. Women's Soccer," ESPN, December 6, 2004, http://sports.espn.go.com/espn/wire?section= soccer&id=1940064.

6. Foudy, "Julie Foudy Hall of Fame Induction Speech."

7. J. Lavine (producer), *Dare to Dream: The Story of the U.S. Women's Soccer Team*, video documentary (New York: HBO, 2005).

8. Christopher, *On the Field with . . . Julie Foudy,*

9. Ibid., 20.

10. Ibid.

11. J. Lavine, *Dare to Dream.*

12. J. Foudy, personal communication, April 19, 2013. Unless otherwise indicated, all "told me" references in this chapter are from this source.

13. J. Lavine, *Dare to Dream.*

14. J. Foudy, *Achievement and Overcoming Obstacles* [video file], 2009, http:// www.youtube.com/watch?feature=player_detailpage&v=WR_l-13a7BU.

15. J. Lavine, *Dare to Dream.*

16. Ibid.

17. Ibid.

18. D. Zirin, *A People's History of Sports in the United States: 250 Years of Politics, Protest, People and Play* (New York: The New Press, 2005).

19. J. Lavine, *Dare to Dream.*

20. Ibid.

21. J. Savage, *Julie Foudy: Soccer Superstar* (Minneapolis: Lerner Sports, 1999).

22. Here's one place where she says almost exactly that: http://www.allreadable .com/vid/gold-medalist-julie-foudy-on-title-ix-1742421.html.

23. K. Whiteside, "Foudy Is Captain, Conscience of U.S. Team," *USA Today*, September 8, 2003, http://www.usatoday.com/sports/soccer/national/2003-09-08- cover-foudy_x.htm.

24. J. Foudy, "GlobalGirl Media Kick It Up! Project Launch," video (Culver City, CA: 2010), http://www.youtube.com/watch?v=BxHtDm2rFt0.

25. Whiteside, "Foudy Is Captain, Conscience of U.S. Team."

26. J. Lavine, *Dare to Dream.*

27. Ibid.

28. J. Foudy, "Kickin' It with Julie Foudy," video (Hillsborough, NC: 2009), http:// www.youtube.com/watch?v=at7fycNwehI.

29. J. Foudy, interview by J. Thompson, "Julie Foudy: Leadership in Sports," podcast, July 2, 2010, https://www.responsiblesports.com/media/podcasts-1.

30. J. Foudy, "20 People to Watch: Julie Foudy on Things She Is Proud Of," video (Arlington, VA: The Century Council, 2011), http://www.youtube.com/watch?v=HPbR5b9J1B8.

31. J. Foudy, personal communication, March 26, 2014.

32. Foudy, interview by J. Thompson.

33. Foudy, "20 People to Watch."

Chapter 6

1. B. Springsteen, "Bruce Springsteen Accepts—Rock and Roll Hall of Fame Induction Speech," Waldorf Astoria Hotel, New York, March 15, 1999, transcript, https://rockhall.com/inductees/bruce-springsteen/transcript/bruce-springsteen-accepts/.

2. E. Alterman, *It Ain't No Sin to Be Glad You're Alive: The Promise of Bruce Springsteen* (New York: Little, Brown and Company, 1999), 13.

3. Springsteen, "Bruce Springsteen Accepts."

4. For a description of Springsteen's physical transformation during this period, see Alterman, *It Ain't No Sin.*

5. D. Remnick, "We Are Alive: Bruce Springsteen at Sixty-Two, *New Yorker,* July 30, 2012, http://www.newyorker.com/reporting/2012/07/30/120730fa_fact_remnick?currentPage=all.

6. R. Kirkpatrick, *The Words and Music of Bruce Springsteen* (Westport, CT: Greenwood Publishing Group, 2007).

7. S. Michaels, "Madonna's MDNA Is Highest-Grossing Tour of 2012," *Guardian,* December 17, 2012, http://www.guardian.co.uk/music/2012/dec/17/madonna-highest-grossing-tour-2012.

8. For Springsteen's take on his nickname, see Alterman, *It Ain't No Sin.*

9. Remnick, "We Are Alive."

10. B. Child, "Bruce Springsteen Describes Making of *Darkness on the Edge of Town,*" *Guardian,* October 29, 2010, http://www.guardian.co.uk/music/2010/oct/30/bruce-springsteen-darkness-edge-town.

11. B. Springsteen, interview by D. Marsh, *Live from E Street Nation,* SiriusXM Internet Radio Channel 20, January 10, 2014.

12. B. Springsteen, "Chords for Change," *New York Times,* op-ed, August 5, 2004, http://www.nytimes.com/2004/08/05/opinion/05bruce.html.

13. For Springsteen's description of his mother, see "The Backstreet Phantom of Rock," *Time,* October 27, 1975, p. 62.

14. Remnick, "We Are Alive."

15. Alterman, *It Ain't No Sin.*

16. B. Springsteen, interview, in "Bruce Springsteen," *VH1 Storytellers* (New York: Columbia, 2005), http://www.youtube.com/watch?v=hVGAUTfBuyA&feature=related.

17. Remnick, "We Are Alive."

18. B. Springsteen, "Bruce Springsteen's SXSW 2012 Keynote Speech," Austin Convention Center, Austin, Texas, March 18, 2012, http://www.npr.org/2012/03/16/148778665/bruce-springsteens-sxsw-2012-keynote-speech.

19. D. Marsh, *Two Hearts: Bruce Springsteen, the Definitive Biography, 1972–2003* (New York: Routledge, 2004).

20. B. Springsteen, interview, in "Bruce Springsteen," *VH1 Storytellers.*

21. Alterman, *It Ain't No Sin.*

22. "The Backstreet Phantom of Rock."

23. Marsh, *Two Hearts*.

24. Springsteen, "Bruce Springsteen's SXSW 2012 Keynote Speech."

25. J. Landau, "Growing Young with Rock and Roll," *The Real Paper*, May 22, 1974, http://all-the-wine.blogspot.com/2010/04/growing-young-with-rock-and-roll-jon.htm.

26. Alterman, *It Ain't No Sin*, 60.

27. Details of the recording process from "The Backstreet Phantom of Rock."

28. G. Marcus, "Bruce Springsteen: Born to Run," *Rolling Stone*, October 9, 1975, http://www.rollingstone.com/music/albumreviews/born-to-run-19851001.

29. Marsh, *Two Hearts*, p. 125.

30. Alterman, *It Ain't No Sin*.

31. Remnick, "We Are Alive."

32. Ibid.

33. The offer was reported to be as much as $12 million. See Kirkpatrick, *The Words and Music of Bruce Springsteen*, p. 105.

34. Springsteen, in "Bruce Springsteen," *VH1 Storytellers*.

35. R. Wiersema, *Walk Like a Man: Coming of Age with the Music of Bruce Springsteen* (Berkeley, CA: D&M Publishers, 2011).

36. N. Strauss, "My Life Lessons from Springsteen, Gaga and Clapton," *Telegraph*, April 26, 2011, http://www.telegraph.co.uk/culture/8465755/My-life-lessons-from-Springsteen-Gaga-and-Clapton.html.

37. B. Springsteen, interview by J. Stewart, *The Daily Show*, March 19, 2009 (New York: Comedy Central), http://www.thedailyshow.com/watch/thu-march-19-2009/bruce-springsteen---interview.

38. B. Springsteen, interview by E. Bradley, *60 Minutes*, CBS, January 21, 1996, http://www.cbsnews.com/video/watch/?id=3340303n&tag=segementExtraScroller; housing.

39. Wiersema, *Walk Like a Man*.

40. B. Springsteen, interview by J. Levy, "Bruce Springsteen: The Rolling Stone Interview," *Rolling Stone*, November 1, 2007, http://www.rollingstone.com/music/news/bruce-springsteen-the-rolling-stone-interview-2007110.

41. S. Hochman, "Bruce Springsteen is on Fire for MusiCares," February 9, 2013, http://www.grammy.com/blogs/bruce-springsteen-is-on-fire-for-musicares.

42. B. Springsteen, "Bruce's Speech from MusiCares 2013," February 13, 2013, video, http://brucespringsteen.net/news/2013/bruces-speech-from-musicares-2013.

43. Editors of Rolling Stone, The, *Bruce Springsteen: The Rolling Stone Files* (New York: Hyperion, 1996), 204.

44. E. Kirschbaum, (2008, July 15). "Memories of How Springsteen Rocked Berlin," Reuters, July 15, 2008, http://www.reuters.com/article/2008/07/16/us-germany-springsteen-idUSL1334031920080716; and P. A. Carlin, *Bruce* (New York: Simon & Schuster, 2012), 443.

45. The 2013 film *Springsteen and I* is a fascinating testament to this idea.

46. Springsteen, interview by E. Bradley, *60 Minutes*.

47. Springsteen, "Bruce Springsteen's SXSW 2012 Keynote Speech."

48. Although Christie cried with joy that night, later events have changed their relationship yet again. The scandal involving Christie's staff having allegedly caused traffic jams at the George Washington Bridge entrance for the purposes of political revenge against the mayor of Fort Lee, New Jersey, caused Springsteen and *Late Night* host Jimmy Fallon to mercilessly spoof Christie. The video of their sarcastic remake of *Born to Run* went massively viral.

49. At the 2014 Rock and Roll Hall of Fame induction ceremony for The E Street Band, its members spoke directly to how "profoundly inspiring" it was to be part of his relentless drive for greatness, to this day, after 40 years; how good it was to know that "nothing was off limits" every performance; and how gratifying it felt to be "entrusted

with the responsibility to use our musical instincts and our particular vision to create" when they are called into the studio to record. "2014 Rock and Roll Hall of Fame Induction Ceremony," April 10, 2014.

50. Alterman recounted how Springsteen explained the sources of his musical aspirations: "I had locked into what was pretty much a hectic obsession, which gave me enormous focus and energy and fire to burn, because it was coming out of pure fear and self-loathing and self-hatred." Alterman, *It Ain't No Sin.*

51. "2014 Rock and Roll Hall of Fame Induction Ceremony," April 10, 2014.

Chapter 8

1. For the benefits of envisioning a future ideal self, see R. E. Boyatzis and K. Akrivou, "The Ideal Self as the Driver of Intentional Change," *Journal of Management Development* 25, no. 7 (2006), 624–642. And see R. F. Baumeister, "The Self," in *The Handbook of Social Pyschology*, eds. D. T. Gilbert, S. T. Fiske, and G. Lindzey (New York: McGraw-Hill, 1998), 680–740, on the distinction between "ideal" and "ought."

2. See Boyatzis and Akrivou, "The Ideal Self as the Driver of Intentional Change," and C. R. Snyder, "Hope Theory: Rainbows in the Mind," *Psychological Inquiry* 13, no. 4 (2002): 249–275, who define hope as a motivational state resulting from an individual's pathway and agency thoughts in pursuit of a goal. K. Reivich and A. Shatté, *The Resilience Factor: 7 Essential Skills for Overcoming Life's Inevitable Obstacles* (New York: Broadway Books, 2002), describe how both kinds of thoughts can be derailed when one jumps to conclusions about one's abilities without considering all relevant data.

3. I describe this further in S. D. Friedman, *Total Leadership: Be a Better Leader, Have a Richer Life* (Boston: Harvard Business School Publishing, 2008).

4. For a useful source on how one can better synthesize work and caregiving roles, see E. E. Kossek, R. A. Noe, and B. J. DeMarr, "Work-Family Role Synthesis: Individual and Organizational Determinants," *International Journal of Conflict Management* 10, no. 2 (1999): 102–129, http://search.proquest.com/docview/199041184?accountid=14707.

5. See W. James, "Habit," in *Principles of Psychology: Briefer Course* (Cambridge, MA: Harvard University Press, 1984) 125–138, for more on new habits. James describes how actions must be repeated many times for new neural pathways reflecting the desired change to be created and how, at the point when an action becomes a habit, less work is required to sustain it.

6. K. M. Sheldon and A. J. Elliot, "Goal Striving, Need Satisfaction, and Longitudinal Well-Being: The Self-Concordance Model," *Journal of Personality and Social Psychology* 76, no. 3 (1999): 482–497. See also M. Csikszentmihalyi, *The Evolving Self: A Psychology for the Third Millenium* (New York: HarperCollins, 1993), who defines a good personal goal as one that is harmonious with an individual's sense of self and involves purposeful activity leading to the satisfaction of uniquely personal desires. See also H. T. Reis, K. M. Sheldon, S. L. Gable, J. Roscoe, and R. M. Ryan, "Daily Well-Being: The Role of Autonomy, Competence, and Relatedness," *Personality and Social Psychology Bulletin* 26, no. 4 (2000): 419–435, and K. W. Brown and R. M. Ryan, "Fostering Healthy Self-Regulation from Within and Without: A Self-Determination Theory Perspective," in *Positive Psychology in Practice*, eds. P. A. Linley and S. Joseph (Hoboken, NJ: Wiley, 2004), 105–124, on goals and self-determination.

7. See W. James, "Will," in *Principles of Psychology* (Cambridge, MA: Harvard University Press, 1981), 1098–1193, and M. Csikszentmihalyi, *Flow* (New York: HarperCollins, 1990), who defines optimal experience, or a "state of flow," as "when the information that keeps coming into awareness is congruent with goals." The "want to want to" exercise gives you the opportunity to focus attention on how your values can be expressed better through your behavior.

8. For more on telling, understanding, and conveying your emotional journey line and crucible experiences, see N. M. Tichy and E. Cohen, *The Leadership Engine: How Winning Companies Build Leaders at Every Level* (New York: Harper Collins, 1997), and R. J. Thomas, *Crucibles of Leadership* (Boston: Harvard Business School Publishing, 2008), who describe the benefits of analyzing significant events in your life as a catalyst for learning from experience. See J. A. Singer, "Narrative Identity and Meaning Making across the Adult Lifespan: An Introduction," *Journal of Personality* 72, no. 3 (2004): 437–459, on how the narratives individuals tell themselves and others about their own life experiences lead to the development of self-concepts, beliefs about others, and ideas about how the world works.

9. See P. Guber, "The Four Truths of the Storyteller," *Harvard Business Review* 85, no. 12 (2007): 52–59, on practicing how to make connections between stories and values.

10. See S. Lyubomirsky, *The How of Happiness* (New York: Penguin Books, 2007), and H. G. Halvorson, *Succeed: How We Can Reach Our Goals* (New York: Hudson Street Press, 2010), L. B. Pham and S. E. Taylor, "From Thought to Action: Effects of Process-Versus Outcome-Based Mental Simulations on Performance," *Personality and Social Psychology Bulletin* 25, no. 2 (1999): 250–260, and K. M. Sheldon and S. Lyubomirsky, "How to Increase and Sustain Positive Emotion: The Effects of Expressing Gratitude and Visualizing Best Possible Selves," *Journal of Positive Psychology* 1, no. 2 (2006): 73–82.

11. For more on public commitments and goal attainment, see Lyubomirsky, *The How of Happiness*.

12. For more on goal-setting, see E. A. Locke and G. P. Latham, "Building a Practically Useful Theory of Goal Setting and Task Motivation: A 35-Year Odyssey," *American Psychologist* 57, no. 9 (2002): 705–717.

13. On the impact of actions in reducing anxiety associated with not having pursued a goal in the past, see Lyubomirsky, *The How of Happiness*, and in generating positive emotion, see B. Fredrickson, *Positivity: Groundbreaking Research Reveals How to Embrace the Hidden Strength of Positive Emotions, Overcome Negativity, and Thrive* (New York: Random House, 2009).

Chapter 9

1. M. S. Knowles, E. F. Holton, and R. A. Swanson, *The Adult Learner: The Definitive Classic in Adult Education and Human Resource Development* (Amsterdam: Elsevier, 2005), 6.

2. Learn about the benefits of high-quality connections and how to achieve them in J. E. Dutton and E. D. Heaphy, "The Power of High-Quality Connections," in *Positive Organizational Scholarship: Foundations of a New Discipline*, eds. K. S. Cameron, J. E. Dutton, and R. E. Quinn (New York: Oxford University Press, 2003), 244–256; J. E. Dutton, *Energize Your Workplace: How to Create and Sustain High-Quality Connections at Work* (San Francisco: Jossey-Bass, 2003), and B. Fredrickson, *Positivity: Groundbreaking Research Reveals How to Embrace the Hidden Strength of Positive Emotions, Overcome Negativity, and Thrive* (New York: Random House, 2009).

3. See, for example, C. D. Bateson, "How Social an Animal? The Human Capacity for Caring," *American Psychologist* 45 (1990): 336–346.

4. See A. M. Grant, *Give and Take: A Revolutionary Approach to Success* (New York: Viking, 2013).

5. For more on the positive social consequences of helping others, see S. Lyubomirsky, *The How of Happiness* (New York: Penguin Books, 2007); S. Lyubomirsky, K. M. Sheldon, and D. Schkade, "Pursuing Happiness: The Architecture of Sustainable Change," *Review of General Psychology* 9, no. 2 (2005): 111–131;

and J. A. Piliavin, "Doing Well by Doing Good: Benefits for the Benefactor," in *Flourishing: Positive Psychology and the Life Well-Lived*, edited by C. L. M. Keyes and J. Haidt (Washington, DC: American Psychological Association, 2003), 227–247.

6. For more on social perceptions of asking for and giving help, see F. J. Flynn, "What Have You Done for Me Lately? Temporal Adjustments to Favor Evaluations," *Organizational Behavior and Human Decision Processes* 91, no. 1 (2003): 38–50; F. J. Flynn and V. K. B. Lake, "If You Need Help, Just Ask: Underestimating Compliance with Direct Requests for Help," *Journal of Personality and Social Psychology* 95, no. 1 (2008): 128–143; and Grant, *Give and Take*. Although people often rely on help from others in pursuit of their goals, assistance doesn't usually occur spontaneously or without some form of provocation. People are hesitant to ask for help because they tend to underestimate others' willingness to provide support.

7. See Grant, *Give and Take* and A. M. Grant and J. M. Berg, "Prosocial Motivation at Work: When, Why, and How Making a Difference Makes a Difference," in *Handbook of Positive Organizational Scholarship*, eds. K. Cameron and G. Spreitzer (New York: Oxford University Press, 2010), 28–44.

8. For more on the process of capitalizing on your unique character strengths, see R. Biswas-Diener, T. B. Kashdan, and G. Minhas, "A Dynamic Approach to Psychological Strength Development and Intervention," *Journal of Positive Psychology* 6, no. 2 (2011): 106–118; R. M. Niemiec, "OK, Now What? Taking Action," Via Institute, 2009, http://www.viacharacter.org/www/AwareExploreApply/tabid/249/language/en-US/Default.aspx; VIA Institute, "VIA Institute on Character," *VIAPro Character Strengths Profile Practitioner's Guide*, 2011, http://www.viacharacter.org; and M. E. P. Seligman, T. A. Steen, N. Park, and C. Peterson, "Positive Psychology Progress: Empirical Validation of Interventions," *American Psychologist* 60, no. 5 (2005): 410–421, who observed that by using their identified strengths in new ways, people experienced increases in happiness and decreases in depression.

9. Maggie Jackson's *Distracted* (Amherst, NY: Prometheus Books, 2008) provides a useful overview.

10. B. E. Ashforth, G. E. Kreiner, and M. Fugate, "All in a Day's Work: Boundaries and Micro Role Transitions," *Academy of Management Review* 25, no. 3 (2000): 472–491, studied role transitions, or the boundary-crossing action in disengaging from one role and engaging in another, and observed that people are inclined to minimize the difficulty of navigating these transitions. The authors suggest that "role schemas" be used to make switching easier—to be mindful, that is, of the expectations associated with each role as you move from one to another.

11. See E. E. Kossek, M. N. Ruderman, P. Brady, and K. Hannum, "Work-Nonwork Boundary Management Profiles: A Person-Centered Approach," *Journal of Vocational Behavior* 81, no. 1 (August 2012): 112–128 for a survey that measures this. See also A. Ollier-Malaterre, N. Rothbard, and J. Berg, "When Worlds Collide in Cyberspace: How Boundary Work in Online Social Networks Impacts Professional Relationships," *Academy of Management Review* 38, no. 4 (October 2013): 645–669.

12. G. E. Kriener, E. C. Hollensbe, and M. L. Sheep, "Balancing Borders and Bridges: Negotiating the Work-Home Interface via Boundary Work Tactics," *Academy of Management Journal* 52, no. 4 (2009): 704–730, suggest strategies for each type of boundary. Behavioral strategies include enlisting other people to support your efforts and allowing "differential permeability": letting some work behaviors seep through because they are acceptable at home, and filtering out those that should not cross that boundary into home life. Temporal strategies include controlling work time and finding respite from its strains. Physical strategies include manipulating space and artifacts by, for example, making it clear that your home office is a place of work and only work. Communicative strategies include setting expectations, such as defining

when you are not available, and confronting violators by telling them that they've crossed a line.

13. See L. M. Roberts, J. E. Dutton, G. M. Spreitzer, E. D. Heaphy, and R. E. Quinn, "Composing the Reflected Best-Self Portrait: Building Pathways for Becoming Extraordinary in Work Organizations," *Academy of Management Review* 30, no. 4 (2005): 712–736, who discuss how people can construct their lives in ways that allow them to use their reflected strengths to achieve goals aligned with their core values.

14. P. Sims and P. Lorenzi, *The New Leadership Paradigm: Social Learning and Cognition in Organizations* (Thousand Oaks, CA: Sage Publications, 1992).

Chapter 10

1. D. Kahneman and A. Tversky, eds., *Choices, Values, and Frames* (New York: Cambridge University Press and the Russell Sage Foundation, 2000).

2. See A. Wrzesniewski and J. E. Dutton, "Crafting a Job: Revisioning Employees as Active Crafters of Their Work," *Academy of Management Review* 26, no. 2 (2001): 179–201, who describe job crafting as "the physical and cognitive changes individuals make in the task or relational boundaries of their work." This can involve physically changing task boundaries (where and when you do things), cognitively changing task boundaries (to see your job in a new light in its significance for others), or modifying interactions with coworkers to make them more meaningful and rewarding.

3. See, for example, T. L. Jacobs et al, "Self-Reported Mindfulness and Cortisol during a Shamatha Meditation Retreat," *Health Psychology* 32, no. 10 (October 2013): 1104–1109, and A. Caelleigh, "Naps," *Academic Medicine* 75, no. 6 (June 2000): 601 on napping.

4. K. E. Weick, "Small Wins: Redefining the Scale of Social Problems," *American Psychologist* 39, no. 1 (1984): 40–49.

5. For a discussion of the role of creativity and of enlisting others to participate in the creative process, see T. Harding, "Fostering Creativity for Leadership and Leading Change," *Arts Education Policy Review* 111, no. 2 (2010): 51–53.

6. See I. Chen and J. Chen, "Creativity Strategy Selection for the Higher Education System," *Quality and Quantity* 46, no. 3 (2012): 739–750, for more on ways to enahance personal creativity. See A. Hiam, "9 Obstacles to Creativity—and How You Can Remove Them," *Futurist* 32, no. 7 (1998): 30–34, who identifies nine habits that inhibit innovation.

7. See A. J. Mento, P. Martinelli, and R. M. Jones, "Mind Mapping in Executive Education: Applications and Outcomes," *Journal of Management Development* 18, no. 4 (1999): 390–407.

8. Mento, Martinelli, and Jones, ibid., asked individuals who had completed mind maps variations on these same questions about the experience of mind mapping. The questions reinforced new learning and spurred creativity.

9. See K. Reivich and A. Shatté, *The Resilience Factor: 7 Essential Skills for Overcoming Life's Inevitable Obstacles* (New York: Broadway Books, 2002).

10. See W. Umiker, "How to Prevent and Cope with Resistance to Change," *Health Care Manager* 15, no. 4 (1997): 35–41, on how false perception based on lack of information, misinterpretation of information, or irrational thinking can lead to resistance to change.

11. See G. M. Spreitzer and R. E. Quinn, "Empowering Middle Managers to Be Transformational Leaders," *Journal of Applied Behavioral Science* 32, no. 3 (1996): 237, on how poor self-esteem contributes to an individual's resistance to change, and Reivich and Shatté, *The Resilience Factor*, on how resilience results from an individual's belief that he has the power to control events. To increase resilience, individuals should identify their beliefs and challenge the ones inhibiting growth.

12. See T. M. Amabile, E. A. Schatzel, G. B. Moneta, and S. J. Kramer, "Leader Behaviors and the Work Environment for Creativity: Perceived Leader Support," *Leadership Quarterly* 15, no. 1 (2004): 5–32, who found that leaders who remain open to and appreciative of others' ideas, who are skilled at communicating, and who use interpersonal networks masterfully to think outside the box, promote environments in which innovation thrives.

13. For more on this method, see D. L. Cooperrider, D. Witney, and J. M. Stavros, *Appreciative Inquiry Handbook: For Leaders of Change*, 2nd ed. (Brunswick, OH: Crown Custom Publishing, 2008).

Conclusion

1. B. L. Fredrickson, K. M. Grewen, K. A. Coffey, A. B. Algoe, A. M. Firestine, J. J. G. Srevalo, J. Ma, and S. W. Cole, "A Functional Genomic Perspective on Human Well-Being." *Proceedings of the National Academy of Sciences* (2013): 1–6.

2. J. Lovell, "George Saunders's Advice to Graduates," *New York Times*, July 31, 2013.

Bibliography

A&E Networks. *Bruce Springsteen.* n.d. http://www.youtube.com/watch?v=w4vlIX9Y5Jc.

A&E Networks. *Bruce Springsteen: Biography.* 2012. http://www.biography.com/people/bruce-springsteen-9491214?page=1.

Abrams, J. J. Personal communication. June 10, 2013.

"Acceptable Fate of Facebook, The." *The Economist,* July 23, 2011.

Acocella, J. "East Room Recital." *New Yorker,* October 4, 2010. http://www.newyorker.com/talk/2010/10/04/101004ta_talk_acocella.

Alt, D. "Eric Greitens: Public Servant." *Ladue News,* January 27, 2011. http://www.laduenews.com/living/special-features/eric-greitens/article_f3a9929e-4a2e-5416-8604-677af6098270.html?mode=story.

Alterman, E. *It Ain't No Sin to Be Glad You're Alive: The Promise of Bruce Springsteen.* New York: Little, Brown and Company, 1999.

Amabile, T. M., E. A. Schatzel, G. B. Moneta, and S. J. Kramer. "Leader Behaviors and the Work Environment for Creativity: Perceived Leader Support." *Leadership Quarterly* 15, no. 1 (2004):5–32.

Ashforth, B. E., G. E. Kreiner, and M. Fugate. "All in a Day's Work: Boundaries and Micro Role Transitions." *Academy of Management Review* 25, no. 3(2000): 472–491.

Associated Press. "Retiring Trio Major Players in Golden Era of U.S. Women's Soccer." ESPN. December 6, 2004. http://sports.espn.go.com/espn/wire?section=soccer&id=1940064.

AthleticCapital. "Be Your Own Hero Spotlight April 2011—Eric Greitens." YouTube video. April 24, 2011. http://www.youtube.com/watch?v=MJiyq7EuPqQ.

Auletta, K. "A Woman's Place: Can Sheryl Sandberg Upend Silicon Valley's Male-Dominated Culture?" *New Yorker,* July 11, 2011. http://www.newyorker.com/reporting/2011/07/11/110711fa_fact_auletta.

"Backstreet Phantom of Rock, The." *Time,* October 27, 1975, 62.

Baer, S. "U2's Bono in Washington." *Washingtonian,* March 1, 2006. http://www.washingtonian.com/articles/people/1707.html.

Bandura, A. "Social Cognitive Theory: An Agentic Perspective." *Annual Review of Psychology* 52(2001): 1–26.

Barnett, E., and R. Blackden. "Meet Sheryl Sandberg: The Woman Who Holds Mark Zuckerberg's Purse Strings." *The Telegraph,* January 8, 2011. http://www.telegraph.co.uk/technology/facebook/8247838/Meet-Sheryl-Sandberg-the-woman-who-holds-Mark-Zuckerburgs-purse-strings.html.

Bateson, C. D. "How Social an Animal? The Human Capacity for Caring." *American Psychologist* 45 (1990): 336–346.

Baumeister, R. F. "The Self." *The Handbook of Social Pyschology,* edited by D. T. Gilbert, S. T. Fiske, and G. Lindzey, 680–740. New York: McGraw-Hill, 1998.

Baumeister, R. F., M. Gailliot, C. N. DeWall, and M. Oaten. "Self-Regulation and Personality: How Interventions Increase Regulatory Success, and How Depletion

Moderated the Effects of Traits on Behavior." *Journal of Personality* 74, no. 6 (2006): 1773–1801.

Bennett, J. "Sheryl Sandberg on the Power of Facebook." *Daily Beast*, April 11, 2011. http://www.thedailybeast.com/articles/2011/04/11/sheryl-sandberg-talks-facebook-china-and-women-in-tech.html.

Biden, J., and M. Obama, "Remarks by the First Lady and Dr. Biden Discussing Military Spouse Employment at National Governors Association Annual Meeting." February 27, 2012. Transcript. http://www.whitehouse.gov/the-press-office/2012/02/27/remarks-first-lady-and-dr-biden-discussing-military-spouse-employment-na.

Biswas-Diener, R., T. B. Kashdan, and G. Minhas. "A Dynamic Approach to Psychological Strength Development and Intervention." *Journal of Positive Psychology* 6, no. 2 (2011): 106–118.

Bodden, V. *Michelle Obama: First Lady and Role Model*. Edina, MN: ABDO Publishing Company, 2009.

BookTV. "Eric Greitens, *The Heart and the Fist*." YouTube video. October 5, 2011. http://www.youtube.com/watch?v=cuIIuivBQwE.

Boyatzis, R. E., and K. Akrivou. "The Ideal Self as the Driver of Intentional Change." *Journal of Management Development* 25, no. 7 (2006), 624–642.

Bradach, J. Personal communication. February 16, 2013.

Bradach, J., T. Tierney, and N. Stone. "Delivering on the Promise of Nonprofits." *Harvard Business Review*, December 2008. http://www.svpcharlotte.org/downloads/HBRArticleDeliveringonthePromiseofNonprofits.pdf.

Breger, E. "University Releases Obama 85's Senior Thesis." *Daily Princetonian*, February 26, 2008. http://www.dailyprincetonian.com/2008/02/26/20258/.

Brill, M. T. *Michelle Obama: From Chicago's South Side to the White House*. Minneapolis, MN: Lerner Publications Company, 2009.

Brooks-Bertram, P., and B. A. S. Nevergold. *Go, Tell Michelle: African American Women Write to the First Lady*. Albany, NY: University of New York Press, 2009.

Brophy, D. B. *Michelle Obama: Meet the First Lady*. New York: HarperCollins Publishers, 2009.

Brown, C., G. Dance, J. Ellis, B. Gerst, T. Jackson, M. Sharpe, and S. Wheaton. "Michelle Obama's Speech at the Democratic National Convention." *New York Times* interactive video. August 25, 2008. http://elections.nytimes.com/2008/president/conventions/videos/20080825_OBAMA_SPEECH.html.

Brown, K. W., and R. M. Ryan. "Fostering Healthy Self-Regulation from Within and Without: A Self-Determination Theory Perspective." In *Positive Psychology in Practice*, edited by P. A. Linley and S. Joseph, 105–124. Hoboken, NJ: Wiley, 2004.

Bruce Springsteen and the E Street Band. Press conference from the 2009 Super Bowl, January 9, 2009. YouTube video. http://www.youtube.com/watch?v=b5-nERmAwo8&feature=related.

Buford, B. *Finishing Well: What People Who Really Live Do Differently*. Nashville, TN: Thomas Nelson, Inc., 2004.

"Business 100 Profiles: Thomas J. Tierney." *Irish America Magazine*, 2009. http://irishamerica.com/2012/04/thomas-j-tierney/.

Caelleigh, A. "Naps." *Academic Medicine* 75, no. 6 (June 2000): 601.

Carlin, P. A. *Bruce*. New York: Simon & Schuster, Inc., 2012.

Carlson, M. "Michelle Obama's Charm Offensive." *Daily Beast*, February 5, 2012. http://www.thedailybeast.com/articles/2012/02/05/michelle-obama-s-charm-offensive.html.

Caroli, B. B. *First Ladies: From Martha Washington to Michelle Obama*. New York: Oxford University Press, Inc., 2010.

CenturyCouncil. "Mia Hamm and Julie Foudy Highlight Video." YouTube video. March 1, 2007. http://www.youtube.com/watch?v=zwHSWLj1oCw.

Chen, I., and J. Chen. "Creativity Strategy Selection for the Higher Education System." *Quality and Quantity* 46, no. 3 (2012): 739–750.

Child, B. "Bruce Springsteen Describes Making of *Darkness on the Edge of Town.*" *The Guardian*, October 29, 2010. http://www.guardian.co.uk/music/2010/oct/30/bruce-springsteen-darkness-edge-town.

Christopher, M. *On the Field with . . . Julie Foudy.* New York: Little, Brown Young Readers, 2000.

Colbert, D. *Michelle Obama: An American Story.* Boston: Sandpiper, 2009.

Collie, A. J. "Louder Than Bombs." *Soccer Digest*, 2005.

Collins, L. "One Year: The Two Mrs. Obamas." *New Yorker*, January 20, 2010. http://www.newyorker.com/online/blogs/newsdesk/2010/01/one-year-the-two-mrs-obamas.html.

———. "The Other Obama: Michelle Obama and the Politics of Candor." *New Yorker*, March 10, 2008. http://www.newyorker.com/reporting/2008/03/10/080310fa_fact_collins?currentPage=all

Conley, K. "Sheryl Sandberg: What She Saw at the Revolution." *Vogue*, April 15, 2010. http://www.vogue.com/magazine/article/sheryl-sandberg-what-she-saw-at-the-revolution/.

Cook, M. "A Couple in Chicago." *New Yorker*, January 19, 2009. http://www.newyorker.com/reporting/2009/01/19/090119fa_fact_cook#ixzz2BeuCKwGy.

Cooperrider, D. L. "The Concentration Effect of Strengths: How the Whole System AI Summit Brings Out the Best in Human Enterprise." *Organizational Dynamics* 42, no. 2 (April 2012).

Cooperrider, D. L., D. Witney, and J. M. Stavros. *Appreciative Inquiry Handbook: For Leaders of Change*, 2nd ed. Brunswick, OH: Crown Custom Publishing, 2008.

Crombie, N. "Portland Weather: Clouds Today, Sunshine Tomorrow." *Oregonian*, November 9, 2011. http://www.oregonlive.com/weather/index.ssf/2011/11/portland_weather_clouds_today.html.

Csikszentmihalyi, M. *The Evolving Self: A Psychology for the Third Millenium.* New York: HarperCollins, 1993.

———. *Flow.* New York: HarperCollins, 1990.

Dao, J. "In Veterans' Aid, Growth Pains." *New York Times*, November 8, 2012. http://www.nytimes.com/2012/11/09/giving/after-war-more-veterans-find-more-help.html?pagewanted=1&_r=2&ref=philanthropy&adxnnlx=1352473244-7yAlH8OAk0b5xG/cpNXb5Q.

Delo, C. "Facebook Files for IPO; Reveals $1 Billion in 2011 Profit." *Advertising Age*, February 1, 2012. http://adage.com/article/digital/facebook-files-ipo-reveals-1-billion-2011-profit/232484/.

DeRue, D. S., and S. J. Ashford, "Power to the People: Where Has Personal Agency Gone in Leadership Development?" *Industrial and Organizational Psychology: Perspectives on Science and Practice* 3, no. 1(2010): 24–27. doi:10.1111/j.1754-9434.2009.01191.x.

Donahoe, J. Personal communication. February 1, 2013.

Dutton, J. E. *Energize Your Workplace: How to Create and Sustain High-Quality Connections at Work.* San Francisco: Jossey-Bass, 2003.

Dutton, J. E., and E. D. Heaphy. "The Power of High-Quality Connections." *Positive Organizational Scholarship: Foundations of a New Discipline,* edited by K. S. Cameron, J. E. Dutton, and R. E. Quinn, 244–256. New York: Oxford University Press, 2003.

Editors of Rolling Stone, The. *Bruce Springsteen: The Rolling Stone Files.* New York: Hyperion, 1996.

Edwards, J. R., and N. P. Rothbard. "Work and Family Stress and Well-Being: An Integrative Model of Person-Environment Fit Within and Between the Work and Family Domains." In *Work and Life Integration: Organizational, Cultural, and Individual Perspectives*, edited by E. E. Kossek and S. J. Lambert, 211–242. Mahwah, NJ: Lawrence Erlbaum Associates Publishers, 2005.

"ESPN's Julie Foudy Scores One for the Girls." Video. June 28, 2010. http://espn. go.com/high-school/girls-soccer/video/clip?id=6571465.

"Executive Bios." *Facebook.com*. https://www.facebook.com/press/info.php?execbios.

Farhi, P. "Michelle Obama's Target Trip: Critics Take Aim." *Washington Post*, October 2, 2011. http://www.washingtonpost.com/lifestyle/style/michelle-obamas-target-trip-critics-take-aim/2011/10/02/gIQATrMLGL_story.html.

"Fellowship FAQs." The Mission Continues. 2012. http://missioncontinues.org/ fellowships/fellowship-faqs.

"50 Most Powerful Women in Business." *Fortune*, October 8, 2012. From CNN Money website. http://money.cnn.com/magazines/fortune/most-powerful-women/2012/ full_list/.

Fleishman, J. Personal communication. January 23, 2013.

Fleishman, J., and T. Tierney. "Joel L. Fleishman and Thomas J. Tierney on Their Book *Give Smart*." Interview by C. Rose. *Charlie Rose*. Video. June 13, 2011. http://www. charlierose.com/view/interview/11728.

―――. "Avoiding the Madonna Effect in Philanthropy." *Harvard Business Review Blog Network*, April 5, 2011. http://blogs.hbr.org/cs/2011/04/avoiding_ the_madonna_effect_in.html.

―――. "As Government Helps Less, Let's Do Good Better." *National Journal*, April 28, 2011. http://www.nationaljournal.com/politics/ as-government-helps-less-let-s-do-good-better-20110422.

―――. *Give Smart: Philanthropy That Gets Results*. New York: Public Affairs, 2011.

Fletcher, J. K., and L. Bailyn, "The Equity Imperative: Redesigning Work for Work-Family Integration." In *Work and Life Integration: Organizational, Cultural, and Individual Perspectives*, edited by E. E. Kossek and S. J. Lambert, 171–189. Mahwah, NJ: Lawrence Erlbaum Associates Publishers, 2005.

Flynn, F. J. "What Have You Done for Me Lately? Temporal Adjustments to Favor Evaluations." *Organizational Behavior and Human Decision Processes* 91, no. 1 (2003): 38–50.

Flynn, F. J., and V. K. B. Lake. "If You Need Help, Just Ask: Underestimating Compliance with Direct Requests for Help." *Journal of Personality and Social Psychology* 95, no. 1 (2008): 128–143.

Foudy, J. "Achievement and Overcoming Obstacles." YouTube video. April 7, 2009. http://www.youtube.com/watch?feature=player_detailpage&v=WR_l-13a7BU.

―――. "Dare to Dream: Interview with Julie Foudy." Transcript. HBO. n. d. http:// www.hbo.com/sports/dare-to-dream-us-womens-soccer-team/interview/julie-foudy.html.

―――. "Empower Youth to Lead." Lecture presented at the Play On 2010 Conference at Columbia University in New York, New York. October 21, 2010. YouTube video. http://www.youtube.com/watch?v=cs47hjT2gBo.

―――. "Get in the Game." YouTube video. July 9, 2011. http://www.youtube.com/ watch?v=t0F2H5qtG-I.

―――. "GlobalGirl Media Kick It Up! Project Launch." Culver City, CA: GlobalGirl Media, 2010. YouTube video. http://www.youtube.com/watch?v=BxHtDm2rFt0.

―――. "Hall of Fame Induction Speech." Presented in Oneonta, New York, August 26, 2007. YouTube video. http://www.youtube.com/watch?v=RdDjP9Uq9PA.

―――. Interview at 2008 NSCAA Convention in Baltimore, MD, February 29, 2008. YouTube video. http://www.youtube.com/watch?v=bEybNd-0KzI.

_____. "Julie Foudy: Leadership in Sports." Interview by J. Thompson. Podcast. July 2, 2010. https://www.responsiblesports.com/media/podcasts-1.

_____. "Julie Foudy: Leadership in Sports." Podcast. n.d. http://responsiblesports. com/media_library/podcasts.aspx?id=21.

_____. "Julie Foudy Responds to Mia Hamm's Challenge: 'Heck Ya Athletes Have an Obligation!'" YouTube video. December 4, 2009. http://www.youtube.com/ watch?v=DptTymsaPjM.

_____. "Julie Foudy Sports Leadership Academy." YouTube video. October 9, 2010. http://www.youtube.com/watch?v=U-PPs5KC8eA.

_____. "Julie Foudy Talking About *Girl Talk*." Interview by K. O'Connor. YouTube video. August 28, 2007. http://www.youtube.com/ watch?v=91-836FWp9k&feature=related.

_____. "Jule Foudy Talks Title IX." ESPN, May 10, 2012. YouTube video. http://www. youtube.com/watch?v=j4IgGLzZZKM.

_____. "Kickin' It with Julie Foudy." Interview by Soccer.com. YouTube video. 2009. http://www.youtube.com/watch?v=at7fycNwehI.

_____. "Olympic Soccer Gold Medalist Julie Foudy Chats w/Jim Clash." The Adventurer with Jim Clash." *Forbes* video. Posted on YouTube March 19, 2008. http://www.youtube.com/watch?v=PDDv7f8_GTg&feature=related.

_____. "1 on 1—Julie Foudy." Interview by M.Gaschk. YouTube video. March 11, 2011. http://www.youtube.com/watch?v=xDjNZMG_3a4.

_____. Personal communication. April 19, 2013.

_____. "Public Service Announcement 2." YouTube video. 2010. http://www.youtube. com/watch?v=i3uhlif7LpI.

_____. "20 People to Watch: Julie Foudy on Her Inspiration." YouTube video. Arlington, VA: The Century Council, April 4, 2011. http://www.youtube.com/watch? v=2JXGi8yqTDE.

_____. "20 People to Watch: Julie Foudy on Things She Is Proud Of." YouTube video. Arlington, VA: The Century Council, April 4, 2011. http://www.youtube.com/ watch?v=HPbR5b9J1B8.

_____. "Text of Julie Foudy's Letter to Title IX Commission." *USA Today*, February 20, 2003. http://usatoday30.usatoday.com/sports/college/2003-02-24-titleix-foudy-letter_x.htm.

_____. "30 Sec AYSO Spot." YouTube video. February 10, 2009. http://www.youtube. com/watch?v=zQlnOa_g2xQ.

_____. "U.S. Women's Soccer: Julie Foudy." YouTube video. Park City, UT: Park City Television, April 8, 2010. http://www.youtube.com/watch?v=wQ85zbWCe2g.

Fredrickson, B. *Positivity: Groundbreaking Research Reveals How to Embrace the Hidden Strength of Positive Emotions, Overcome Negativity, and Thrive.* New York: Random House, 2009.

Fredrickson, B. L., K. M. Grewen, K. A. Coffey, A. B. Algoe, A. M. Firestine, J. M. G. Arevalo, J. Ma, and S. W. Cole. "A Functional Genomic Perspective on Human Well-Being." *Proceedings of the National Academy of Sciences* (2013).

Fricke, D. "Bringing It All Back Home." *Rolling Stone*, Februrary 5, 2009.

Friedman, S. D. *Baby Bust: New Choices for Men and Women in Work and Family.* Philadelphia: Wharton Digital Press, 2013.

_____. *Total Leadership: Be a Better Leader, Have a Richer Life.* Boston: Harvard Business School Publishing, 2008.

Friedman, S. D., and J. H. Greenhaus. *Work and Family—Allies or Enemies? What Happens When Business Professionals Confront Life Choices.* New York: Oxford University Press, 2000.

Friedman, S. D., and S. Lobel. "The Happy Workaholic: A Role Model for Employees." *Academy of Management Executives* 17, no. 3 (2005): 87–98.

Friedman, S. D., J. DeGroot, and P. Christensen, eds. *Integrating Work and Life: The Wharton Resource Guide*. New York: Pfeiffer, 1998.

Gable, S. L., G. C. Gonzaga, and A. Strachman. "Will You Be There for Me When Things Go Right? Supportive Responses to Positive Event Disclosures." *Journal of Personality and Social Psychology* 91, no. 5 (2006): 904–917.

Gable, S. L., H. T. Reis, E. A. Impett, and E. R. Asher. "What Do You Do When Things Go Right? The Intrapersonal and Interpersonal Benefits of Sharing Good Events." *Journal of Personality and Social Psychology* 87, no. 2 (2004): 228–245. doi:10.1037/0022-3514.87.2.228.

Gallagher, M. *CMF News Wire*. June 6, 2011. http://www.michiganfoundations.org/s_cmf/doc.asp?CID=335&DID=48698.

Gaudin, S. "Facebook IPO Shines Light on Revenue, User Growth." *Computerworld*, February 1, 2012. http://www.computerworld.com/s/article/9223906/Facebook_IPO_shines_light_on_revenue_user_growth?taxonomyId=169&pageNumber=1.

Ghosn, C. "Words of Wisdom from Sheryl Sandberg." The Levo League. November 2, 2011. http://www.levoleague.com/powwow/words-of-wisdom-from-sheryl-sandberg/.

Goldfein, J., V. Jarrett, T. G. Ranzetta, J. Herrin, and S. Sandberg. "Women in Technology Panel Discussion." Presented in Palo Alto, CA, April 22, 2011. YouTube video. http://www.youtube.com/watch?v=T44XdGH5s-8.

Goldman, D. "Facebook Tops 900 Million Users." *CNN Money*, April 23, 2012. http://money.cnn.com/2012/04/23/technology/facebook-q1/index.htm.

Goldman, R. Personal communication. April 15, 2013.

Gordon, M. "NYU Professor Speaks on the Finance of the First Lady's Fashion." *State Press*, January 10, 2012. http://www.statepress.com/2012/01/10/nyu-professor-speaks-on-the-finance-of-the-first-ladys-fashion/.

Graham, J. "Facebook COO Sheryl Sandberg Talks Personal Tech." *ABC News*. October 3, 2011. http://abcnews.go.com/Technology/facebook-coo-sheryl-sandberg-talks-personal-tech/story?id=14655312#.TtN9H7JFtRc.

Grant, A. M., and J. M. Berg. "Prosocial Motivation at Work: How Making a Difference Makes a Difference." In *Handbook of Positive Organizational Scholarship*, edited by K. Cameron and G. Spreitzer. New York: Oxford University Press, 2010.

Greene, A. "Occupy E Street: Inside Springsteen's New Album." *Rolling Stone*, March 15, 2012.

Greenhaus, J. H., and N. J. Beutell. "Sources of Conflict Between Work and Family Roles." *Academy of Management Review* 10, no.1 (1985): 76–88.

Greitens, E. "Book Discussion on *The Heart and the Fist*." C-SPAN video. August 31, 2011. http://www.c-spanvideo.org/program/Fist.

———. "Building the Future: How Iraq, War, and the Humanitarian Ethic Are Shaping the Next Generation of American Leadership." Speech delivered at the Missouri Court of Appeals, St. Louis, MO. Video. June 20, 2007. C-SPAN video. http://www.c-spanvideo.org/program/AmericanLeader.

———. Commencement speech delivered at Tufts University, Medford, Massachusetts, May 20, 2012. Transcript. http://now.tufts.edu/commencement-address-eric-greitens.

———. "Conversations with Eric Greitens." *Charlie Rose*. PBS. May 27, 2011. http://www.charlierose.com/view/interview/11697.

———. "CPL Interview with Eric Greitens." Harvard Kennedy School Center for Public Leadership. YouTube video. February 25, 2012. http://www.youtube.com/watch?v=RIpwqzifjJk.

———. "Eric Greitens Addressing Walden Students." YouTube video. May 14, 2010. http://www.youtube.com/watch?v=pJ-nudvepXw.

———. "Eric Greitens: *The Heart and the Fist*." Interview by S. Page. *The Diane Rehm Show*. Transcript. American University Radio. July 26, 2011. http://thedianerehm show.org/shows/2011-07-26/eric-greitens-heart-and-fist/transcript.

———. "Eric Greitens: *The Heart and the Fist*." The Pritzker Military Library Presents series. Chicago: Jumpmaster Productions, 2011. http://www.pritzkermilitarylibrary. org/Home/eric-greitens.aspx.

———. "Eric Greitens on *The Heart and the Fist*." Harvard Kennedy School Center for Public Leadership. YouTube video. June 21, 2012. http://www.youtube.com/ watch?feature=player_embedded&v=Iql6V60d1mM.

———. "Eric Greitens Speaking—Compass." YouTube video. October 22, 2012. http://www.youtube.com/watch?feature=player_embedded&v=MCNHd3_auVo.

———. "Eric Greitens Speaking—Courage." YouTube video. October 22, 2012. http:// www.youtube.com/watch?feature=player_embedded&v=l8BSbmmqGLA,

———. "Eric Greitens Speaking—Friendship." YouTube video. October 22, 2012. http://www.youtube.com/watch?feature=player_embedded&v=_mwe700ghTY.

———. "Founder & CEO Eric Greitens' Congressional Testimony." The Mission Continues. YouTube video. March 27, 2012. http://www.youtube.com/watch? v=vXhY5x-tQfY.

———. Guest lecture presented at the Leading Authorities headquarters in Washington, DC. YouTube video. August 11, 2008. http://www.youtube.com/ watch?v=-sOW0mXzDXU.

———. *The Heart and the Fist: The Education of a Humanitarian, the Making of a Navy SEAL*. Boston: Houghton Mifflin Harcourt, 2011.

———. "Helping Recent Vets Find Meaning in New Jobs." Interview by N. Conan. Audio file. *Talk of the Nation*. NPR. August 27, 2012. http://www.npr.org/2012/ 08/27/160120142/helping-recent-vets-find-meaning-in-new-jobs.

———. Interview by T. Brokaw. *NBC Nightly News*. New York: MSNBC. March 4, 2010. http://www.youtube.com/watch?v=W8MwfO6rbc0.

———. Interview by S. Colbert. *ColbertNation*. May 11, 2011. http://www.colbertnation. com/the-colbert-report-videos/386088/may-11-2011/eric-greitens.

———. "An Interview with Eric Greitens." Interview by A. Murphy. Transcript. December 10, 2012. http://www.ncoc.net/TheWarriorsHeart.

———. Interview by B. Williams. *NBC Nightly News with Brian Williams*. NBC. n.d. http://www.ericgreitens.com/nbc-nightly-news-with-brian-williams/.

———. "KSDK Interviews Eric Greitens." YouTube video. March 4, 2010. http:// www.youtube.com/user/TheGreitensGroup?blend=22&ob=5#p/a/u/1/ WRWI8D8JsQM.

———. "Lieutenant Commander US Navy SEAL Eric Greitens." Interview by A. Monica. Audio file. *ABC Local*. May 6, 2011. http://www.abc.net.au/sundayprofile/ stories/3209403.htm.

———. "A Navy SEAL Recounts a Story of Combat and Compassion." Interview by T. Hall. *Today*. NBC. April 14, 2011. http://www.today.com/id/42555983/site/ todayshow/ns/today-books/t/navy-seal-recounts-story-combat-compassion/#. UTVy0DA4u90.

———. Personal communication. April 2, 2013.

———. "Point Person: Our Q&A with Eric Greitens." Interview by T. Robberson. Transcript. *Dallas Morning News*, January 6, 2012. http://www.dallasnews.com/ opinion/sunday-commentary/20120106-point-person-our-qa-with-eric-greitens.ece.

———. Résumé. n.d. http://siproject.missouri.edu/files/truman/vitaes/eric_greitens_ resume.pdf.

————. "The SEAL Sensibility." *Wall Street Journal*, May 7, 2011. http://online.wsj.
com/article/SB10001424052748703992704576307021339210488.html.

————. *Strength & Compassion: Photographs and Essays*. Washington, DC: Leading
Authorities Press, 2009.

————. "This Veterans Day, Their Mission Continues Coast to Coast." *Huffington
Post*, November 9, 2012. http://www.huffingtonpost.com/eric-greitens/veterans-
day-2012_b_2096303.html.

————. "U.S. Navy SEAL Training to Kill Osama Bin Laden." Interview by E. Pedro.
C-SPAN video. May 7, 2011. http://www.c-spanvideo.org/program/LTr.

————. "Veterans Advocate Urges Iraq War Awareness." Audio file. *All Things
Considered*. NPR. April 4, 2008. http://www.npr.org/templates/story/story.
php?storyId=89388190.

————. *The Warrior's Heart: Becoming a Man of Compassion and Courage*. Boston:
Houghton Mifflin Harcourt, 2012.

Greitens Group, The. "Eric Greitens: Leadership, Purpose, Inspiration." 2012. http://
www.ericgreitens.com/bio/.

Guber, P. "The Four Truths of the Storyteller." *Harvard Business Review*, December
2007.

"Ian Darke and Julie Foudy Post-Game Remarks 2011 World Club US vs. Brazil
Hope Solo." *WomensFootballUSA*. Video. July 10, 2011. http://www.youtube.com/
watch?v=ke8XNArZvVU.

Halvorson, H. G. *Succeed: How We Can Reach Our Goals*. New York: Hudson Street
Press, 2010.

Handel, S. "Michelle LaVaughn Robinson Obama." *Talk of the Nation*. NPR. August 25,
2008. http://www.npr.org/blogs/talk/2008/08/michelle_lavaughn_robinson_oba.
html.

Harbaugh, K. Personal communication. April 11, 2013.

Harding, T. "Fostering Creativity for Leadership and Leading Change." *Arts Education
Policy Review* 111, no. 2 (2010): 51–53.

Harvard Business School Newsroom. "Thomas Tierney (MBA 1980) Named Chair of
HBS Social Enterprise Initiative Advisory Board." Press release. January 5, 2009.
http://www.hbs.edu/news/releases/thomastierney.html.

"The Heart and the Fist by Eric Greitens." Book trailer. YouTube video. United States:
Circle of Seven Productions, 2011. http://www.youtube.com/user/TheGreitensGro
up?blend=22&ob=5#p/u/2/sDuVQG_xBIY.

Helft, M. "Mark Zuckerberg's Most Valuable Friend." *New York Times*, October 3,
2010. http://www.nytimes.com/2010/10/03/business/03face.html?pagewanted=all.

Hempel, J. "Meet Facebook's New Number Two." *CNN Money*, April 12, 2008. http://
money.cnn.com/2008/04/11/technology/facebook_sandberg.fortune/index.htm.

Hertz, N. *The Debt Threat: How Debt Is Destroying the Developing World*. New York:
Harper Collins, 2005. http://www.atu2.com/news/book-excerpt-the-debt-threat-
how-debt-is-destroying-the-developing-world-pt-1.html.

Heywood, L. *Built to Win: The Female Athlete as Cultural Icon*. Minneapolis, MN:
University of Minnesota Press, 2003.

Hiam, A. "9 Obstacles to Creativity—and How You Can Remove Them." *Futurist* 32,
no. 7 (1998): 30–34.

Hinman, K. "Captain America." *Riverfront Times*, April 9, 2008. http://www.
riverfronttimes.com/2008-04-09/news/navy-seal-eric-greitens-has-come-home-
to-st-louis-to-help-fellow-iraq-vets/.

Hochman, S. "Bruce Springsteen Is on Fire for MusiCares." February 9, 2013. http://
www.grammy.com/blogs/bruce-springsteen-is-on-fire-for-musicares.

Hogshead-Makar, N., and A. Zimbalist. *Equal Play: Title IX and Social Change*.
Philadelphia: Temple University Press, 2007.

Holzman, D. C. "Diet and Nutrition: White House Proposes Healthy Food Financing Initiative." *Environmental Health Perspectives* 118, no. 4(2010), 156. http://www. ncbi.nlm.nih.gov/pmc/articles/PMC2854743/.

Humax Networks. 2010. http://www.humaxnetworks.com/default.asp

Hunter-Gault, C. "The Root: Michelle Brings Hope, Exposure to Africa." *National Public Radio.* June 24, 2011. http://www.npr.org/2011/06/24/137391155/ the-root-michelle-brings-hope-exposure-to-africa.

Izzi, L. (director/producer). *Soccer: Julie Foudy Leadership Academy.* YouTube video. November 18, 2007. http://www.youtube.com/watch?v=5iqrAPRcmXo.

Jacobs, P. "Q&A: Tackling a Brave New World: Bain & Company's Tom Tierney." *Harvard Business School Bulletin,* October 2000. http://www.alumni.hbs.edu/ bulletin/2000/october/qanda.html.

Jacobs, T. L. et al. "Self-Reported Mindfulness and Cortisol during a Shamatha Meditation Retreat." *Health Psychology* 32, no. 10 (October 2013): 1104–1109.

James, W. "Will." In *Principles of Psychology,* 1098–1193. Cambridge, MA: Harvard University Press, 1981.

———. "Habit." In *Principles of Psychology: Briefer Course,* 125–138. Cambridge, MA: Harvard University Press, 1984.

Julie Foudy Sports Leadership Academy. "More about Julie Foudy." http://www. juliefoudyleadership.com/About_us/Staff/About_Julie_Foudy.html.

Kahneman, D., and A. Tversky, eds. *Choices, Values, and Frames.* New York: Cambridge University Press and the Russell Sage Foundation, 2000.

Kantor, J. "First Lady Strives for Caring Image above Partisan Fray." *New York Times,* September 3, 2012. http://www.nytimes.com/2012/09/04/us/politics/michelle-obamas-role-in-presidents-re-election-bid.html?pagewanted=all&_r=0.

———. *The Obamas.* New York: Penguin Group, Inc., 2012.

Kantor, J., and R. L.Swarns. "In First Lady's Roots, a Complex Path from Slavery." *New York Times,* October 7, 2009. http://www.nytimes.com/2009/10/08/us/ politics/08genealogy.html.

Khan, S., E. Greitens, S. Mukherjee, and P. Farmer. "Conversations with Salman Khan, Eric Greitens, Siddhartha Mukherjee, and Paul Farmer." *Charlie Rose.* PBS. August 30, 2011. http://www.charlierose.com/view/interview/11870.

King, L. A. "The Health Benefits of Writing about Life Goals." *Personality and Social Psychology Bulletin* 27, no. 7(2001): 798–807. doi:10.1177/0146167201277003

Kirkpatrick, R. *The Words and Music of Bruce Springsteen.* USA: Greenwood Publishing Group, Inc., 2007.

Kirschbaum, E. "Memories of How Springsteen Rocked Berlin." Reuters. July 15, 2008. http://www.reuters.com/article/2008/07/16/us-germany-springsteen-idUSL1334031920080716.

Klein, J. "Can Service Save Us?" *Time,* June 20, 2013. http://nation.time. com/2013/06/20/can-service-save-us/.

Knowles M.S., E. F. Holton, and R. A. Swanson. *The Adult Learner: The Definitive Classic in Adult Education and Human Resource Development.* Amsterdam: Elsevier, 2005.

Kossek, E. E., R. A. Noe, and B. J. DeMarr. "Work-Family Role Synthesis: Individual and Organizational Determinants." *International Journal of Conflict Management* 10, no. 2 (1999): 102–129. http://search.proquest.com/docview/199041184? accountid=14707.

Kossek, E. E., M. N. Ruderman, P. Brady, and K. Hannum. "Work–Nonwork Boundary Management Profiles: A Person-Centered Approach." *Journal of Vocational Behavior* 81, no. 1 (August 2012): 112–128.

Kriener, G. E., E. C. Hollensbe, and M. L. Sheep. "Balancing Borders and Bridges: Negotiating the Work-Home Interface via Boundary Work Tactics." *Academy of Management Journal* 52, no. 4 (2009): 704–730.

Kympton, S. Personal communication. April 12, 2013.

Landau, J. "Growing Young with Rock and Roll." *The Real Paper*, May 22, 1974. http://all-the-wine.blogspot.com/2010/04/growing-young-with-rock-and-roll-jon.html.

Lavine, J. (producer). *Dare to Dream: The Story of the U.S. Women's Soccer Team*. HBO video.December 11, 2005.

Let's Move! "Let's Move! Two Years of Healthy Changes for Our Nation's Kids." Blog post. February 3, 2012. http://www.letsmove.gov/blog/2012/02/03/let%E2%80%99s-move-two-years-healthy-changes-our-nation%E2%80%99s-kids.

Li, C., and S. Sandberg. "Facebook COO Sheryl Sandberg in Conversation with Altimeter Group Founder Charlene Li." YouTube video. October 15, 2009. http://www.youtube.com/watch?v=feqty0DhULU&feature=related.

Lightfoot, E. *Michelle Obama: First Lady of Hope*. Guilford, CT: The Lyons Press, 2008.

Locke, E. A., and G. P. Latham. "Building a Practically Useful Theory of Goal Setting and Task Motivation: A 35-Year Odyssey." *American Psychologist* 57, no. 9 (2002): 705–717.

Longman, J. "Women's World Cup; Foudy Is the U.S. Team's Renaissance Midfielder." *New York Times*, June 16, 1999. http://www.nytimes.com/1999/06/16/sports/women-s-world-cup-foudy-is-the-us-team-s-renaissance-midfielder.html.

Lorsch, J., and T. Tierney. "Build a Life, Not a Resume." *Bain & Company Insights*, September 1, 2002. http://bain.com/publications/articles/build-a-life-not-a-resume.aspx.

Lovett, E. "Facebook Is Friend to Jobless and Small Business, Says Company COO." *ABC News*. September 15, 2011. http://abcnews.go.com/Business/facebook-friend-jobless-small-business-creates-jobs-coo/story?id=14521237#.TtN-MbJFtRc.

Lovell, J. "George Saunders's Advice to Graduates." *New York Times*, July 31, 2013.

Lyubomirsky, S. *The How of Happiness*. New York: Penguin Books, 2007.

Lyubomirsky, S., K. M. Sheldon, and D. Schkade. "Pursuing Happiness: The Architecture of Sustainable Change." *Review of General Psychology* 9, no. 2(2005): 111–131.

MacMillan, D. "Facebook's Sandberg Friends Gaga to Obama en Route to IPO." *Bloomberg*. January 31, 2012. http://www.bloomberg.com/news/2012-01-31/facebook-s-sandberg-friends-gaga-to-obama-as-social-media-ipo-nears-tech.html.

Mahoney, R. "Julie Foudy Finds Another Forum." *Soccer America*, September 7, 2007. http://www.socceramerica.com/article/23355/julie-foudy-finds-another-forum.html.

Mahoney, S. "Giving Wounded and Disabled Veterans a New Mission." *TravelsOfJohn.com*. 2010. http://travelsofjohn.com/interviews/general/eric-greitens/.

Marcus, G. "Bruce Springsteen: *Born to Run*." *Rolling Stone*, October 9, 1975. http://www.rollingstone.com/music/albumreviews/born-to-run-19851001.

Marsh, D. *Two Hearts: Bruce Springsteen, the Definitive Biography, 1972–2003*. New York: Routledge, 2004.

Marvin, C. Personal communication. April 12, 2013.

McKay, M. M., J. P. Forsyth, and G. H. Eifert. *Your Life on Purpose*. Oakland, CA: New Harbinger Publications, Inc., 2010.

Mehra, S., A. D. Joyal, and M. Rhee. "On Adopting Quality Orientation as an Operations Philosophy to Improve Business Performance in Banking Services." *e International Journal of Quality & Reliability Management* 28, no. 9 (2011): 951–968.

Meister, J. *Learning from the CEO: How Chief Executives Shape Corporate Education*. New York: Forbes Custom Publishing, 2000.

Mento, A. J., P. Martinelli, and R. M. Jones. "Mind Mapping in Executive Education: Applications and Outcomes." *Journal of Management Development* 18, no. 4 (1999): 390–407.

Michaels, S. "Madonna's MDNA Is Highest-Grossing Tour of 2012." *The Guardian*, December 17, 2012. http://www.guardian.co.uk/music/2012/dec/17/madonna-highest-grossing-tour-2012.

"Michelle Obama." *Biography.com*. 2011. http://www.biography.com/people/michelle-obama-307592.

Miller, C. C., and N. Perlroth. "The $1.6 Billion Woman, Staying on Message." *New York Times*, February 4, 2012. http://www.nytimes.com/2012/02/05/business/sheryl-sandberg-of-facebook-staying-on-message.html?pagewanted=all&_r=0.

"Mind Maps Chart the Way to Business Efficiency." *Education & Training* 40, nos. 4/5 (1998): 173–174.

"Mission Continues, Goldman Sachs Launch $20M Coalition." *St. Louis Business Journal*, December 9, 2010. http://www.bizjournals.com/stlouis/news/2010/12/09/mission-continues-forms-20m-coalition.html?page=all.

Morrell, K., A. Nanda, and P. L. Fagan. *Tom Tierney's Reflections*. Boston: Harvard Business School Publishing, 2003.

Morris, M. L., and S. R. Madsen. "Advancing Work-Life Integration in Individuals, Organizations, and Communities." *Advances in Developing Human Resources* 9, no. 4, (2007): 439–454.

Mundy, L. *Michelle: A Biography*. New York: Simon & Schuster Paperbacks, 2008.

Myrie, J., and K. Daly. "The Use of Boundaries by Self-Employed, Home-Based Workers to Manage Work and Family: A Qualitative Study in Canada." *Journal of Family and Economic Issues* 30, no. 4(2009): 386–398. doi:10.1007/s10834-009-9166-7.

Nanda, A., and P. L. Fagan. *Tom Tierney at Bain & Company (A)*. Boston: Harvard Business School Publishing, 1999.

Nanda, A., and P. L. Fagan. *Tom Tierney at Bain & Company (B)*. Boston: Harvard Business School Publishing, 1999.

Nanda, A., and P. L. Fagan. *Tom Tierney at Bain & Company (C)*. Boston: Harvard Business School Publishing, 1999.

National Military Family Association. "26 States Support Military Spouse Career Portability." 2012. http://www.militaryfamily.org/feature-articles/26-states-support-military.html.

Nauffts, M. "Tom Tierney, Chairman/Co-Founder, Bridgespan Group: Philanthropy That Gets Results." *Philanthropy News Digest*, May 6, 2011. http://foundationcenter.org/pnd/newsmakers/nwsmkr.jhtml?id=339200006.

Niemiec, R. M. "OK, Now What? Taking Action." Via Institute. 2009. http://www.viacharacter.org/www/AwareExploreApply/tabid/249/language/en-US/Default.aspx.

Nippert-Eng, C. "Calendars and Keys: The Classification of 'Home' and 'Work.'" *Sociological Forum* 11, no. 3 (1996): 563–582.

Norwood, M. *Michelle Style: Celebrating the First Lady of Fashion*. New York: Harper Collins, 2009.

NPR staff. "For a Navy SEAL, Balance Between 'Heart' and 'Fist.'" *Weekend Edition*. NPR. June 11, 2011. http://www.npr.org/2011/06/11/137108125/for-a-navy-seal-balance-between-heart-and-fist.

Obama, B. *Kennedy Center Honors Address*. YouTube video.2009. http://www.youtube.com/watch?v=oS1-BLl_H30.

Obama, M. "Extended Interview with Michelle Obama by Soledad O'Brien." CNN video. February 1, 2008. http://www.youtube.com/watch?v=JSkd0xrhcQ8.

Obama, M. "First Lady Michelle Obama Delivers Remarks at the 2011 International Women of Courage Awards." YouTube video. March 8, 2011. http://www.youtube.com/watch?v=wided5-BtpI&feature=related.

Obama, M. Interview by David Letterman. *Late Show with David Letterman*, CBS.
    September 7, 2012.

Obama, M. "Mrs. Obama 'Confident' in Her Husband's Campaign." Interview
    by G. King. *CBS This Morning*. January 11, 2012. http://www.youtube.com/
    watch?v=M8MF9vT0VAM.

Obama, M. Remarks by the First Lady at Joining Forces Veterans Hiring Event
    delivered at the Mayport Naval Station in Mayport, FL, August 22, 2012.
    Transcript. http://www.whitehouse.gov/the-press-office/2012/08/22/remarks-
    first-lady-joining-forces-veterans-hiring-event.

O'Connor, C. "How Sheryl Sandberg Helped Make an Entrepreneur's Big Decision."
    equentia. September 27, 2011. http://portal.eqentia.com/techvc/permalink/
    81339713-How-Sheryl-Sandberg-Helped-Make-An-Entrepreneurs-Big-Decision.

O'Connor, E. "Chris Christie Wept over Springsteen Hug." *Time*, November 7, 2012.
    http://newsfeed.time.com/2012/11/07/chris-christie-wept-over-springsteen-hug/.

Oliphant, J. "Conservatives Dig into Michelle Obama's Anti-Obesity Program." *Los
    Angeles Times*, February 26, 2011. http://articles.latimes.com/2011/feb/26/nation/
    la-na-michelle-obama-obesity-20110227.

Ollier-Malaterre, A., N. Rothbard, and J. Berg. "When Worlds Collide in Cyberspace:
    How Boundary Work in Online Social Networks Impacts Professional Relationships."
    Academy of Management Review 38, no. 4 (October 2013): 645–669.

Osburg, B. Personal communication. April 18, 2013.

"Other Women to Watch, The." *Wall Street Journal*, November 19, 2007. http://online.
    wsj.com/article/SB119517314579995043.html.

Pennebaker, J. W. "Conflict and Canned Meat." *Psychological Inquiry* 9, no.
    3(1998):219–220. doi:10.1207/s15327965pli0903_6

Peterson, C. *A Primer in Positive Psychology*. New York: Oxford University Press, 2006.

Peterson, C., and M. E. P. Seligman. *Character Strengths and Virtues: A Handbook and
    Classification*. New York: Oxford University Press, 2004.

Pham, L. B., and S. E. Taylor. "From Thought to Action: Effects of Process- Versus
    Outcome-Based Mental Simulations on Performance." *Personality and Social
    Psychology Bulletin* 25, no. 2 (1999): 250–260.

Piliavin, J. A. In *Doing Well by Doing Good: Benefits for the Benefactor*, edited by
    C. L. M. Keyes and J. Haidt, 227–247. Washington, DC: American Psychological
    Association, 2003.

"Powerful Women: How They Do It All." *CNN Money*. September 14, 2009. http://
    money.cnn.com/2009/09/10/news/companies/work_life_balance_women.fortue/
    index.htm.

Rath, T., and B. Conchie. *Strengths Based Leadership: Great Leaders, Teams, and Why
    People Follow*. New York: Gallup Press, 2008.

Reis, H. T., K. M. Sheldon, S. L. Gable, J. Roscoe, and R. M. Ryan. "Daily Well-Being:
    The Role of Autonomy, Competence, and Relatedness." *Personality and Social
    Psychology Bulletin* 26, no. 4 (2000): 419–435.

Reivich, K., and A. Shatté. *The Resilience Factor: 7 Essential Skills for Overcoming
    Life's Inevitable Obstacles*. New York: Broadway Books, 2002.

Remnick, D. *The Bridge: The Life and Rise of Barack Obama*. New York: Random
    House Digital, Inc., January 4, 2011.

———. "State of the Union: A New Book on the First Marriage." *New Yorker*,
    January 16, 2012. http://www.newyorker.com/arts/critics/books/2012/01/
    16/120116crbo_books_remnick?currentPage=all.

———. "We Are Alive: Bruce Springsteen at Sixty-Two." *New Yorker*, July 30,
    2012. http://www.newyorker.com/reporting/2012/07/30/120730fa_fact_
    remnick?currentPage=all.

Road Trip: 40 Years of the Boss. Video. United States: Music Video Distributors, 2009.

Roberts, L. M., J. E. Dutton, G. M. Spreitzer, E. D. Heaphy, and R. E. Quinn. "Composing the Reflected Best-Self Portrait: Building Pathways for Becoming Extraordinary in Work Organizations." *Academy of Management Review* 30, no. 4 (2005): 712–736.

Roberts, L. M., G. Spreitzer, J. Dutton, and R. Quinn. "How to PLAY to Your Strengths." *Harvard Business Review*, January 2005.

Robinson, M. L. "Princeton-Educated Blacks and the Black Community." Senior thesis, Princeton University, 1985. http://www.politico.com/pdf/080222_MOPrincetonThesis_1–251.pdf.

Rogak, L. *Michelle Obama: In Her Own Words*. New York: Public Affairs, 2009.

Rutherford, D. "Biography: Sheryl Sandberg." *Helium*. July 19, 2011. http://www.helium.com/items/2201201-biography-sheryl-sandberg.

Samakow, J. "Adele Sandberg, Sheryl Sandberg's Mom, Inspired Daughter to 'Lean In from Childhood until Today.'" *Huffington Post*, May 7, 2013. http://www.huffingtonpost.com/2013/05/07/adele-sandberg-sheryl-sandberg-mom-tribute_n_3230540.html.

Sandberg, A. Personal communication. April 4, 2013.

Sandberg, S. "Changing the World." *Daily Beast*, October 3, 2008. http://www.thedailybeast.com/newsweek/2008/10/03/changing-the-world.html.

———. "The Charity Gap." *Wall Street Journal*, April 4, 2007.

———. Commencement speech presented at Barnard College, New York, New York, May 17, 2011. Video. http://barnard.edu/headlines/facebook-executive-barnard-graduates-world-needs-you-run-it.

———. "Facebook COO Sheryl Sandberg at Nielson Consumer 360." YouTube video. June 15, 2010. http://www.youtube.com/watch?v=Gm8NdNy4wOM.

———. Facebook status update. November 4, 2011. https://www.facebook.com/sheryl?fref=ts.

———. "Facebook's Sheryl Sandberg on What Makes Women Succeed." Interview by P. Sellers. Transcript. *CNN Money*. October 4, 2011. http://management.fortune.cnn.com/2011/10/04/facebook-sheryl-sandberg/.

———. "FORA.tv Speaker—Sheryl Sandberg." FORA.tv. http://fora.tv/speaker/2286/Sheryl_Sandberg.

———. "IC2011 Conversation with Sheryl Sandberg." Interview by P. Mitchell. Video. September 16, 2011. http://www.paleycenter.org/ic-2011-la-livestream/.

———. Keynote address at the Grace Hopper celebration of women in computing. Video. November 10, 2011. http://www.livestream.com/fbtechtalks/video?clipId=pla_e6b1a965-8cc5-4ef9-9ac8c2048d612e96&utm_source=lslibrary&utm_medium=ui-thumb&time=1.

———. Keynote address at the 2010 BLC breakfast. Video. March 5, 2010. http://www.jewishfed.org/community/page/blcvideos#Sandberg.

———. *Lean In: Women, Work, and the Will to Lead*. New York: Alfred A. Knopf, 2013.

———. "Leaving Work at 5:30pm." Video. 2013. http://www.makers.com/sheryl-sandberg/moments/leaving-work-530pm.

———. "A Public Failure." Video. 2013. http://www.makers.com/sheryl-sandberg/moments/public-failure.

———. "Reaching Women around the World." *Huffington Post*, November 24, 2009. http://www.huffingtonpost.com/sheryl-sandberg/reaching-women-around-the_b_369636.html.

———. "Sheryl Sandberg on Career Growth." YouTube video. http://www.youtube.com/watch?v=inA7W4C7F5E

————. "Sheryl Sandberg on Facebook's Future." Interview by S. J. Adler. *Bloomberg BusinessWeek*, April 8, 2009. http://www.businessweek.com/stories/2009-04-08/sheryl-sandberg-on-facebooks-futurebusinessweek-business-news-stock-market-and-financial-advice.

————. "Sheryl Sandberg at the London School of Economics: It's All about People." YouTube video. May 25, 2011. http://www.youtube.com/watch?feature=player_embedded&v=eL2S4sESc1E.

————. "Sheryl Sandberg: Not Heeding Own Advice." Video. 2013. http://www.makers.com/sheryl-sandberg/moments/not-heeding-own-advice.

————. "Sheryl Sandberg: Spotlight on Scalability." Entrepreneurial Thought Leader Lecture. *Stanford University eCorner*. Audio podcast. April 22, 2009. http://ecorner.stanford.edu/authorMaterialInfo.html?mid=2214.

————. "Sheryl Sandberg: Starting at Facebook." Interview by H. Blodget. *Business Insider*, December 5, 2011. http://www.businessinsider.com/sheryl-sandberg-facebook-beginning-2011-12.

————. "Sheryl Sandberg's Brilliant Career." Interview by M. Forbes. *Forbes* video. April 8, 2013. http://landing.newsinc.com/forbes/video.html?vcid=24724201&freewheel=91218&sitesection=forbes.

————. Talk and FAQ presented at the Bellevue in Philadelphia, PA, April 4, 2013.

————. "Talking Your Tech—Sheryl Sandberg." Interview by J. Graham. YouTube video. October 3, 2011. http://www.youtube.com/watch?v=q6o3wfT3JAA.

————. "Techcrunch Interviews Sheryl Sandberg, Facebook COO, at the World Economic Forum in Davos, Switzerland." YouTube video. January 2010. http://www.youtube.com/watch?NR=1&v=bG-xK65zOZM.

————. UCLA Anderson School of Management 2011 commencement address. YouTube video. June 16, 2011. http://www.youtube.com/watch?v=NWd_AfnXJBU.

————. "Web 2.0 Summit '09: A Conversation with Sheryl Sandberg." Interview by J. Battelle. YouTube video. October 22, 2009. http://www.youtube.com/watch?v=D8VTPbZGmh4.

————. "Why We Have Too Few Women Leaders." Video. December 21, 2010. http://www.ted.com/talks/sheryl_sandberg_why_we_have_too_few_women_leaders.html.

————. "Women's Guilt." Video. 2013. http://www.makers.com/sheryl-sandberg/moments/womens-guilt.

Sandberg, S., and M. Zuckerberg. "Preview of Mark Zuckerberg and Sheryl Sandberg." Interview by C. Rose. Video. November 7, 2011. http://venturebeat.com2011/11/07/zuckerberg-and-sandberg-on-charlie-rose/.

Savage, J. *Julie Foudy: Soccer Superstar*. Minneapolis, MN: Lerner Sports, 1999.

Schneider, D., and C. J. Schneider. *First Ladies: A Biographical Dictionary*, 3rd ed. New York: Facts on File, Inc., 2010.

Schonfeld, E. "Pre-IPO Filing, Facebook Trading Privately at $84 Billion Valuation." Blog post. *TechCruch*. January 30, 2012. http://techcrunch.com/2012/01/30/facebook-84-billion-valuation/.

Sealey, G. "Does America Buy the Female Athlete?" *ABC News*. September 24, 2003. http://abcnews.go.com/Business/story?id=86036&page=1.

Seligman, M. E. P. "Can Happiness Be Taught?" *Dædalus* 133, no. 2(2004):80–87.

Seligman, M. E. P., and M. Csikszentmihalyi. "Positive Psychology: An Introduction." *American Psychologist* 55, no. 1 (2000): 5–14.

Seligman, M. E. P., T. A. Steen, N. Park, and C. Peterson. "Positive Psychology Progress: Empirical Validation of Interventions." *American Psychologist* 60, no. 5 (2005): 410–421.

Sellers, P. "Facebook COO Sheryl Sandberg: Unedited." *CNN Money*. October 5, 2009. http://postcards.blogs.fortune.cnn.com/2009/10/05/facebook-coo-sheryl-sandberg-unedited/.

_____. "How Facebook's Sheryl Sandberg Learned to Love Power." *CNN Money.* July 5, 2011. http://postcards.blogs.fortune.cnn.com/2011/07/05/how-facebooks-sheryl-sandberg-learned-to-love-power/.

_____. "The New Valley Girls." *CNN Money.* January 26, 2009. http://money.cnn.com/2008/09/25/news/newsmakers/sellers_valleygirls.fortune/index.htm.

Severson, L. "The Mission Continues." *Religion & Ethics Newsweekly,* November 9, 2012. http://www.pbs.org/wnet/religionandethics/episodes/november-9-2012/the-mission-continues/13724/.

"Sheena Chestnut, Eric Greitens." *New York Times,* August 5, 2011. http://www.nytimes.com/2011/08/07/fashion/weddings/sheena-chestnut-eric-greitens-weddings.html?_r=0.

Sheldon, K. M., J. Arndt, and L. Houser-Marko. "In Search of the Organismic Valuing Process: The Human Tendency to Move Towards Beneficial Goal Choices." *Journal of Personality* 71, no. 5. (2003): 835–869. doi:10.1111/1467-6494.7105006.

Sheldon, K. M., and A. J. Elliot. "Goal Striving, Need Satisfaction, and Longitudinal Well-Being: The Self-Concordance Model." *Journal of Personality and Social Psychology* 76, no. 3 (1999): 482–497.

Sheldon, K. M., and S. Lyubomirsky. "How to Increase and Sustain Positive Emotion: The Effects of Expressing Gratitude and Visualizing Best Possible Selves." *Journal of Positive Psychology* 1, no. 2 (2006): 73–82.

Shumate, M., and J. Fulk. "Boundaries and Role Conflict When Work and Family Are Colocated: A Communication Network and Symbolic Interaction Approach." *Human Relations* 57, no. 1(2004): 55–74.

Sims P. and P. Lorenzi. *The New Leadership Paradigm: Social Learning and Cognition in Organizations.* Thousand Oaks, CA: Sage Publications, 1992.

Singer, J. A. "Narrative Identity and Meaning Making across the Adult Lifespan: An Introduction." *Journal of Personality* 72, no. 3 (2004): 437–459.

Slaughter, A. "Why Women Still Can't Have It All." *Atlantic,* June 2012.

Snyder, C. R. "Hope Theory: Rainbows in the Mind." *Psychological Inquiry* 13, no. 4 (2002): 249–275.

Sorensen, C. "Facebook's Best Friend: Sheryl Sandberg Has Bold Plans to Transform the Social Networking Site into an Advertising Juggernaut." *Maclean's,* November 11, 2010. http://www2.macleans.ca/2010/11/15/facebooks-best-friend/.

Spreitzer, G. M., and R. E. Quinn. "Empowering Middle Managers to Be Transformational Leaders." *Journal of Applied Behavioral Science* 32, no. 3 (1996): 237.

Springsteen, B. "American Skin (41 Shots)." On *Live in New York City,* by Bruce Springsteen and the E Street Band. New York: Sony Records, 2001.

_____. "Bruce's Speech from MusiCares 2013." Video. February 13, 2013. http://brucespringsteen.net/news/2013/bruces-speech-from-musicares-2013.

_____. "Bruce Springsteen Accepts—Rock and Roll Hall of Fame Induction Speech." Waldorf Astoria Hotel, New York. Transcript. March 15, 1999. https://rockhall.com/inductees/bruce-springsteen/transcript/bruce-springsteen-accepts/.

_____. "Bruce Springsteen: The Rolling Stone Interview." Interview by J. Levy. *Rolling Stone,* November 1, 2007. http://www.rollingstone.com/music/news/bruce-springsteen-the-rolling-stone-interview-20071101.

_____. *Bruce Springsteen: Songs.* New York: Avon Books, Inc., 1998.

_____. "Bruce Springsteen's State of the Union." Interview by J. Stewart. Transcript. *Rolling Stone,* March 29, 2012.

_____. "Bruce Springsteen Interview from July 9, 1978." Interview by D. Herman. Audio file. http://www.wolfgangsvault.com.

_____. "Chords for Change." *New York Times,* August 5, 2004. http://www.nytimes.com/2004/08/05/opinion/05bruce.html.

————. "Classic Bruce Springsteen Interview: How Born to Run Saved the Boss." Interview by D. Marsh. *The Quietus*. http://thequietus.com/articles/04027-bruce-springsteen-interview-born-to-run-creem-magazine.

————. Interview by E. Bradley. *60 Minutes*. CBS. January 21, 1996. http://www.cbsnews.com/video/watch/?id=3340303n&tag=segmentExtraScroller;housing.

————. "Bruce Springsteen." *VH1 Storytellers*. New York: Columbia, 2005. http://www.youtube.com/watch?v=hVGAUTfBuyA&feature=related.

————. Interview by David Letterman. *Late Show with David Letterman*. CBS. 2007. http://www.youtube.com/watch?v=UDowjavKNUo.

————. Interview by E. Norton. *Fresh Air*. WHYY. November 15, 2010. http://www.npr.org/2010/11/12/131272103/ed-norton-interviews-bruce-springsteen-on-darkness.

————. Interview by J. Stewart. *The Daily Show*. March 19, 2009. http://www.thedailyshow.com/watch/thu-march-19-2009/bruce-springsteen---interview.

————. Interview by B. Williams. *NBC Nightly News with Brian Williams*. MSNBC. 2010. http://vodpod.com/watch/4622536-bruce-springsteen-interview-brian-williams-nbc-30-mn-version.

————. "Interview: Bruce Springsteen." Interview by S. Sennett. *Sydney Morning Herald*, March 3, 2012. http://www.smh.com.au/entertainment/music/interview-bruce-springsteen-20120301-1u3xp.html.

————. "Interview with Bruce Springsteen." By Rock and Roll Hall of Fame. Audio file. http://rockhall.com/media/assets/files/INT548904.mp3.

————. "Interview with Bruce Springsteen." By V. Scelsa. Audio file. http://www.youtube.com/watch?v=MPgWNDUPDWg.

————. "Live from E Street Nation." Interview by D. Marsh. SiriusXM Internet Radio Channel 20. January 10, 2014.

————. "The 1995 Molly Meldrum Interview." Video. 1995. http://video.google.com/videoplay?docid=7449216374190055334.

————. "SXSW 2012 Keynote Speech." Presented at the Austin Convention Center, Austin, TX, March 15, 2012. http://www.npr.org/2012/03/16/148778665/bruce-springsteens-sxsw-2012-keynote-speech.

Steele, R., and T. Tierney. *The Donor-Grantee Trap: How Ineffective Collaboration Undermines Philanthropic Results for Society, and What Can Be Done About It*. Boston: The Bridgespan Group, October 7, 2011. http://www.givesmart.org/grant-ees/The-Donor-Grantee-Trap.aspx.

Stone, B. "Everybody Needs a Sheryl Sandberg." *Bloomberg BusinessWeek*, May 12, 2011. Audio podcast. http://www.businessweek.com/mediacenter/podcasts/cover_stories/covercast_05_12_11.htm.

Stone, B. "Why Facebook Needs Sheryl Sandberg." *BusinessWeek*, May 12, 2011. http://www.businessweek.com/magazine/content/11_21/b4229050473695.htm?chan=magazine+channel_top+stories.

Strauss, N. "My Life Lessons from Springsteen, Gaga and Clapton." *The Telegraph*, April 26, 2011. http://www.telegraph.co.uk/culture/8465755/My-life-lessons-from-Springsteen-Gaga-and-Clapton.html.

Sutton, K. L., and R. A. Noe. "Family-Friendly Programs and Work-Life Integration: More Myth Than Magic?" In *Work and Life Integration: Organizational, Cultural, and Individual Perspectives*, edited by E. E. Kossek and S. J. Lambert, 151–169. Mahwah, NJ: Lawrence Erlbaum Associates Publishers, 2005.

Swisher, K. "Sandberg Tidbits." Video. March 5, 2005. http://allthingsd.com/20080305/sandberg-tidbits/.

————. "Telling Employees He Hasn't 'Walked the Talk,' Cisco's John Chambers Leans In on Women in the Workplace Issue." *All Things D*, March 13, 2013. http://allthingsd.com/20130313/telling-employees-hes-not-walked-the-talk-ciscos-john-chambers-leans-in-on-women-in-the-workplace/.

Tapper, J. "Rush Limbaugh Says First Lady Was Booed Partly Because NASCAR Fans Hate Her 'Uppityism.'" *ABC News.* November 21, 2011. http://abcnews.go.com/blogs/politics/2011/11/rush-limbaugh-says-first-lady-was-booed-partly-because-nascar-fans-hate-her-uppityism/.

"Thomas J. Tierney Profile." *Forbes.com.* http://people.forbes.com/profile/thomas-j-tierney/28236.

"Thomas J. Tierney Profile." *The Bridgespan Group.* http://www.bridgespan.org/about/teammemberdetails.aspx?id=276.

Thomas, R. J. *Crucibles of Leadership.* Boston: Harvard Business School Publishing, 2008.

Thompson, K. "The Leading Lady: Michelle Obama." *Essence Magazine,* September 28, 2011. http://www.essence.com/2011/09/28/the-leading-lady-michelle-obama/.

Thompson, R. "The Transformers." *Harvard Business School Alumni Bulletin,* December 2010. http://www.alumni.hbs.edu/bulletin/2010/december/transformers.html.

Tichy, N. M., and E. Cohen. *The Leadership Engine: How Winning Companies Build Leaders at Every Level.* New York: Harper Collins, 1997.

Tierney, K. Personal communication. January 25, 2013.

Tierney, T. "Collaborating for the Common Good." *Harvard Business Review,* July 2011. http://hbr.org/2011/07/column-collaborating-for-the-common-good/ar/1.

———. "The Fourth Annual Ray Murphy Lecture." Speech presented at the Lir Theater, Dublin. December 8, 2011. Video. http://www.siliconrepublic.com/special-events/the-4th-annual-ray-murphy-lecture/.

———. "Give Smart." Speech presented at the Maine Community Foundation's Inspiring Philanthropy Event, University of Southern Maine, Portland, ME, November 16, 2011. Video. http://www.mainecf.org/ipnov2011.aspx.

———. "Give Smart: Philanthropy That Gets Results." Speech presented at the 2011 Annual Philanthropy Roundtable meeting, October 28, 2011. Audio file. http://www.philanthropyroundtable.org/site/print/2011_annual_meeting_resources.

———. Guest lecture. University of Pennsylvania, Philadelphia. Video. April 10, 2008.

———. "Helping Leaders Find Their Way." Interview transcript. The Philanthropy Roundtable. http://www.philanthropyroundtable.org/topic/excellence_in_philanthropy/helping_leaders_find_their_way.

———. "How Is American Higher Education Measuring Up? An Outsider's Perspective." San Jose: The National Center for Public Policy and Higher Education, 2006. http://www.highereducation.org/reports/hunt_tierney/Hunt_Tierney.pdf.

———. "How Philanthropy's Bad Habits Shortchange America." Transcript. Speech presented at the Manhattan Institute for Policy Research, New York, NY, December 3, 2009. http://www.manhattan-institute.org/pdf/simon2009.pdf.

———. "IMPACT Speaker Tom Tierney." Lecture presented at Georgia Institute of Technology College of Management, Atlanta, January 25, 2012. YouTube video. http://www.youtube.com/watch?v=J5PoE53oa2.

———. "Interview with Tom Tierney." California Community Foundation. Transcript. n.d. https://www.calfund.org/page.aspx?pid=1138.

———. "An Interview with Tom Tierney, Co-author of *Give Smart: Philanthropy That Gets Results.*" Interview by R. Kanani. *Huffington Post,* May 15, 2011. http://www.huffingtonpost.com/rahim-kanani/an-interview-with-tom-tie_b_862049.html.

———. "Interview with Tom Tierney, MBA 1980." *Harvard Business School Institutional Memory* website. 2010. http://institutionalmemory.hbs.edu/leadership/interview_with_tom_tierney_mba_1980.html.

————. Keynote address presented at the 2009 Purpose Prize Summit, Stanford University, Stanford, CA, November 1, 2009. YouTube video. http://www. youtube.com/watch?v=rKg9ei23aQM and http://www.youtube.com/ watch?v=SzlHU-HiVho&feature=endscreen&NR=1.

————. "The Leadership Deficit." *Stanford Social Innovation Review,* Summer 2006. http://www.ssireview.org/articles/entry/the_leadership_deficit.

————. "The Nonprofit Sector's Leadership Deficit." Boston: The Bridgespan Group. 2006. http://www.bridgespan.org/getattachment/a74c3ca1-3837-45c3-aa7b-1876a73e80fd/The-Nonprofit-Sectors-Leadership-Deficit.aspx.

————. Personal communication. January 16, 2013.

————. "Philanthropy That Gets Results." Audio podcast, hosted by K. Boyd. *Think.* April 11, 2011. http://podcastdownload.npr.org/anon.npr-podcasts/podcast/77/510036/135330716/KERA_135330716.mp3?_kip_ipx=1050792548-1332593085.

————. "Philanthropy's Road Less Traveled—and How It Makes All the Difference." *Harvard Business School Alumni* website. 2011. http://www.alumni.hbs.edu/careers/philanthropy.html.

————. Speech presented at the 2006 Annual Philanthropy Roundtable meeting, Charleston, SC, November 2006. http://www.bridgestar.org/Library/LeadershipDeficitAudio.aspx.

————. "Success vs. Significance." Interview by P. Cubeta. YouTube video. February 2012. http://www.youtube.com/watch?v=LTiXlca9Zyo.

————. "Tom Tierney: Staying Grounded in Who I Am." Interview by S. D. Friedman. Video. 2008. http://www.totalleadership.org/tltv/.

————. "Tom Tierney: You're a Steamroller." Interview by S. D. Friedman. Video. 2008. http://www.totalleadership.org/tltv/.

————. "Tom Tierney: It's Easy to Ignore the Soul." Interview by S. D. Friedman. Video. 2008. http://www.totalleadership.org/tltv/.

————. "The 'Third Rail' of Nonprofits: Overhead." Interview by V. Dagher. Transcript. 2011. http://online.wsj.com/article/SB10001424052970203611404577046171703664012.html.

————. "Tom Tierney in Conversation with John Kobara." Interview by J. Kobara. Video. http://vimeo.com/28346864. June 29, 2011.

————. Welcome Address—2011 Nonprofit Leadership Summit, Sepember 26, 2011. YouTube video. http://www.youtube.com/watch?v=nIlYnYJ8OD0&feature=related.

Tierney, T., and A. Tuck. "To Succeed, Philanthropy Needs to Be Rooted in Deep Personal Beliefs." *Chronicle of Philanthropy,* February 20, 2011. http://philanthropy.com/article/How-HeadHeart-Must-Blend/126413/.

Total Leadership, Inc. "My Total Leadership Skills." 2008. http://www.totalleadership.org/resources/performance-tools/.

Turak, A. "Leadership Secrets from a Navy SEAL." *Forbes,* September 16, 2011. http://www.forbes.com/sites/augustturak/2011/09/16/leadership-secrets-from-a-navy-seal/?utm_source=allactivity&utm_medium=rss&utm_campaign=20110916.

Umiker, W. "How to Prevent and Cope with Resistance to Change." *Health Care Manager* 15, no. 4 (1997):35–41.

United States Army Combined Arms Center. Center for Army Lessons Learned, http://usacac.army.mil/cac2/call/thesaurus/toc.asp?id=33978.

University of Chicago Medical Center. "University of Chicago and University of Chicago Medical Center Accomplishment Fact Sheet." http://www.uchospitals.edu/pdf/uch_018012.pdf.

"Veterans." Official website of the White House and President Barack Obama. http://www.whitehouse.gov/issues/veterans.

VIA Institute. "VIA Institute on Character." *VIAPro Character Strengths Profile Practitioner's Guide.* 2011. http://www.viacharacter.org.

Wall, C. A. "On Dolls, Presidents and Little Black Girls." *Signs* 34, no. 4(2010): 796–801. http://www.jstor.org/pss/10.1086/651034.

Weick, K. E. "Small Wins: Redefining the Scale of Social Problems." *American Psychologist* 39, no. 1 (1984): 40–49.

Wheeler, J. C. *Michelle Obama.* Edina, MN: ABDO Publishing Company, 2010.

White House, Office of the Vice President. "America's Social Workers Join Dr. Jill Biden to Launch 'Social Work and Service Members: Joining Forces to Support Veterans and Military Families.'" Press release. July 25, 2012. http://www.whitehouse.gov/the-press-office/2012/07/25/americas-social-workers-join-dr-jill-biden-launch-social-work-and-servic.

———. "AACTE, MCEC Join Dr. Jill Biden to Celebrate Milestone for Joining Forces Commitment 'Operation Educate the Educators.'" Press release. October 3, 2012. http://www.whitehouse.gov/the-press-office/2012/10/03/aacte-mcec-join-dr-jill-biden-celebrate-milestone-joining-forces-commitm.

White House (Poster). "The First Lady on International Women's Day." YouTube video. March 8, 2011. http://www.youtube.com/user/whitehouse#p/search/28/WMI7-6RLow8.

———. "First Lady Michelle Obama Addresses Young African Women Leaders." YouTube video. June 23, 2011. http://www.youtube.com/user/whitehouse#p/search/1/MzczmosdT_M.

———. "First Lady Michelle Obama Answers Your Questions on Let's Move!" YouTube video. July 13, 2011. http://www.youtube.com/watch?v=rUbJZGrnV3w&feature=related.

———. "First Lady Michelle Obama on Leadership and Mentoring in Detroit." YouTube video. May 27, 2010. http://www.youtube.com/user/whitehouse#p/search/38/MYIhFzcOgwc.

———. "First Lady Michelle Obama Speaks to Youth in Mexico City." YouTube video. April 15, 2010. http://www.youtube.com/user/whitehouse#p/search/17/x-BRxuw96lA.

———. "The First Lady Previews Holidays at the White House." YouTube video. December 2, 2009. http://www.youtube.com/user/whitehouse#p/search/99/nFtz7ymi8XI.

———. "First Lady Speaks to American Servicewomen." YouTube video. March 9, 2009. http://www.youtube.com/user/whitehouse#p/search/110/iK7_ULP2hPY.

Whiteside, K. "Foudy Is Captain, Conscience of U.S. Team." *USA Today*, September 8, 2003. http://www.usatoday.com/sports/soccer/national/2003-09-08-cover-foudy_x.htm.

Wiersema, R. *Walk Like a Man: Coming of Age with the Music of Bruce Springsteen.* Berkeley, CA: D&M Publishers, 2011.

Wolfe, R. "Barack's Rock." *Newsweek*, February 16, 2008. http://www.thedailybeast.com/newsweek/2008/02/16/barack-s-rock.html.

Womack, K., J. Zolten, and M. Bernhard. *Bruce Springsteen, Cultural Studies and the Runaway American Dream.* Farnham, UK: Ashgate Publishing, Ltd., 2012.

Wrzesniewski, A., and J. E. Dutton. "Crafting a Job: Revisioning Employees as Active Crafters of Their Work." *Academy of Management Review* 26, no. 2 (2001): 179–201.

Yeager, H. "The Heart and Mind of Michelle Obama." *O magazine*, November 2007. http://www.oprah.com/world/The-Heart-and-Mind-of-Michelle-Obama/1.

Zirin, D. *A People's History of Sports in the United States: 250 Years of Politics, Protest, People and Play.* New York: The New Press, 2005.

Index

Acknowledgments

The six stories in this book have highlighted an eternal truth; without a doubt, no one makes it on their own. I'm very pleased to take this moment to thank those who've provided me with that most precious thing, their help, in producing this book.

I am most grateful to the many people who expressed their skepticism about the essential idea in *Total Leadership*—that work and the rest of life are locked in combat with a guaranteed loser in the end—for they propelled me to write it. I hope that *Leading the Life You Want* persuades a few of them to think again about the possibilities for four-way wins over the course of a life.

But despite my keen interest in demonstrating that great achievement in the sphere of work is the result of commitments and resources we derive from other parts of life, I would not have had the wherewithal to take up the cudgels were it not for Melinda Merino, my editor at Harvard Business Review Press, who asked, as soon as *Total Leadership* was done, "OK, what's the next one?" "Are you kidding?" I exclaimed, "I'm exhausted!" She corralled my oft-wandering attention and inspired me to take the collection of biographies I'd been gathering for years, make my argument, and use the biographies to show others how these people achieved both greatness and goodness in their lives. The brilliant Scott Cooper gave me invaluable pointers for how to pitch the book's initial structure and start to organize the raw material on the biographies. Then, after all the stuff was in one place, my captain, the incomparably talented editor, Connie Hale, took me by the hand and walked me through the arduous tasks of composition, step by step, with grace, exquisite taste, and just the right amount of edge. But the sculpting of the biographies themselves would not have happened without the journalistic prowess of Jessie Scanlon, who, with kind and knowing hands, worked her magic with the giant slab of clay I'd thrown on the table.

Producing that slab of clay was the result of many dedicated hands, starting with the hundreds of Wharton MBA students in my Total Leadership class who, over the past decade, have written short narratives about the people they admired, using the principles of the class as the lens through which to view these exemplary lives. (You can view some of these at http://www.slideshare.net/totalleadership/presentations.) Their impassioned explorations of the meaning of these lives fueled my conviction with evidence. The specific suggestion for four of the six profiles came from these students: Chris Marvin, who wrote persuasively about Eric Greitens; Wendy Guthrie, who connected me to Julie Foudy; Jessica Wang, who suggested Sheryl Sandberg (years before she became a household name); and Lara Gitlin, who demonstrated why Michelle Obama was a great case in point. (I chose Tom Tierney and Bruce Springsteen on my own.) Amrita Singh and Emily Weinstein did invaluable research in culling the many biographical studies and helping me think through how these exemplars demonstrated the principles and skills of Total Leadership. Once I'd narrowed the list, a small group of student researchers, under the wise and patient direction of another student, Alice Zhou, gathered everything we could find about our subjects. Christie Irizarry unearthed all available information about Julie Foudy, Karen Okigbo gathered tons of information on Michelle Obama, and the incomparable Molly Reed brought together the material on Greitens, Sandberg, Springsteen, and Tierney. Sarah Fu, Alex Lim, and Vandit Shah researched three subjects who were ultimately excluded from this volume.

I had the good fortune and great pleasure to speak directly with people who helped me put flesh on the bones of these stories. In addition to my own observations and conversations with the principals, I benefited enormously from chronicles kindly offered by J. J. Abrams, Jeff Bradach, John Donahoe, Joel Fleishman, Rebecca Goldman, Lawrence Green, Ken Harbaugh, Kaj Larsen, Reggie Love, Chris Marvin, Barb Osburg, Adele and Joel Sandberg, and Karen Tierney.

Part II of this book is the result of a rich collaboration with two people from whom I learned a great deal about the skills needed for integrating work and the rest of life, and how to teach them: organizational psychologist Alyssa Westring, of DePaul University, and positive psychology coach Katie Comtois. Alyssa has brought her remarkable insight and deep knowledge of the literature to researching these skills with me for many years. For this book, she gathered information on many specific practices and described their evidentiary basis. Katie, for her thesis in Penn's Master of Applied Psychology program, did the same. After substantial winnowing, I asked alumni of my Total Leadership class to provide feedback on the exercises we'd collected, and over sixty of them did so, vastly refining the description and rationale for the two exercises I ultimately chose for each skill. I was very fortunate to have the able assistance of Gabriel Friedman, my son, in harvesting a heap of inspiring quotations, for flavor.

I am blessed to have the chance to work with my dedicated team of colleagues at Total Leadership, who bring to life our mission, which is to increase the capacity of leaders in all walks of life to perform in ways that create maximum value for themselves and for society. My wife and business partner, clinical psychologist Hallie Friedman, is not only my love and inspiration; she also drives our strategy, provides editorial guidance, and employs her substantial expertise as a researcher and clinician in analyzing all the thorny questions we encounter in trying to apply our core ideas and methods. Our head of client services, the magical Michelle Rajotte, was a student in my MBA for Executives class a while back, after having served our nation as an Air Force captain, and, to my great fortune, now brings her tireless enthusiasm and care to making it possible for thousands of students and clients to benefit from Total Leadership solutions. I am grateful, too, to Ryan Findley, the gracious and resourceful engineer who runs our online operations, and his team at Neomind Labs, especially the late Justin Broglie, for his creative talent and generous spirit.

I would be nowhere without the love and tolerance of my family: words cannot describe the gratitude I feel, though poorly express, each day for Hallie, Gabriel, Harry, and Lody. And before them, my remarkable parents, the inspiring artists, Vic and Leah Friedman.

About the Author

Stew Friedman joined the Wharton School faculty in 1984. He became the Management Department's first Practice Professor in recognition of his work on the application of theory and research to the real challenges facing organizations. He is the founding director of both the Wharton Leadership Program and the Wharton Work/Life Integration Project. In 2001, Stew concluded a two-year assignment (while on leave from Wharton) at Ford Motor Company, where he was the senior executive for leadership development. In partnership with the CEO, he launched a corporate-wide portfolio of initiatives to transform Ford's culture, in which over twenty-five hundred managers per year participated. Following these efforts, a research group (ICEDR) described Ford as a "global benchmark" in leadership development.

Stew's writings on leadership development and succession, work/life integration, and the dynamics of change include the widely cited *Harvard Business Review* articles "Work and Life: The End of the Zero-Sum Game" (coauthored with Perry Christensen and Jessica DeGroot) and "Be a Better Leader, Have a Richer Life," and, in the *Academy of Management Executive*, "The Happy Workaholic: A Role Model for Employees" (with Sharon Lobel). His books include *Integrating Work and Life: The Wharton Resource Guide*, in which he co-edited (with Jessica DeGroot and Perry Christensen) the first collection of learning tools for building leadership skills that integrate work with the rest of life. *Work and Family—Allies or Enemies?*

(coauthored with Jeff Greenhaus) was recognized by the *Wall Street Journal* as one of the field's best. His national bestseller, *Total Leadership: Be a Better Leader, Have a Richer Life*, has sold over sixty thousand copies, is now available in six languages, and is the basis for a massive open online course (MOOC) that reaches tens of thousands worldwide (on coursera.org). Stew's latest book, *Baby Bust: New Choices for Men and Women in Work and Family*, is a landmark twenty-year longitudinal study that revealed surprising differences between Gen Xers and Millennials.

Stew has advised many organizations, including the US Departments of Labor and State, the U.N., and two White House administrations. He gives high-energy keynote speeches, conducts interactive workshops, and is an award-winning teacher. The *New York Times* cited the "rock star adoration" he inspires in his students. He was chosen by *Working Mother* as one of America's twenty-five most influential men in having made things better for working parents and by Thinkers50 as one of the "world's top 50 business thinkers." The Families and Work Institute honored him with a Work Life Legacy Award in 2013. Follow him on Twitter @StewFriedman. Tune in to his show, *Work and Life*, on SiriusXM 111, "Business Radio Powered by the Wharton School," Tuesdays at 7:00 p.m. (EST).

Stew played music and drove a taxi in New York during college and for a year thereafter, then worked for five years as a mental health professional in Vermont and New York before earning his PhD (1984) in organizational psychology from the University of Michigan.

www.totalleadership.org

Improving performance in all aspects of life—work, home, community, and the private self (mind, body, spirit)—by creating mutual value among them

- Access tools you can use
- Learn about inspiring experiments others have done
- View alumni and other videos
- Keep up-to-date: blogs, research, media coverage, news, events, and more

Compose and share your four circles
at myfourcircles.com

- What my four circles say:
  Size the circles to show the relative importance of your domains then click and drag them to show their alignment

- What I'm working on:
  Identify experiments to improve alignment and score a four-way win

- Ask your community:
  Get help from others on the design and implementation of your experiments

Stew Friedman | Founder, Total Leadership

Stew brings inspiring passion and practical ideas for action.

With his worldwide experience as a successful leader of change in organizations for three decades—he's an award-winning educator, widely cited researcher, accomplished executive, sought-after consultant, high-impact coach, and dynamic speaker—he knows how to help people in organizations produce sustainable results.

Invite Stew to your group or organization to improve performance at work, at home, in the community, and for the private self (mind, body, and spirit). He will show you how to score four-way wins with Total Leadership in a way that makes sense for you and the most important people in your life.

info@totalleadership.org
610.664.2387 (USA)
www.totalleadership.org